Law Meets Film

AF722321

Art and Law

Editors-in-Chief

Tiziana Andina (*University of Turin*)
Gianmaria Ajani (*University of Turin*)
Werner Gephart (*University of Bonn*)

Associate Editors

Angela Condello (*University of Messina*)
Davide Dal Sasso (*Scuola IMT Alti Studi Lucca*)

Editorial Board

Mark Antaki (*McGill University*)
Emanuele Conte (*University of Roma Tre*)
David Davies (*McGill University*)
Alessandra Donati (*University of Milano Bicocca*)
Thomas Dreier (*Karlsruhe Institute for Technology (KIT) and University of Freiburg*)
Maurizio Ferraris (*University of Turin*)
Pierpaolo Forte (*Museo Madre, Naples* and *University of Sannio*)
Peter Goodrich (*Cardozo School of Law*)
Paolo Heritier (*University of Turin*)
Desmond Manderson (*Australian National University*)
Sabine N. Meyer (*University of Osnabrück*)
Stewart Motha (*University of Birkbeck School of Law*)
Alberto Oddenino (*University of Turin*)
Greta Olson (*Justus-Liebig-Universität Giessen*)
Andreas Philippopoulos-Mihalopoulos (*Westminster School of Law*)
Reinold Schmücker (*University of Münster*)
Peter Schneck (*University of Osnabrück*)
Eva Schürman (*Otto-von-Guericke-Universität Magdeburg*)
John Searle (*University of California at Berkeley*)
Alberto *Voltolini* (*University of Turin*)
Michel Wieviorka (*École des hautes études en sciences sociales*)

The titles published in this series are listed at *brill.com/rpals*

Law Meets Film

Taxonomy of an Encounter

Edited by

Gianmaria Ajani
Lucie Bader
Walter Stoffel

BRILL

ISSN 2468-4295
ISBN 978-90-04-76169-8
ISBN 978-90-04-76170-4 (PDF)
DOI https://doi.org/10.1163/9789004761704

Library of Congress Control Number: 2026936603

© 2026 the author(s)/editor(s), published by Koninklijke Brill BV, Plantijnstraat 2, 2321 JC Leiden, The Netherlands

All rights reserved. No part of this publication may be reproduced, translated, stored in a retrieval system, or transmitted in any form or by any means, electronic, mechanical, photocopying, recording or otherwise, without prior written permission from the publisher. Text and datamining for commercial purposes requires the publisher's permission.

Brill and Koninklijke Brill BV are part of De Gruyter Brill.
www.degruyterbrill.com

Questions about General Product Safety Regulation: productsafety@degruyterbrill.com

Cover illustration: Opening of the film OPPENHEIMER, Santa Barbara U.S.A., 24th July, 2023 (Amy Katz/ ZUMA Press Wire)

Contents

PART 4
Perspectives

Preface

Art knows no limits. The law sets rules, and limits. According to the most recurrent representations, Law is characterized by predictability, certainty, and a remarkable formal rigor. Law represents and defines the rules for the management of social relationships, in the different places where we act. Said more extensively, the primary role of law in human society is to prevent violent interpersonal conflicts, to provide a third and impartial solution to private disputes, to support the founding concept of democracy, that is, the equality of all before the rules approved by our political representatives.

Art, at least since the aesthetic revolution that accompanied the 20th century and continues in the present days, asserts itself as free from formal constraints; it is the artist's autonomy to choose the formal canon of reference (or not to choose any, while creating her own). Surprise and uncertainty characterize artistic productions. Even art that, at a certain time or place, can be qualified as "illegal", remains art. Indeed, it is precisely the recognition of an action, a work, as an artistic one, that can create a space of "legal immunity".

So, why combine Film and Law? Is there any added value in producing scholarly work on Law and Film, beside the most elementary recourse to movie-watching for teaching purposes? Film-making, like all visual arts, contributes to representing and defining the social and cultural identity of our time.

More generally, the practice of investigating the contributions of visual arts to the understanding of Law as a cultural phenomenon has long been established under various names (Law & Literature, Law & Arts, Law & Culture). It is within that area of research that this volume is placed, an area that has been widely investigated, being the subject of study and teaching both in the Department of Law of the University of Turin and at the Law Faculty of the University of Fribourg. In fact, partnership and cooperation in teaching and research programs between these two academic institutions are well established.

The texts composing this volume were presented in a preliminary version at the international colloquium Law meets Film, held at the Law Department of the University of Turin on November 25, 2024. The main aim of the colloquium was to encourage an interdisciplinary dialogue among law professionals, film experts, and filmmaker(s).

My co-editors in this publication have devoted brilliant pages (see, below, Law meets Film: Who Meets Whom, by Walter Stoffel and Lucie Bader) to the similarities and differences between Law and Film. We can, therefore, contain this Foreword to highlight the methodological result achieved at the Colloquium and now offered to the readers of this volume: a contribution to clarify the role that Film can play in understanding and investigating the role of Law within human societies. A role activated by three main modes of human interaction—observation, discussion, interrogation—that are spelt out in the Introduction following the Foreword, as well as all throughout this publication.

The colloquium and this volume were made possible by the support of several institutions: together with the Law Faculties of the Torino and Fribourg University, the "School for Advanced Studies Ferdinando Rossi" at the Torino University, and the "Cinematographic Scenography and Digital Technology Chair" at the Torino Academy of Fine Arts.

Special acknowledgements are deserved by all chairpersons, contributors and discussants, who actively accepted the cultural challenge we proposed: an articulation of different perspectives on the Law meeting Films.

We also would like to thank our Colleagues in Comparative legal studies, Michele Graziadei and Simona Novaretti, whose support in the making of the Colloquium was crucial.

A very special "close-up" to Dorianne Cattoen (Student at Bangor University in the LL.M. in International Human rights law and International Criminal Law, Graduate of a double degree in French and English law and a Master in EU law): her competence, patience and reliability in the editing and revision of all contributions and other texts in this volume were far beyond a valuable professional commitment.

Gianmaria Ajani

Figures

Notes on Contributors

Gianmaria Ajani

Professor of Law and past Rector, University of Turin. Teaches and researches Law and Arts, Comparative Law and Economics, Artists' rights, Law & technology. Publications include *The Artificial Author*, Brill, 2020. Co-founder *Brill Research Perspectives in Art and Law*. Doctor h.c., Université de Savoie, Guest Professor, University of Bergen, Norway, Honorary Professor, Shanghai Normal University, PRC.

Emin Alper

Turkish filmmaker and historian. He holds a Ph.D. in Modern Turkish History and teaches at Istanbul Technical University. His films *Tepenin Ardi* (Beyond the Hill), *Abluka* (Frenzy) and *A Tale of Three Sisters*, received many awards. His latest work *Burning Days* (Kurak Günler) has been presented in numerous festivals including Cannes in the section Un Certain Regard.

Lucie Bader

Studies in journalism, film and media management in Zurich, Washington D.C. and Linz. Professor in film and co-director of the Master's program, Zurich University of the Arts, 1992–2012. Member of the Swiss Film Academy, jury member in film festivals. Since 2013, Director of *outreach gmbh* (media and science communication), lecturer at the University of Fribourg (*Law in the Movies*).

Elisabeth Bronfen

Cultural scientist, author and freelance curator. Global Distinguished Professor New York University. Emerita University of Zurich, since 2023. Literature and visual culture, femininity and death, cross-mapping as a hermeneutic process, TV dramas, Shakespeare and seriality. Monographs, anthologies, essays and contributions to exhibition catalogues. A cookery memoir and a novel.

Naomi Mezey

Law professor at Georgetown University. Teaches civil procedure, jurisprudence, gender & sexuality, law & popular culture, and nationalism. Interdisciplinary scholarship on legal regulation of sexual, gender, racial, and national identities, film and visuality, and sovereignty. B.A. from Wesleyan University, a M.A. in American Studies from the University of Minnesota, and a J.D. from Stanford Law School.

Stefan Machura
Dr. rer. soc., Dr. rer. pol. habil., is Professor emeritus of Criminology and Criminal Justice at Bangor University (UK). Publications include *Law and Film* (co-edited with Peter Robson, 2001), *Recht im Film* (co-edited with Stefan Ulbrich, 2002), *Krieg im Film* (co-edited with Rüdiger Voigt, 2005) and *Law and War in Film* (editor, 2024).

Ferdinando Spina
Ph.D., is Associate Professor of Sociology of Law at the University of Salento, where he teaches courses on the sociology of law, sociology of crime, crime and media. His most recent publications include the book *Vigilante Justice in Society and Popular Culture. A Global Perspective*, edited with P. Robson, and the book *La legge nelle proprie mani* (*The Law in One's Own Hands*).

Agata Fijalkowski
Reader-in-Law at Leed Beckett University Law School (UK) is an interdisciplinary scholar writing in the field of Law and Humanities. Her publications include *Law, Visual Culture, and the Law* (Routledge 2023) and has been awarded an MA in Screenwriting from the Northern Film School.

Michael Randall
Senior Teaching Fellow University of Strathclyde School of Law (2016–Present). Michael is the coordinator of the *Law, Film and Popular Culture* and *Law in the Context of Contemporary Culture* modules at Strathclyde. His publications include *Taylor Swift: Authenticity and The Influence of Popular Culture Icons In Law*.

Peter Robson
LL.B. (St. Andrews University); Ph.D. (Strathclyde); Solicitor; Judge (1992–2022); Professor of Social Welfare Law. University of Strathclyde (1992–2019). Numerous books on law and film, including *Film and the Law: the cinema of justice* (2010), *From Bloodbaths to Parody—Western Cinema's Uneasy Relationship with Rape Revenge Themes—a fresh approach?* (2024).

Walter Stoffel
Professor at the Faculty of Law of the University of Fribourg (Switzerland), 1986–2020. Dean 1998–2000. Academic Co-director Center for Transnational Legal Studies (CTLS), London, 2020–2022. Organizer and founder *Law in the Movies*, University of Fribourg (since 2013), with Lucie Bader. Ombudsman, University of Fribourg. Professor at UniDistance Brigue (distance learning university).

CHAPTER 1

"Law Meets Film": Who Meets Whom?

Walter Stoffel and Lucie Bader

1 Distinctions

The following series of articles is presented under the title *Law meets Film*. It distinguishes between three categories of legal films: *Films on legal procedure* (courtroom dramas), *Films on legal problems*, and *Films mirroring law*. This taxonomy is based on how films and filmmakers explicitly or implicitly refer to law, legal protagonists or concepts of justice. The distinctions are the result of recurrent observations made in a film cycle called *Law in the Movies*, which has been presented by the authors at the University of Fribourg in Switzerland and the Center for Transnational Legal Studies (CTLS) in London over the last 12 years.[1]

Why *Law meets Film*? Would *Film meets Law* be more appropriate? Are we interested in law as it approaches film? Or rather the way in which filmmakers approach the law? Perhaps the encounter works both ways.

At the outset, a (lawyerly) thought on definitions is required. What is film? The proposal made by the American film critic James Monaco is one we like: "Poetry is what you can't translate. Art is what you can't define. Film is what you can't explain. But we are going to try, anyway."[2] And what is law? In our context, we propose the following definition: law is the systematic analysis of authoritative decisions made in the past to resolve conflicts in a society. While film is intuitive, non-hierarchical, and image-based, the law is organised, hierarchical and text-based.

Beyond this, there are numerous similarities as well as important differences between law and the art of film. Let's start with the common ground.

- Most obviously, there are similarities in the visual set up of a process in a courtroom and an action on the set: in both cases, we have a performance stage.

1 Université Fribourg (Switzerland), 'Archives Recht im Film / Le droit dans le cinéma / Law in the movies' (*Université Fribourg*) <https://events.unifr.ch/droitcinema/de/archiv/> accessed 27 February 2025.

2 James Monaco, *How to read a film: The World of Movies, Media and Multimedia* (3rd edn, Oxford University Press USA 2000) 65.

© 2026 THE AUTHOR(S) | HTTPS://DOI.ORG/10.1163/9789004761704-002

- Lawyers in the courtroom and filmmakers are story oriented.
- Both must capture a slice of human existence in a short period of time and a limited space.
- The lawyers and the filmmakers invite the court, and the audience to see a story from the perspective they choose, which is one of many possibilities.
- Both decide which facts to include and which to leave out, as well as when to appeal to emotion and when to appeal to reason.[3]

The differences between law and film seem to be more important, at least at first glance:

- In a film, we see only what the director presents to us. Our field of perception is limited to the screen.
- When watching a film, our eyes cannot wander around in space, remain at a place for a while, and then go on again as we wish.
- A film has additional layers. It includes music, sound, and rhythm, not just talking heads and language.
- We may see more in a film than in a specific place in the real world (e.g. a courtroom), because a film has many different angles of view. It can use long shots and close-ups, it can depict parallel events and flashbacks, etc.

The three categories we propose—*Films on legal procedures, Films on legal problems, and Films mirroring law*—can be limiting, but they also allow for an interdisciplinary approach to cinematic form and content and its relevance for law and society. They also make it possible to widen the scope of these discussions to include different regions and their cinematic as well as legal cultures.

2 Films on Legal Procedures (Courtroom Dramas)

We begin with films on legal procedures, generally referred to as courtroom dramas.

2.1 In General

In historical terms, this category comes first. It also takes priority because it corresponds best to the similarities between law and film. Courtroom dramas combine the authority of the law with the power of moving images.

The examples are numerous:

3 David A. Black, *Law in Film: Resonance and Representation* (University of Illinois Press 1999) 61, citing judge Alex Kozinski, Foreword, p. xi, to Paul Bergman and Michael Asimow, *Reel Justice: The Courtroom Goes to the Movies* (Andrews and McMeel 1996).

- Twelve Angry Men (1957, Sydney Lumet)
- Anatomy of a Murder (1959, Otto Preminger)
- Judgment at Nuremberg (1961, Stanley Kramer)
- The Seventh Juror (Le 7e juré) (1962, Georges Lauthner)
- Cleveland V. Wall Street (2010, Jean-Stéphane Bron)
- Denial (2016, Mick Jackson)
- The Children Act (2017, Richard Eyre)
- The Girl with a Bracelet (La fille au bracelet) (2019, Stéphane Demoustier)
- Anatomy of a Fall (Anatomie d’une chute) (2023, Justine Triet)
- Juror #2 (2024, Clint Eastwood)

Most films are narrative, almost by definition.[4] It is not surprising that narrative topics hold a particular—almost natural—attraction for filmmakers. Courtroom dramas are very much narrative topics: here we see the importance of storytelling, the visual similarity between a courtroom setting and a stage or a film set, and the fact that a trial respectively a courtroom drama ends with a verdict. A courtroom is a narrative hotspot.[5]

This is particularly true if the courtroom drama takes place in a legal system which has jury trials. A jury trial allows the filmmaker to evaluate the case by giving the different jurors a voice and by presenting their arguments in a dramatic and often emotional discussion. Will the jurors do what the viewers think that they should do? Or are they handing down an unjust verdict because of the failure of individual jurors or even for systemic reasons? We think, of course, of Twelve Angry Men (1957, Sydney Lumet), The Seventh Juror (1962, Georges Lauthner), or most recently Juror #2 (2024, Clint Eastwood), which builds on these two famous predecessors.

Films on legal procedures give access to a space which is normally inaccessible to most people. The courtroom is for judges, lawyers and the parties, but not for lay people. It is true that, in principle, the public can attend most proceedings, especially criminal cases. But few people who are not legal professionals follow legal proceedings in a real courtroom. Films are therefore

4 The notion of narration is debated, and films can, exceptionally, be non-narrative like films observing nature, films on animals or experimental films. According to the Wikipedia definition: “Narrative film, fictional film or fiction film is a motion picture that tells a fictional or fictionalized story, event or narrative […] Non-narrative film is an aesthetic of cinematic film that does not narrate, or relate “an event, whether real or imaginary”. It is usually a form of art film or experimental film, not made for mass entertainment.” See ‘Narrative film’ (*Wikipedia*) <https://en.wikipedia.org/wiki/Narrative_film> accessed 06 March 2025.

5 David A. Black, *Law in Film: Resonance and Representation* (n 3) 61.

the only real way for most people to gain access to this space. Well informed observers of the genre find that most filmmakers of courtroom dramas devote significant time and resources to researching courts and lawyers, and try to give an accurate picture of what they find.[6] In the eyes of most lawyers, the result rarely corresponds to the reality, but the desire for accuracy by the filmmakers is clear.

There is another aspect to the fascination of courtroom dramas. Court proceedings tell a story that has happened in the world, but can no longer be observed directly. The sequence of events is uncertain or disputed, and this is precisely what the proceedings are about. The court proceedings consist in the retelling of the story. The film, for its part, recounts this retelling. It presents it again and in its own narrative.[7] This double refraction of reality produces a sense of artistic, intellectual and philosophical freedom for both the filmmaker and the audience. It is an additional reason for the attraction of courtroom dramas. ANATOMY OF A FALL (2023, Justine Triet), discussed in two contributions to the present volume,[8] is an outstanding example.

2.2 Myths and Challenges of Courtroom Dramas

Courtroom dramas take legal procedures as their very object. Legal protagonists are combating each other: we see a protagonist and an antagonist, and we have a story unfolding under our eyes. The set-up is emotional, sometimes as breathtaking as a thriller. In courtroom dramas we admire (or despise) the power of law, and we question its impact on society. In this perspective, on the first level of refraction, we can see courtroom dramas as illustrations of otherwise abstract legal questions.

On the second level of refraction, courtroom dramas, while depicting legal procedures, reflect social perceptions of the legal system and the notions of justice. From this point of view, they *challenge* the ability of the law to respond to societal questions. The courtroom drama shows a certain image of the place of law in our society. This image can be positive or negative. The film may advocate a function the law is expected to perform. Or it may challenge the way the law performs. In both cases, the courtroom drama shapes the expectations in the collective mind.

6 Thibault de Ravel d'Esclapon, *La justice au cinéma* (Dalloz 2023).

7 David A. Black, *Law in Film: Resonance and Representation* (n 3).

8 See Stefan Machura, 'The process is the punishment: Anatomy of a Fall in the context of the courtroom drama genre' in Gianmaria Ajani, Lucie Bader and Walter Stoffel (eds), *Law meets Film: Taxonomy of an encounter* (Brill 2026); Agata Fijalkowski, 'Anatomy of a Fall: Interpersonal Drama as a Courtroom Drama' in Gianmaria Ajani, Lucie Bader and Walter Stoffel (eds), *Law meets Film: Taxonomy of an encounter* (Brill 2026).

Courtroom dramas—like films in general—are *myth* carriers. On the one hand, they transport classical myths (biblical stories, Greek tragedies, etc.), and on the other they create their own myths.[9] Such myths produced by the film itself include not only certain narrative structures that have grown into prototypes of film genres (like western, thriller etc.), but also the iconic heroic figures reproduced by the cinema and the star system associated with them.[10]

It is not only the peculiarities of courtroom narratives which are decisive for the appeal for the myth building effects of these dramas, but also the way in which the film is staged. According to Marcus Stiglegger's theory of seduction, it is the images, the editing, the movements, the sounds and the stories in which law-related motifs are treated that seduce the audience both on the intellectual as well as on the emotional levels.[11]

Filmmakers of courtroom dramas are aware of these effects. Whether positive or negative, they intend to shape the vision we have of a courtroom and of the law. The drama comes with a value judgment. This judgment is historically one of a liberal judicial system which may take time and effort to come to grips with a problem, but in the end hands down a rule-based and globally satisfying decision.[12] Although this positive appreciation is not as strong as it once was,[13] it is still present in contemporary courtroom dramas.

The mixture of *illustration* and *challenge* is responsible for the fascination of the genre of the courtroom drama amongst lawyers. They are often used as law school teaching tools, loved by many academics and students alike.[14]

2.3 A Landmark Courtroom Drama and a Legacy

One courtroom drama stands out in all these respects: JUDGMENT AT NUREMBERG (1961, Stanley Kramer). The film was made in the same period as TWELVE ANGRY MEN (1957, Sidney Lumet) and ANATOMY OF A MURDER

9 Marcus Stiglegger, *Ritual & Verführung, Spektakel und Sinnlichkeit im Film* (Bertz und Fischer 2006).

10 Fabian Odermatt, *Das Recht im filmischen Spiegel—Verführung, Mythos und Performanz* (Nomos 2023) 84.

11 Marcus Stiglegger, 'Die Seduktionstheorie des Films' in Markus S. Kleiner and Michael Rappe (eds), *Methoden der Populärkulturforschung: Interdisziplinäre Perspektiven auf Film, Fernsehen, Musik, Internet und Computerspiele* (LIT Verlag 2012) 85–113.

12 David Ray Papke, 'Law, Cinema, and Ideology: Hollywood Legal Films of the 1950s.' (2001) 48 UCLA L. Rev. 1473.

13 Peter Robson and Michael Randall, 'The Future of Law and Film In Context' in Gianmaria Ajani, Lucie Bader and Walter Stoffel (eds), *Law meets Film: Taxonomy of an encounter* (Brill 2026).

14 Ibid.

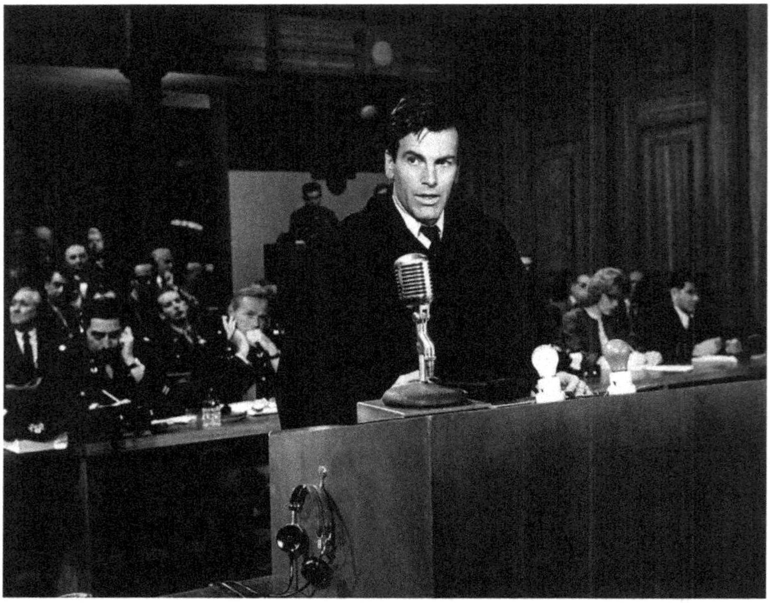

FIGURE 1.1 Defense attorney Hans Rolfe (Maximilian Schell) represents the main defendant Ernst Janning in court (Film still by United Artists)

(1959, Otto Preminger). Its legacy is of particular importance. The film constitutes an individual drama of sanction and punishment for "ordinary" crimes. But in addition, the film presents the procedure as a public drama involving exceptional war crimes. As such it became part of a secular legacy of fair trial and justice.[15]

In JUDGMENT AT NUREMBERG Stanley Kramer, the director, and Ernest Laszlo, the cameraman, gave the courtroom drama a new form which set the tone for later courtroom dramas. For the courtroom sequences, they used a single camera set up in a 360 degrees circling mode. This revolving camera allowed the director to move from the lawyers and defendants to the judges without cutting. The different courtroom chapters (four in number) were followed and interrupted by relatively long scenes of "real" life: in the kitchen of the mansion, the prison, the town, at parties and dinners and so on.

15 Walter Stoffel and Lucie Bader, 'Jugement à Nuremberg (Judgement at Nuremberg)' in Matthieu Perrin (ed), *100 films à voir (ou à revoir) lorsque l'on est juriste* (Mare et Martin 2025) 91–93.

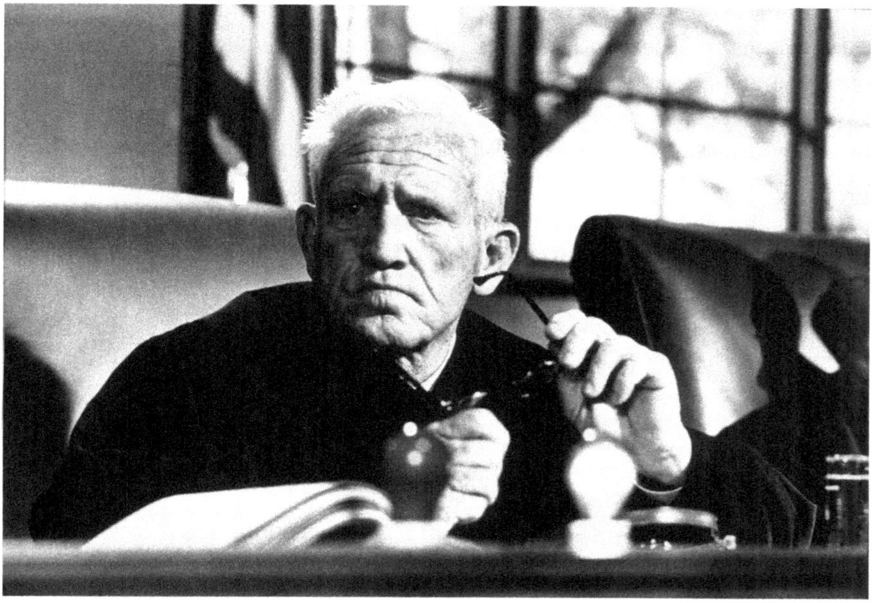

FIGURE 1.2 Judge Dan Heywood (Spencer Tracey) listens to the attorney (Film still by United Artists)

"The circling camera saved us photographically," said Kramer. It prevented the image from becoming "slow and cerebral"[16] and resulted in a lively film, full of suspense until the end, despite its great length of almost three hours. The film thus set a standard for the views that could be shown, the stories to be told and the protagonists to be portrayed.

This form gave a weight to the content that its message carries to this day. Justice was done by the judges after a fair trial even for persons accused of war crimes. That there should be no verdict without a fair trial was far from self-evident at the time the film was made, still less at the time the Nuremberg trials were held: the British would have preferred a summary judgment, the Russians a show trial. But the Americans insisted that a formal trial took place. In the film itself, the verdicts were not as obvious as the viewer might expect. The judges in the dock were accused of relatively minor crimes (allowing forced sterilisation, convicting the innocent), rather than the huge crimes

16 Cited after a post "Behind the Scenes" by Brian Hannan. See Brian Hannan, 'Behind the Scenes: "Judgement at Nuremberg" (1961)' (*The Magnificent 60s*, 30 October 2023) <https://themagnificent60s.com/2023/10/30/behind-the-scenes-judgement-at-nuremberg-1961/> accessed 17 September 2025.

of the Nazi concentration camps, but the prosecutor made the link between these crimes and the camps by presenting the horrific images of the liberation of the Bergen-Belsen camp filmed by the British army.

Through its cinematic form, JUDGMENT AT NUREMBERG was instrumental in creating a general awareness that a fair trial is necessary in every circumstance. This became the normative legacy of Nuremberg: societies based on the belief that a fair process can bring truth and justice to light.[17] Without JUDGMENT AT NUREMBERG and the courtroom dramas that followed it, this awareness may not have been possible.

This returns us to one of our initial questions: when it comes to courtroom dramas, we can say quite firmly that *film is meeting law*, not the other way around.

2.4 Do Courtroom Dramas Have a Male Gaze?

For most of its history, the film industry has been dominated by men. It is therefore not surprising that courtroom dramas are dominated by a "male gaze"[18] too. JUDGMENT AT NUREMBERG is no exception: men wrote the script, directed the film, defined its visual concept and produced it. JUDGMENT AT NUREMBERG, and courtroom dramas in general, are part of a legacy that shaped the public understanding of the law, including the invisibility of women in court proceedings. The main characters were male and were played by male actors.[19] The male gaze places the male characters in a position of power, and women are portrayed as bearers rather than producers of meaning. "Men act, women appear."[20] Even actresses like Marlene Dietrich appear as witnesses or in supporting roles, not as lawyers or judges.

In film, men are almost always doing the *looking*, with women left in the weaker position of being *looked at*, as Alicia Malone puts it when she asks how

17 (n 12).

18 "The male gaze is a feminist theory that states that cinema narratives and portrayals of women in cinema are constructed in an objectifying and limiting manner to satisfy the psychological desires of men, and more broadly, of patriarchal society. [...] The theory, developed by filmmaker and theorist Laura Mulvey, considers the ways that three different perspectives, or looks, are combined in cinema to sustain a symbolic order that privileges men." See Igor Rodriguez and Deborah Teasley, 'Laura Mulvey's Male Gaze Theory | Definition & Examples' (*Study.com*, 21 November 2023) <https://study.com/academy/lesson/the-male-gaze-definition-theory.html> accessed 07 February 2025.

19 Laura Mulvey, 'Visual Pleasure and Narrative Cinema' (1975) 16 Screen 3, 6–18.

20 John Berger, *Ways of Seeing: based on the BBC television series with John Berger* (British Broadcasting Corporation and Penguin Books 1972) 47.

the world looks through female eyes.[21] It is only very recently that we observe a shift to a "female gaze", with female directors, female protagonists, female main actors and female perspectives on courtroom dramas which "broaden the spectrum [on] justice and injustice".[22] Examples are RBG (2018, Betsi West and Julie Cohen), a documentary on the career of the US Supreme Court Justice Ruth Bader Ginsburg; and GOD EXISTS, HER NAME IS PETRUNYA (2019, Teona Strugar Mitovski), which presents a young Macedonian woman throwing herself into a traditionally men-only ceremony, kicking up a ruckus and standing her ground in front of the police and church authorities.[23]

The French courtroom dramas SAINT OMER (2022, Alice Diop) and ANATOMY OF A FALL (2023, Justine Triet), discussed later in this volume,[24] feature stories about accused women whose personalities are complex and self-determined: they are active agents, not passive and certainly not submissive. Future courtroom dramas as well as other legal films may well continue to pursue such rich social, legal and gender perspectives.

3 Films on Legal Problems

3.1 In General

The second category concerns films on legal problems. Rather than depicting legal proceedings, films can have legal questions as their object. The theme of these films is not a legal proceeding, or the law itself, but a topic with a legal component, or a social problem for which the law could or should be a solution.

---

21 Alicia Malone, *The Female Gaze: Essential Movies Made by Women* (Mango Publishing Group 2022) 9.

22 "It's also not just women who are victims of the system; feminism is about equality for all. So, I think it is very important to broaden the spectrum when you talk about justice and injustice. When I write the scenarios, I always try to sort of show the variety and diversity of aspects of human existence." Bernadette Kolonko, 'Conversation with Teona Strugar Mitevska' in Bernadette Kolonko (ed), *Unsichtbares und Ungesagtes, 10 Female Feminist Gazes* (Schüren Verlag 2023) 187.

23 Lucie Bader and Walter Stoffel, 'Dieu existe, son nom est Petrunya (Gospod postoi, imeto i' e Petrunija) (2019)' in Matthieu Perrin (ed), *100 films à voir (ou à revoir) lorsque l'on est juriste* (Mare et Martin 2025) 385–387.

24 See Stefan Machura, 'The process is the punishment: Anatomy of a Fall in the context of the courtroom drama genre' (n 8) and Agata Fijalkowski, 'Anatomy of a Fall: Interpersonal Drama as a Courtroom Drama' (n 8).

When talking about films on legal problems, we move away from the similarities between law and cinema and come closer to the differences. Such legal films do not take place in the courtroom. Rather, they involve legal protagonists acting outside of the courtroom. Or they present dramas involving heroes (and anti-heroes) acting in a plot that makes visible a societal problem linked to law, but that is not resolved in a legal proceeding before the camera.

In the most direct form, these films present a problem which is caused by the law itself. The law is shown as the reason for malfunction and suffering or, worse still, as an instrument of oppression and the abuse of power. The films then advocate a change to the existing law, hence the term "advocacy films".

In a less direct form, a film on legal problems shows a social problem which a change in the law might solve; or the law being silent where it should be vocal; or law that is in place but poorly or not applied by the judges, the lawyers, the police or other legal protagonists. The film invokes the law as a positive, empowering instrument and is often, but not always, an advocacy film.

In this sense, advocacy films on legal problems illustrate a legal norm or a judicial decision that, in the filmmaker's view, should be changed. This is the reason why, like courtroom dramas, such films are often used in legal education. The illustration must be clear, but it can be made without mentioning the law or showing legal protagonists. It is sufficient that the structure underlying the social problem presented by the film is a legal one. The reference to law is indirect. Such films are films on legal problems in the same way as those that make no explicit reference to law.

Here is a list of examples for such films:
- The Wind that Shakes the Barley (2006, Ken Loach)
- The Secret in their Eyes (El secreto de sus ojos) (2009, José Campanella)
- Hot Coffee (2011, Susan Salandoff)
- The Other Son (Le fils de l'autre) (2012, Lorraine Lévy)
- The Big Short (2015, Adam McKay)
- The State vs Fritz Bauer (2015, Lars Kraume)
- The Danish Girl (2015, Tom Hooper)
- Beauty and the Dogs (La belle et la meute) (2016, Kaouther Ban Hania)
- Team Spirit (L'Outsider) (2016, Christophe Barratier)
- On the Basis of Sex (2018, Mimi Leather)
- RBG (2018, Betsy West and Julie Cohen)
- Official Secrets (2019, Gavin Hood)
- Oppenheimer (2023, Christopher Nolan); the film is discussed further in this volume[25]

25 See the contributions on OPPENHEIMER in this volume.

3.2 Advocacy Films and Documentaries

Advocacy films are often thought of in terms of documentary films. This is true and misleading at the same time. Such films do reveal social problems by identifying them in the real world and establishing ("documenting") them to show this part of the real world to the viewers, but there is no such thing as a simple observation or passive reflection of reality through film.

When watching a documentary, we may expect more authenticity, credibility, reliability, reality, truth and facts than in a fiction film, but even documentaries shape and interpret factual material. What characterizes a documentary film as opposed to a fiction film is less a matter of "reality, truth and facts" than cinematic technique: instead of actors playing the parts of the protagonist in contexts of the filmmaker's choice or design, real protagonists are shown in real surroundings.

Documentaries are not reproductions of the world. For the American film theoretician Bill Nichols, a documentary film "is a representation of the world we already occupy. It stands for a particular view of the world, one we may never have encountered before, even if the aspects of the world that is represented are familiar to us."[26]

3.3 Examples

The American documentary filmmaker Michael Moore, for example, presents a certain view of the real world when he examines it in BOWLING FOR COLUMBINE. The film explores American gun culture through the 1999 mass shooting at Colorado's Columbine High School, which left 15 dead and 24 injured. He seeks to explain how the massacre could have occurred, and why the number of gun deaths is so much higher in the US than in other countries. The audience is aware that some scenes are staged and happened before the shooting. This is what makes them so thought provoking. Moore's film won the Oscar for the Best Documentary Feature 2003 and had an international impact on debates about gun laws.

The story a documentary tells is always part fictional; it necessarily relies on the narrative conventions of film. Dramaturgical rules, the condensation of the story, rhythm or the audiovisual form are among the factors that determine the impact of documentary films as well. Sometimes documentarists even re-enact scenes that appear to be documentary. They depict real events that

26 Bill Nichols, *Representing Reality: Issues and Concepts in Documentary* (Indiana University Press 1991) 20.

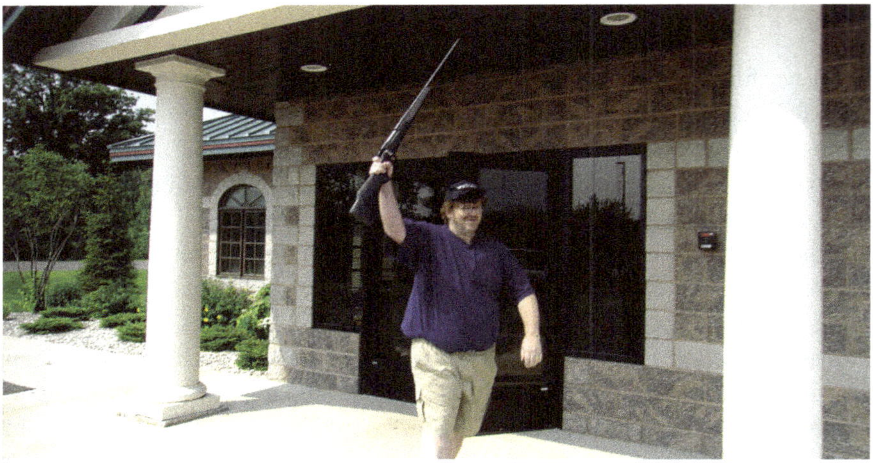

FIGURE 1.3 Michael Moore holding a gun (Film still by Moviestore Collection)

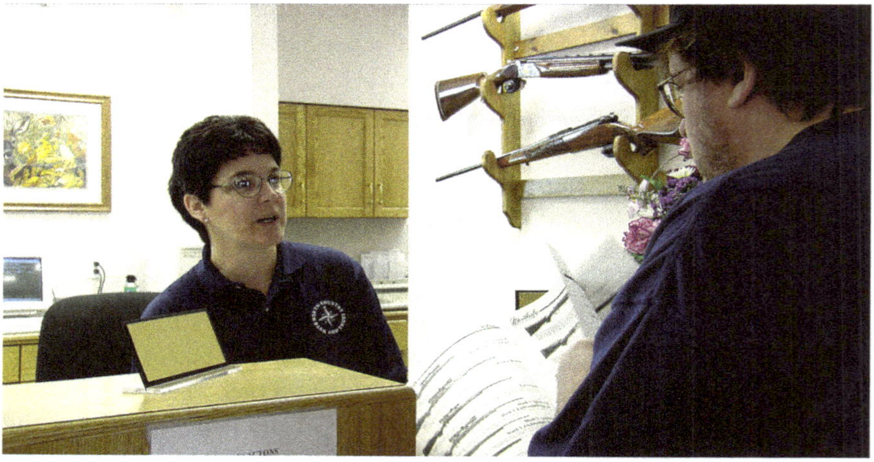

FIGURE 1.4 Michael Moore in a gun shop (Film still by Moviestore Collection)

have happened in the past, or events that cannot be filmed on the spot, in a way that makes them look as if they were filmed as they unfolded.

Another example is THE CLEANERS (2018, Hans Block and Moritz Riesewieck). The film unveils the shadow industry of digital censorship in Manila. The two German filmmakers do not claim to be objective: they take a partisan view and advocate for greater awareness of their theme. The protagonists are content moderators who work to remove thousands of incredibly

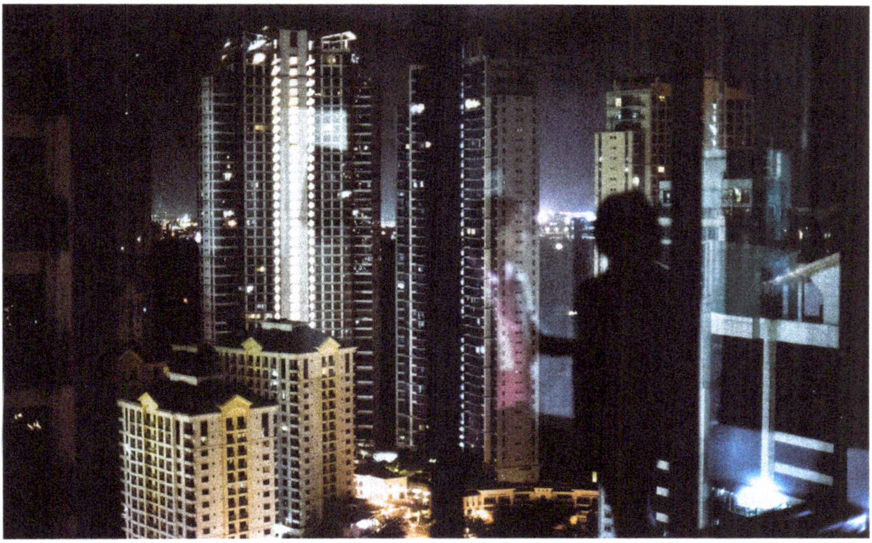

FIGURE 1.5 Content moderator working at night (Film still Gebrueder Beetz Filmproduktion)

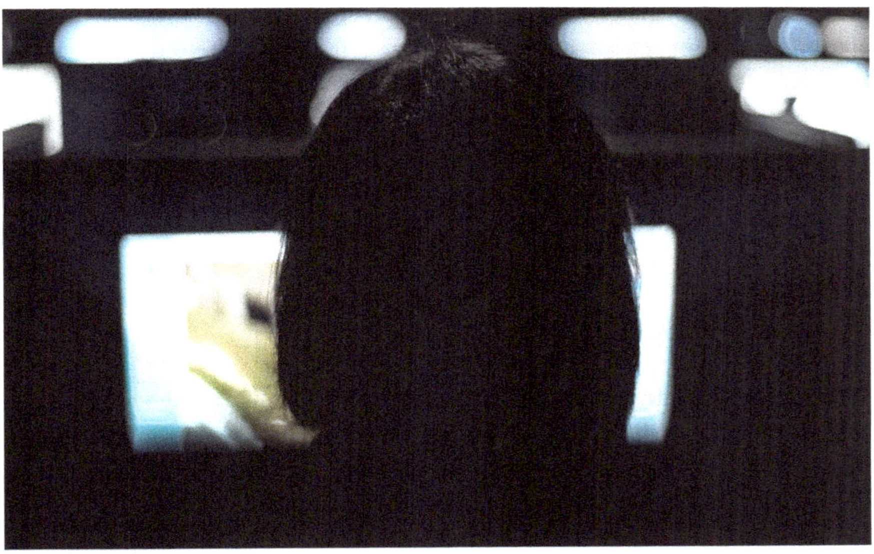

FIGURE 1.6 Content moderator watching the screen (Film still Gebrueder Beetz Filmproduktion)

cruel photos from Facebook and become traumatised in the process. The portrait of the workers shows harsh working situations in a hidden world. Since the filmmakers were unable to shoot the scenes at the real workplace, the filming was done in an ordinary office located elsewhere. The filmmakers took advantage of this restraint and staged these parts of the film in a style reminiscent of a film noir thriller.

"The content moderators deserve our empathy," commented a film critic from the movie journal Variety. "Yet, when (the film directors) Riesewieck and Block follow them home, lingering over footage of fish guts and garbage dumps, the film also seems to question what gives these poor people in this poor country the right to rule the global conversation."[27] The film presents a partisan view and the documentary style is part of its advocacy orientation.

Hot Coffee (2011, Susan Saladoff) is a further example. The movie deals with a famous American case in which a jury awarded punitive damages amounting to several million dollars to a customer for having spilled a hot coffee purchased at a McDonald's drive-in on her clothes. The film shows that although this verdict was overturned on appeal, the coffee had indeed been served at a temperature likely to cause third degree burns to the victim; McDonald's had instructed its franchisees to do so despite their knowing about the dangers of serving coffee at such high temperature; and that the victim—an elderly lady—did not drink her coffee while driving but as a passenger in a halted car pulled over to the side by her nephew. The film argues that the first instance jury verdict was used by a powerful campaigning lobby to discredit the punitive damages regime. The film thus puts an event of the real world (here even a clearly legal world) in a filmed context and tells a story quite different to that promoted by critics of the punitive damage regime. Does it document the reality, or one which the filmmaker chose to show, or both?

3.4 Advocacy Films and Fiction Films

Fiction films can do much the same with other cinematic means. Here the story is invented and played out by actors, rather than "real" protagonists in "real" situations. This presents the filmmaker with more possibilities. The invented story is not limited to social situations in the outside world, but may

27 Amy Nicholson, 'Sundance Film Review: 'The Cleaners' (*Variety*, 24 January 2018) <https://variety.com/2018/film/reviews/the-cleaners-review-1202673932/> accessed 06 March 2025.

also depict inner worlds. Although not limited to their depiction, fiction films are particularly well suited to showing such inner realities.

Many fiction films are "based on true events". The fiction does not merely *select* the parts of reality to be shown, but it creates the world that will be filmed and seen on the screen. It uses a streamlined narrative that fits the purpose perfectly. It is obvious that this technique allows filmmakers to show encounters with law when they choose to do so.

Let us take the films of Jean-Pierre and Luc Dardenne as examples. The Dardenne brothers began with documentaries such as THE SONG OF THE NIGHTINGALE (Le chant du Rossignol, 1978). Their earlier films were strongly rooted in social realism, but the filmmakers turned to fiction in the mid-1980s. They remained committed to making advocacy films, but found that fiction gave them better means to depict "true" reality.[28]

The fictional drama TWO DAYS, ONE NIGHT (2014) is an excellent example. In this film, the Dardenne brothers tell the story of a Belgium factory worker called Sandra. She is laid off after the work assigned to her is distributed to her co-workers in exchange for a EUR 1,000 bonus. Her boss gives her the "chance" to convince her colleagues to renounce to their bonuses, thus allowing her to be re-engaged. She has a weekend (two days, one night) in which to meet her colleagues—twelve in number—and try to win them over one by one.

The story is invented and played by established actors. This allowed the Dardenne brothers to base their fiction on the structure of a jury trial. Their script had been inspired by Sidney Lumet's 12 ANGRY MEN, which also concerned "a process of going to see people to try and change their minds". The jury they designed is composed of co-workers acting in their personal environment, rather than a courtroom or a legal process, but they still reached a "verdict" of sorts. The fiction became particularly real.

3.5 THE SECRET IN THEIR EYES and the Fight for Justice

THE SECRET IN THEIR EYES—El Secreto de sus Ojos—(2009, Juan José Campanella) offers a particularly telling example. The film is a thriller and a melodrama. It is one of the most successful Argentinian movies and winner of the Oscar for the Best Foreign Language Film in 2010. It tells the story of a retired legal counsellor (Ricardo Darín) who writes a novel hoping to find

28 Jean-Pierre Dardenne and Luc Dardenne, *Dardenne par Dardenne: Entretiens avec Michel Simon* (Éditions Le Bord de l'Eau—Collection La Muette 2016).

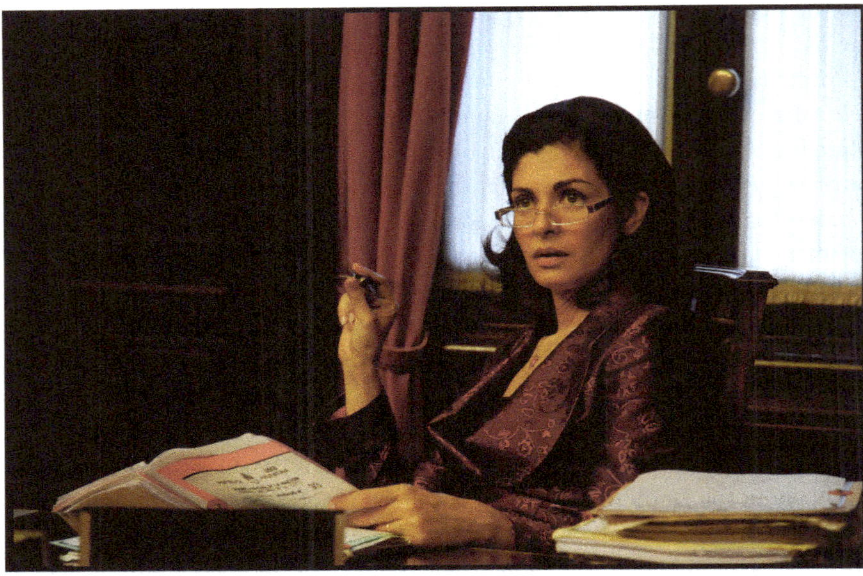

FIGURE 1.7 Judge Irene Hastings (Soledad Villamil) at her desk (Film still by Moviestore Collection)

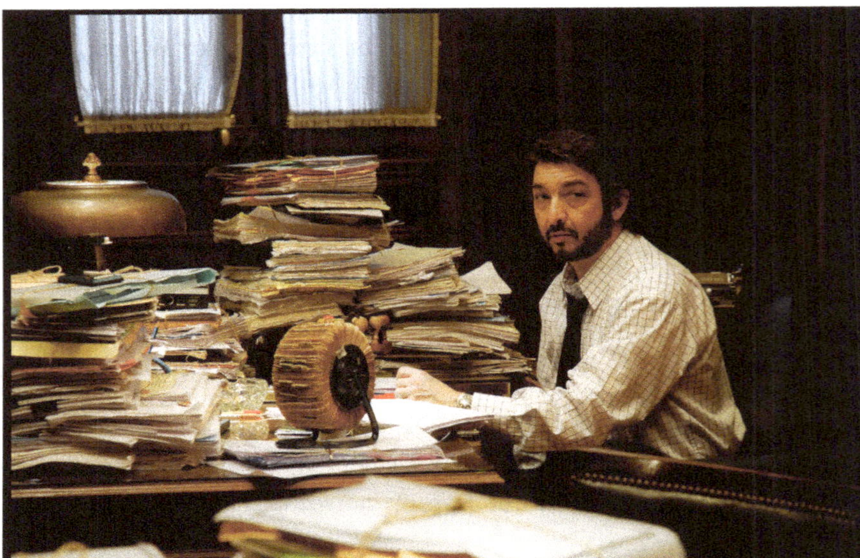

FIGURE 1.8 Legal consular Esposito (Ricardo Darín) in his office (Film still by Moviestore Collection)

closure for one of his past unresolved homicide cases and his unrequited love for his superior—both of which still haunt him decades later.

We experience the story through the eyes of the main character. The eyes have a key dramatic function in the narration and drive the action. Benjamin Esposito, a former legal counsellor worked routinely at the Court when he met Irene (Soledad Villamil), his new boss, and first saw her eyes. He wants to find the perpetrator of a femicide after having been called to the site of the crime and seeing the raped and brutalised body of the victim. The key element in his search will lie in the gaze of the suspect Gomez, a former admirer of the victim, who is eventually found and sentenced. But after the conviction, the regime in Argentina changes. The convicted murderer is released from prison and becomes a collaborator of the regime. Esposito and Irene are shocked when they find out and report to the head of the prosecutor's office what they have seen and ask for the file to be re-opened. The head laughs at them: "It is another time—forget about Gomez!"

Decades later, when Esposito writes his novel, he recalls how he found Gomez, now a prisoner held by the husband of the victim in the dark cellar of an isolated house. And he sees Irene again, the woman who was then his boss, with whom he fell in love without admitting it. The investigation into the case revisits Argentinian history, while also becoming a personal journey into Benjamin's past, his encounter with Irene and the way the two survived the dark years of the dictatorship. Benjamin was looking for (his personal) truth and for justice (in his legal case). The eyes drive the drama, and they look for justice (and for love).

In the middle of this journey, the military launched its coup and took over the government. The law was no longer effective: its texts had hardly changed—rape and murder continued to be crimes—but its enforcement had altered. The murderer was set free, the judges had to hide. The legal protagonists faced a choice. Irene kept her job and arranged herself with the new situation. Esposito was sent far away. Only the husband of the murdered woman continued as a private judge and prison guard.

From an empowering instrument the law became an instrument of state bullying and even terror in the hands, amongst others, of the suspect Gomez, supported by the state when this serves its interests. At the same time, the court system could no longer be trusted. It was left to private power to arrive at private justice on a small scale, through the victim's husband. The film shows private justice as answer to the perverted instrument of power. But this comes at the price of emotional self-destruction of the victim.

Would the course of action have been different if the legal protagonists had openly resisted? Or were they wise to remain in place and do their best on a personal level, possibly at the price of helping to sustain the regime by collaboration (like the judges who were judged at Nuremberg)? Can the fight for justice only be won at the expense of emotional self-sacrifice? Does this mean that personal happiness can only be achieved when the fight for justice is abandoned?

The legal problem in the foreground is presented by the femicide. It is resolved in the end, but privately. The problem in the background is the role of lawyers, when democracy and the rule of law are abolished. Justice may still be done, but not *by* the legal system. The film is *on* a legal problem.

This allows us to return again to the initial question. When it comes to films on legal problems, we must say both that *film is meeting law*, and also that *law is meeting film*.

4 Films Mirroring Law

4.1 In General

This brings us to the last category, films mirroring law. Here we find films which challenge the law and its protagonists but do not appear to deal with legal issues at all with legal issues. Unlike advocacy films, they are not promoting the just resolution of a specific legal problem.

In films mirroring law, the law forms the background against which the plot of the film evolves. The background does not attract the main attention of the viewer. It is just there, untold and barely visible at first sight, becoming apparent only rarely, e.g. when the law eventually changes. But its discrete character makes it particularly powerful. It determines the perception of the law and of the legal professionals even when the film does not talk about either of them. It may be that the law is silent although it should talk, or that the law makes a stand, but takes the wrong side, as it is the case in advocacy films. But here, we are looking at what the film tells us about society's views of law and lawyers, independently of the observation of a courtroom drama or the resolution of a specific legal problem.

Such films say much about the ways in which the law and its protagonists are seen by non-lawyers and the society at large. When we consider such films as lawyers, we are observing ourselves in the mirror of what the films convey about the law and the legal professionals. Films mirroring law are non-legal films on the surface, but become legal films when we see and feel what lies under the surface. This can give us many and sometimes unexpected insights into the unspoken assumptions that underlie the legal fabric of society.[29] It is good for aspiring lawyers and established professionals alike to confront themselves with such questions.

If we are attentive, we will find numerous examples for films mirroring law:

- Citizen Kane (1941, Orson Welles)
- The Man Who Shot Liberty Valance (1962, John Ford)
- Thelma & Louise (1991, Ridley Scott)
- A Separation (2011, Asghar Farhadi)
- The Circle (Der Kreis) (2014, Stefan Haupt)
- Two Nights, One Day (Deux nuits, un jour) (2014, Jean-Pierre et Luc Dardenne)
- Wajib (2016, Annemarie Jacir)
- The Death and Life of Otto Bloom (2016, Cris Jones)
- Three Billboards Outside Ebbing, Missouri (2017, Martin Mc Donagh)
- BlacKkKlansman (2018, Spike Lee)
- Cold War (2018, Pawel Pawlikowski)
- Parasite (2019, Bong Joon Ho)
- Burning Days (Kurak Günler) (2022, Emin Alper)

Looking at the length and the diversity of this list, we are tempted to paraphrase Ross D. Levi's point that if "legal cinema shows us anything, it is that law is everywhere",[30] and say instead: "If **non**-legal cinema shows us anything, it is that law is everywhere."

4.2 Examples

One example is the film The Circle (Der Kreis) (2014, Stefan Haupt), which shows the life of homosexuals in Zurich in the fifties. At this time, the criminal prohibition of homosexuality was still in force in Germany, but had been abolished in Switzerland in 1942. The film tells the story of the circle, a union formed by homosexuals in Zurich, which soon became a meeting point for the homosexuals of neighbouring Germany too. It shows the success of the circle, its meetings and joyous, colourful parties as well as the oppression the young organisation faced in the form of administrative harassment and social disapproval.

There is an obvious legal connotation in the film with respect to the provisions of criminal law. But these provisions are not the main topic: the film

29 See contributions on Burning Days in this volume.

30 Ross D. Levi, *The Celluloid Courtroom: A History of Legal Cinema* (Praeger 2005) 127.

barely mentions them. Instead, the story is about the life of the circle, given the fact that homosexuality was not illegal in Zurich but was so in other parts of the region, and the increasing administrative and social harassment its members faced. The film shows the mixture of soft administrative repression and the sense of social disapproval, still strong at this time, and looks at how the circle deals with these mainly non legal challenges. But at the same time, the film shows how people, including the police, react when the circle reminds them of the legality of their association. They respect the law, albeit grudgingly, as soon as the members of the circle insist on it.

Another example is THREE BILLBOARDS OUTSIDE OF EBBING, MISSOURI (2017, Martin Mc Donagh). The film tells of the desperate situation of a woman (Frances McDormand) whose daughter was raped and murdered when returning home in the small town of Ebbing. The mother fights day and night to get the local police to conduct a thorough investigation. She pins up huge billboards on the highway at the entry of the town, naming and shaming the officers involved. Despite all her efforts, which almost ruin her life, she does not really succeed at the end. But she does get a glimpse of hope when she boards the car together with one the police officers, now on her side, in order to find the presumed culprit in another State.

What the film shows, indirectly, about law is that even when legal norms are in place, their enforcement can be weak because of social and racial prejudice by the police, lack of courage and engagement, or understaffing and insufficient means. The film suggests that if you want to enforce the law, you must put the gun into the truck of the car and see to it yourself. The citizen is the enforcer. The mirror shows a certain image of law enforcement in the society at large. THREE BILLBOARDS OUTSIDE EBBING, MISSOURI echoes THE MAN WHO SHOT LIBERTY VALANCE (1962, John Ford), in which justice had to be enforced by the local cowboy hero, because the idealistic future senator, preaching "statehood" in the Far West, was unable to do it himself.

4.3 PARASITE or Why Is the Law Silent?

Let us look more particularly at another well-known international film, PARASITE (2019, Bong Joon Ho). The film shows the lucky upper-class Park family living in luxury, and the unfortunate, struggling lower-class Kim family living in a tiny and dark apartment.

One of the members of the Kim family obtains a teaching job in the rich household and soon manages to get domestic jobs there for all other family members as well. The Kim family succeeds in infiltrating the lifestyle of

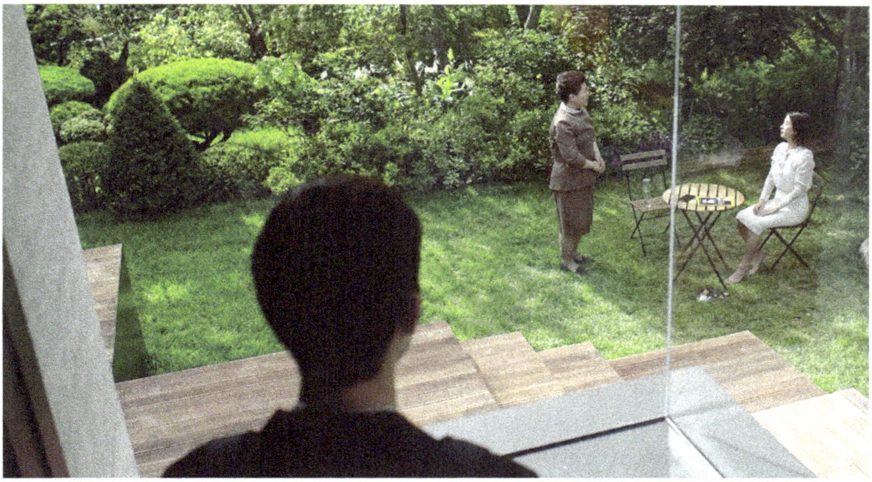

FIGURE 1.9 View from the Park's house down to the garden (Film still by BFA / CJ Entertainment)

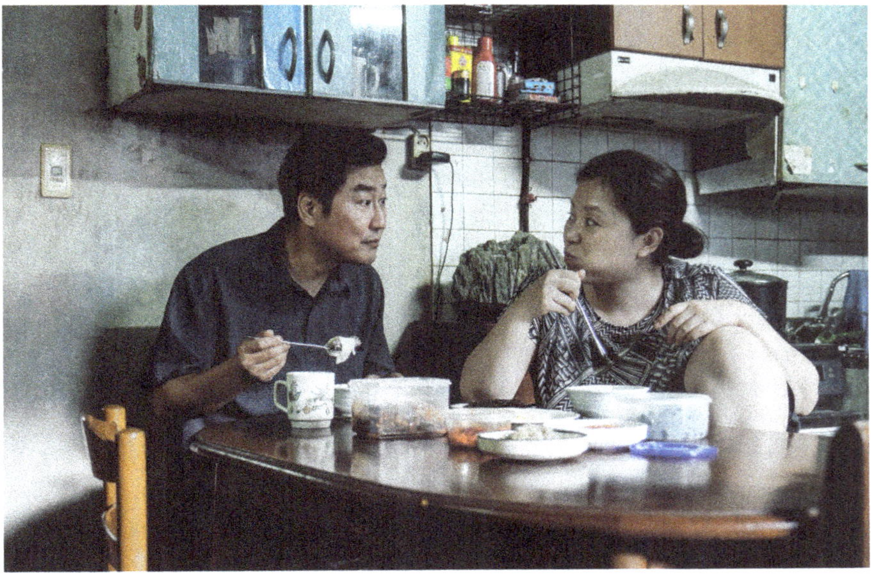

FIGURE 1.10 The Kim's parents eat in their apartment (Film still by Landmark Media)

the rich by finding their way into these positions (like "parasites"), but only after having got rid of those in place before them, and at the price of constant humiliation. Greed and discrimination threaten the newly formed, apparently symbiotic relationship between the wealthy Park family and the destitute Kim clan. This leads to a cataclysmic culmination that destroys them all.

The movie illustrates the inequality in the society in clear visual terms. While the rich Park family resides in a beautiful mansion, the Kim family lives in a dark semi-basement dwelling. The set design as well as the lighting distinguish the two worlds in a subtle way. Even in the shots themselves, the staging is marked by physical lines formed by objects like furniture, windows and the like.

The society is presented as dynamic, forward looking, tolerant towards differences, and aspirational. But social mobility often remains a dream (revolt, dreaming of good marriage) or leads to the kind of cataclysm shown in the film.

The law itself is never mentioned in the film. It seems to be completely absent. In fact, however, the situation is supported by legal rules, framed by an apparent absence of a social security net and of protection against arbitrary layoffs. The lack of rules is part of a legal order. By contrast, notions of property and theft are present. The Park family lives in a luxurious mansion within locked doors, protected by surveillance systems. The Kim family is tapping the mobile network of the neighbours, they live in a constant awareness and fear to be discovered. They are intruders while they try to appear as benevolent friends. At the same time, they know that they are likely to be protected in their wealth should they succeed in attaining it.

Films mirroring the law are often the most intriguing: what makes the law, or the lawyers, like this? Why is the law silent? Why do the lawyers not protest? These questions reveal an attitude towards law, in part of disapproval but also of respect if pressed. This attitude is not the topic of the film, but it is what the film mirrors.

The questions are fundamental, perhaps more philosophical than legal. They may be intellectually and emotionally more satisfying too, as BURNING DAYS (2022, Emin Alper) and several of the aforementioned films showed.[31]

These films are not primarily legal films, but become so when they make an implicit invitation to lawyers to step back for a moment and ask, where are we here? This may allow us to give an answer to our initial question. When it comes to films mirroring law, we might say that the law and the lawyers take the initiative of interrogating themselves, that the *law is meeting film*. And as a parallel movement, the filmmakers react, sometimes anticipate, and turn the mirror to another spot. It becomes a mutual encounter.

31 See contributions on BURNING DAYS in this volume.

5 Conclusion

After an overview of a series of law films with respect to the questions "Who meets Whom" when we are talking about "Law meets Film", three things stand out.

We saw that legal films can give us information about the credibility and fairness that a society attributes to legal methods of conflict resolution. In many films since the end of the Second World War, the rule of law and procedural fairness were the paradigm. As lawyers, we take this as a compliment. This is surely the reason why courtroom dramas are often used as illustrations in legal education.

Legal films can also give us insight into social and economic problems that matter in a society and for which people expect better legal solutions, or legal solutions at all. In this sense, legal films sharpen our problem awareness. They may even prompt action by lawmakers, judges or attorneys. We can call this a sociological approach.

Legal films can also finally confront us with the importance that a society attaches to law, especially when the films do not talk explicitly about law. Looking at the films closely, lawyers and law students will be obliged to take note of the credibility (or the lack thereof) that judges, lawyers and other legal professionals have in society. We ask ourselves about the role and the function of law and lawyers, in what we may call a philosophical approach.

We have presented the films in three categories that correspond to these approaches: *Films on legal procedures* (*courtroom dramas*), *Films on legal problems*, and *Films mirroring law*. Categories are not an end in themselves, but they can serve as tools. The intellectual tool associated with films on legal procedure is "observation". The one associated with films on legal problems is "discussion". And the tool associated with films mirroring law is "interrogation".

We find these distinctions useful, but we are aware that the categories can be very simplifying too. For sure, we always look at the same cathedral.[32] Yet the morning, midnight and sunset lights give a different view of this very same cathedral. The answer to our initial question therefore is not *Law meets Film*, or *Film meets Law*. It is both, to different degrees. But above all, it is an intellectual, artistic and emotional stimulation: a mutual challenge.

32 Reference to the different views of the Rouen Cathedral, painted by Claude Monet.

References

Bader L. and Stoffel W., 'Dieu existe, son nom est Petrunya (Gospod postoi, imeto i' e Petrunija) (2019)' in Matthieu Perrin (ed), *100 films à voir (ou à revoir) lorsque l'on est juriste* (Mare et Martin 2025).

Bergman P. and Asimow M., *Reel Justice: The Courtroom Goes to the Movies* (Andrews and McMeel 1996).

Berger J., *Ways of Seeing: based on the BBC television series with John Berger* (British Broadcasting Corporation and Penguin Books 1972).

Black D.A., *Law in Film: Resonance and Representation* (University of Illinois Press 1999).

Bronfen E., 'Oppenheimer: The Cold War on Trial' in Gianmaria Ajani, Lucie Bader and Walter Stoffel (eds), *Law meets Film: Taxonomy of an encounter* (Brill 2026).

Dardenne J.-P. and Dardenne L., *Dardenne par Dardenne: Entretiens avec Michel Simon* (Éditions Le Bord de l'Eau—Collection La Muette 2016).

de Ravel d'Esclapon T., *La justice au cinéma* (Dalloz 2023).

Fijalkowski A., 'Anatomy of a Fall: Interpersonal Drama as a Courtroom Drama' in Gianmaria Ajani, Lucie Bader and Walter Stoffel (eds), *Law meets Film: Taxonomy of an encounter* (Brill 2026).

Greenfield S., Osborn G. and Robson P., *Film and the Law* (2nd edn, Hart Publishing 2010).

Hannan B., 'Behind the Scenes: "Judgement at Nuremberg" (1961)' (*The Magnificent 60s*, 30 October 2023) <https://themagnificent60s.com/2023/10/30/behind-the-scenes-judgement-at-nuremberg-1961/> accessed 17 September 2025.

Kolonko B., 'Conversation with Teona Strugar Mitevska' in Bernadette Kolonko (ed), *Unsichtbares und Ungesagtes, 10 Female Feminist Gazes* (Schüren Verlag 2023).

Kozinski A., 'Foreword' in Paul Bergman and Michael Asimow (eds), *Reel Justice: The Courtroom Goes to the Movies* (Andrews and McMeel 1996).

Levi R.D., *The Celluloid Courtroom: A History of Legal Cinema* (Praeger 2005).

Machura S., 'The process is the punishment: Anatomy of a Fall in the context of the courtroom drama genre' in Gianmaria Ajani, Lucie Bader and Walter Stoffel (eds), *Law meets Film: Taxonomy of an encounter* (Brill 2026).

Malone A., *The Female Gaze: Essential Movies Made by Women* (Mango Publishing Group 2022).

Mezey N., 'The Fragility of Law & the Politics of Public Memory in Oppenheimer' in Gianmaria Ajani, Lucie Bader and Walter Stoffel (eds), *Law meets Film: Taxonomy of an encounter* (Brill 2026).

Monaco J., *How to read a film: The World of Movies, Media and Multimedia* (3rd edn, Oxford University Press USA 2000).

Mulvey L., 'Visual Pleasure and Narrative Cinema' (1975) 16 Screen 3.

'Narrative film' (*Wikipedia*) <https://en.wikipedia.org/wiki/Narrative_film> accessed 06 March 2025.

Nichols B., *Representing Reality: Issues and Concepts in Documentary* (Indiana University Press 1991).

Nicholson A., 'Sundance Film Review: 'The Cleaners' (*Variety*, 24 January 2018) <https://variety.com/2018/film/reviews/the-cleaners-review-1202673932/> accessed 06 March 2025.

Odermatt F., *Das Recht im filmischen Spiegel—Verführung, Mythos und Performanz* (Nomos 2023).

Papke D.R., 'Law, Cinema, and Ideology: Hollywood Legal Films of the 1950s.' (2001) 48 UCLA L. Rev. 1473.

Robson P. and Randall M., 'The Future of Law and Film In Context' in Gianmaria Ajani, Lucie Bader and Walter Stoffel (eds), *Law meets Film: Taxonomy of an encounter* (Brill 2026).

Rodriguez I. and Teasley D., 'Laura Mulvey's Male Gaze Theory | Definition & Examples' (*Study.com*, 21 November 2023) <https://study.com/academy/lesson/the-male-gaze-definition-theory.html> accessed 07 February 2025.

Spina F., 'The Vulnerability of the Judiciary and the Fragility of the Rule of Law. A Socio-Legal Interpretation of Emin Alper's Burning Days' in Gianmaria Ajani, Lucie Bader and Walter Stoffel (eds), *Law meets Film: Taxonomy of an encounter* (Brill 2026).

Stiglegger M., *Ritual & Verführung, Spektakel und Sinnlichkeit im Film* (Bertz und Fischer 2006).

Stiglegger M., 'Die Seduktionstheorie des Films' in Markus S. Kleiner and Michael Rappe (eds), *Methoden der Populärkulturforschung: Interdisziplinäre Perspektiven auf Film, Fernsehen, Musik, Internet und Computerspiele* (LIT Verlag 2012).

Stoffel W. and Bader L., 'Jugement à Nuremberg (Judgement at Nuremberg)' in Matthieu Perrin (ed), *100 films à voir (ou à revoir) lorsque l'on est juriste* (Mare et Martin 2025).

Université Fribourg (Switzerland), 'Archives Recht im Film / Le droit dans le cinéma / Law in the movies' (*Université Fribourg*) <https://events.unifr.ch/droitcinema/de/archiv/> accessed 27 February 2025.

Filmography (Films Cited in this Essay)

Anatomy of a Fall (Anatomie d'une Chute), France, 2023, director: Justine Triet.

Anatomy of a Murder, USA, 1959, director: Otto Preminger.

A Separation, Iran, 2011, director: Asghar Farhadi.

Beauty and the Dogs (La belle et la meute), Tunisia, 2017, director: Kaouther Ban Hania.

Blackkklansman, USA, 2018, director: Spike Lee.

Bowling for Columbine, USA, 2002, director: Michael Moor.

Burning Days (Kurak Günler), Turkey, 2022, director: Emin Alper.

Citizen Kane, USA, 1941, director: Orson Welles.

Cold War, Poland/France/Great Britain, 2018, director: Pawel Pawlikowski.

Cleveland V. Wall Street, Switzerland, 2010, director: Jean-Stéphane Bron.

Denial, Great Britain/USA, 2016, director: Mick Jackson.

God Exists, Her Name is Petrunya (Gospod postoi, imeto i' e Petrunija), North Macedonia, 2019, director: Teona Strugar Mitevska.

Hot Coffee, USA, 2011, director: Susan Saladoff.

Judgment at Nuremberg, USA, 1961, director: Stanley Kramer.

Juror #2, USA, 2024, director: Clint Eastwood.

Official Secrets, Great Britain, 2019, director: Gavin Hood.

On the Basis of Sex, USA, 2018, director: Mimi Leather.

Oppenheimer, USA/Great Britain, 2023, director: Christopher Nolan.

Parasite, South Korea, 2019, director: Bong Joon Ho.

RBG, USA, 2018, directors: Betsy West and Julie Cohen.

Saint Omer, France, 2022, director: Alice Diop.

Team Spirit (L'Outsider), France, 2016, director: Christophe Barratier.

The Big Short, USA, 2015, director: Adam McKay.

The Children Act, Great Britain/USA, 2017, director: Richard Eyre.

The Circle (Der Kreis), Switzerland, 2014, director: Stefan Haupt.

The Cleaners (Im Schatten der Netzwelt), Germany, 2018, directors: Hans Block and Moritz Riesewieck.

The Danish Girl, Great Britain/USA, 2015, director: Tom Hooper.

The Death and Life of Otto Bloom, Australia, 2016, director: Cris Jones.

The Girl with a Bracelet (La fille au bracelet), France, 2019, director: Stéphane Demoustier.

The Law in these Parts, Israel/USA/Germany, 2011, director: Ra'anan Alexandrowicz.

Thelma and Louise, USA, 1991, director: Ridley Scott.

The Man Who Shot Liberty valance, USA, 1962, director: John Ford.

The Other Son (Le fils de l'autre), France, 2012, director: Lorraine Lévy.

The Secret in their Eyes (El Secreto de sus Ojos), Argentina, 2009, director: José Campanella.

The Seventh Juror (Le Septième Juré), France, 1962, director: Georges Lauthner.

The Song of the Nightingale (Le Chant du Rossignol), Belgium, 1978, directors: Jean-Pierre and Luc Dardenne.

The State vs Fritz Bauer (Der Staat gegen Fritz Bauer), Germany, 2015, director: Lars Kraume.

The Wind that Shakes the Barley, Great Britain, 2006, director: Ken Loach.

THREE BILLBOARDS OUTSIDE EBBING, MISSOURI, USA, 2017, director: Martin McDonagh.

TWELVE ANGRY MEN, USA, 1957, director: Sydney Lumet.

TWO DAYS, ONE NIGHT (Deux Jours, Une Nuit), France, 2014, directors: Jean-Pierre and Luc Dardenne.

WAJIB, Palestine, 2016, director: Annemarie Jacir.

PART 1

Films on Legal Procedures / Courtroom Dramas

CHAPTER 2

The Process Is the Punishment

Anatomy of a Fall in the Context of the Courtroom Drama Genre

Stefan Machura

1 Setting the Scene

The German daily newspaper "Frankfurter Allgemeine Zeitung" has a regular cartoon "Glückskind" (which translates as "lucky child") by the artist Flix. The main characters are a writer, who has moved with his daughter to the countryside, and a streetwise three-legged racoon. The headstrong child lives in a world of her own and has to be reined in or sometimes just advised by the father or her animal friend. The father suffers from severe writer's block and often sits in despair over his laptop. The acclaimed film Anatomie d'une Chute aka Anatomy of a Fall (2023),[1] directed by Justine Triet, has two parents who are writers, a visually impaired son, and his guide dog. Still, the father suffers from writer's block and it was his decision to give up city-life. In a chalet high up in the French Alps, he hopes to find the peace he as author needs. The addition of a mother and wife who is a complicated character adds a different dynamic, not contained in the German cartoon. Not only is she a successful author in contrast to her husband but as a German she feels isolated in the French countryside and deeply resents where she now must live.[2] By the time the film starts, the marriage is at a dead end.

The wife's, Sandra Voiter's, success formula as an author is to take her own challenging life history as material for her books. Her husband, Samuel Maleski, the despairing writer, and otherwise a lecturer, is not able to support the family enough to pay for their lifestyle, especially the cost of renovating their old house. He is forced to work on it himself. Bankruptcy threatens and

---

1 The Internet Movie Database lists 127 prizes, including an Oscar for the best original screen play for writers Justine Triet and Arthur Harari. See 'Anatomy of a Fall awards' (*IMDb*, 2025) <https://www.imdb.com/title/tt17009710/awards/> accessed 27 August 2025.

2 As Agata Fijalkowski discusses in her chapter in this volume, the remote location and the high alpine winter snow surrounding the protagonists during the first part of the film add an atmosphere of cold isolation to many of the scenes.

© 2026 THE AUTHOR(S) | HTTPS://DOI.ORG/10.1163/9789004761704-003

puts additional strain on the marriage. Yet, the alienation between the couple has started much earlier, since when Samuel blames himself for an accident which robbed their son Daniel of his eyesight. Sandra Voiter is the stronger character of the two. Actress Sandra Hüller, for whom the role was written, describes her as "multi-facetted, exact, humorous, hard and not excusing herself".[3] Against Samuel's wishes, Sandra only speaks English with her son, not French. He accuses her of having stolen the key idea of his book project for one of hers. He states to have been "plundered and cheated on".[4] Importantly, Samuel feels that Sandra has thrust the mundane chores of parenting and household work on him. They are no longer sharing the same bedroom and Sandra had sought comfort previously in a lesbian affair. She is drinking heavily and past experiences with drugs are mentioned. Arguments between the parents can turn into violence.

The constellation is set for a serious drama. One day, a female student visits to interview Sandra who, under the influence of alcohol, is talking to her in flirtatious manner. "What do you want to know?" are among the first words heard in the film, the perfect headline for it according to Sandra Hüller, playing the writer.[5] Samuel, working in the attic, starts playing a misogynistic song so loud that conversation becomes impossible and the guest leaves prematurely. The camera then shows Daniel preparing his guide dog Snoop for a walk in the snow and leaving. When he returns, he finds his father lifeless in a puddle of blood in front of the house. This is the setting for a film in the "whodunit" genre. Did Samuel commit suicide under the impression of entrapment in a hopeless situation? Or did his wife shove him out of the attic window? There's a head wound, and the blood splatter on the shed roof under the window forms a suspicious pattern.

On one level ANATOMY OF A FALL is a whodunit and the audience is left with no clear indication as to Sandra's guilt or innocence. Yet, following the proven formula to mix genres, ANATOMY OF A FALL also is a courtroom drama.

---

3 'Die vielen Gesichter der Sandra Hüller. Dokumentation' (*ARD Mediathek*) <https://www.ardmediathek.de/video/dokus-und-reportagen-im-br/die-vielen-gesichter-der-sandra-hueller/br-fernsehen/Y3JpZDovL2JyLmRlL3ZpZGVvLzFhZjFjNWRhLWEwMzItNDBlOC04OTVjLTU2MzRlMWQzMzNkZg> accessed 28 July 2024.

4 Sandra's defence uses the "denial of injury" version of Sykes and Matza's techniques of neutralisation: ideas are free-flowing, anyhow, Sam could have used the idea again etc. See Gresham M. Sykes and David Matza, 'Techniques of neutralization: A theory of delinquency' in Delos H. Kelly (ed), *Criminal behavior: Readings in criminology* (St. Martin's Press 1980) 217–222.

5 Film at Lincoln Centre, 'Justine Triet, Sandra Hüller & Arthur Harari on Anatomy of a Fall | NYFF61' (*YouTube*, 10 October 2023) <https://www.youtube.com/watch?v=IvEhmdPgCgM> accessed 10 August 2024.

Director and script writer Justine Triet wanted to produce one and her favourite courtroom film is none other than Otto Preminger's classic ANATOMY OF A MURDER (USA, 1959).[6] In a courtroom drama, the story finds its solution in a trial. It does not, though, imply that the crime is truly solved, including solved to the satisfaction of the audience. This not the case in both, Preminger's and Triet's film.[7] According to Asimow and Silbey[8] ANATOMY OF A MURDER "hints that a killer avoided legal punishment and that an adulterous spouse got away with her transgression". In ANATOMY OF A FALL, lingering suspicion is left. But, if in doubt, the jury (or the judge) needs to acquit—in dubio pro reo.

2 Trials and Storytelling

The family's house is essentially a building site which can be taken as a visual metaphor for many aspects of the film, including the pair's marriage. But it also highlights the métier of the two authors putting together stories. It alludes as well to the prosecutor forming a condemning line of evidence for his accusation, and for Sandra and her legal team's attempt to counter with their own convincing arguments. As her lawyer, Sandra chose Maître Vincent Renci. They have a past together and it is unclear if they once were just acquaintances or more. From their dialogue, it suggests that he fell for her but was not so special for Sandra. In a key scene, Vincent corrects Sandra: this is about "what we can defend", which is a fall from the balcony to the shed roof, hence the head wound. The irregular blood splatter remains a challenge and needs an expert's explanation. Then: why was her arm bruised? Has there been a fight? Sandra denies that. Suicide is the best defence that is open, declares Vincent. A sound story must be presented to the court. Vincent explains:

> I don't give a fuck about what is reality. You need to start seeing yourself the way others are going to perceive you. A trial is not about the truth. It is about

---

6 Yannick Vely, 'Justine Triet: "Pour 'Anatomie d'une chute', j'ai été fascinée par l'affaire Amanda Knox"' (*Paris Match*, 24 May 2023) <https://www.parismatch.com/culture/cinema/justine-triet-pour-anatomie-dune-chute-jai-ete-fascinee-par-laffaire-amanda-knox-225461> accessed 28 July 2024.

7 For discussion of ANATOMY OF A MURDER: Matthias Kuzina, *Der amerikanische Gerichtsfilm: Justiz, Ideologie, Dramatik* (Vandenhoeck and Ruprecht 2000) 72–79 and Paul Bergman and Michael Asimow, *Reel justice. The courtroom goes to the movies* (Andrews McMeel Publishing 1996) 232–238.

8 Michael Asimow and Jessica Silbey, *Law and popular culture. A course book* (3rd edn, Vandeplas Publishing 2020) 30.

> Sandra interrupts: "I did not know there is a trial".
> Vincent: "Well, there is. (Short pause) Now, what will really count is who you have around you".

Seemingly taking liberty with the "truth", Vincent goes against the ideology of French criminal procedure. As Hodgson explains, "France's is an inquisitorial system, because the model is of a single inquiry in the truth." Yet, "in practice", the parties can bring forward their partisan views.[9] Though, Vincent is interested in truth, we see him investigating the scene of the death, visiting the attic, opening the window to assess the fall.

Lawyers are essentially storytellers. Meyer[10] even suggests that law students should watch courtroom dramas to prepare for their future trade, to see how juries can be swayed. One of the concepts legal scholars have developed to understand trials, is aptly called "the story-model of trial". It draws on the potential persuasiveness of narratives:

> "In short, stories are powerful means of transmitting precise interpretations of distant and complex events to people who either did not witness those events or who did not grasp them from the storyteller's perspective."[11]

And it is nowhere better expressed than in the film AMISTAD (USA, 1997, director Steven Spielberg) in which a seasoned lawyer declares "In court, whoever tells the best story wins". The episode DOUBT of the TV lawyer series THE GOOD WIFE (USA, 2010), like Triet's ANATOMY[12] inspired by the Amanda Knox case in Italy, has a scene in which the despairing client turns to her lawyer who tells her to stick to the truth because that will be best. She does not and, although innocent of the murder, agrees to a plea bargain panicked by the worst-case scenario of a draconian sentence. As it turns out, her sacrifice was unnecessary as the jury was about to acquit her.[13] The Amanda Knox case

---

9 Jacqueline Hodgson cited in: Jessica M. Goldstein, 'A French criminal justice expert answers all our questions about Anatomy of a Fall' (*Vulture*, March 2024) <https://www.vulture.com/article/anatomy-of-a-fall-trial-explained-by-a-french-law-expert.html> accessed 24 August 2024.

10 Philip N. Meyer, *Storytelling for lawyers* (Oxford University Press 2014).

11 W. Lance Bennett, 'Storytelling in criminal trials: A model of social judgment' (1978) 64 Quarterly Journal of Speech 1, 4.

12 On that: Yannick Vely, 'Justine Triet: "Pour 'Anatomie d'une chute', j'ai été fascinée par l'affaire Amanda Knox"' (*Paris Match*, 24 May 2023) (n 6).

13 Stefan Machura and Llewelyn Davies, '"Law is an odd thing"—Liberalism and law in the TV-series "The Good Wife"' (2013) 45 Kriminologisches Journal 279, 292.

is notorious for the press portraying an attractive young woman as killer with an angelic face. There were several trials with different outcomes.[14] Following a formula used by Hollywood cinema, the press in Italy and the UK painted the picture of a "radical disjunction between good and evil co-existent within the female protagonist", Amanda Knox.[15] In ANATOMY OF A FALL, the fact that Sandra is a foreigner, a celebrity writer of fiction, a seemingly violent and non-too-committed wife, and as the prosecutor insinuates: deviant for her bisexuality, threatens to condemn her in the eyes of the public, the judges and jurors.

In the words of Triet, throughout the film, the more we learn about Sandra, the more "opaque" she gets.[16] The viewer is left to at times think she must be innocent and then at other times, that she may have murdered her husband. "Play it like an innocent" was Triet's instruction to Hüller,[17] no doubt contributing to the opaqueness. What becomes clear is that Sandra is trying to hide the sorry state of her marriage and her own questionable behaviour from her lawyers and in court. She wishes to keep up the façade of a conventional marriage. "What do you want to know?", is not in vain Sandra's first sentence. She signals openness but is eager to construct a favourable impression in whoever she deals with: student interviewer, police, lawyers and court.

Openness is a key characteristic of court procedures, distinguishing them from mere rituals in which the outcome is fixed in advance, as Niklas Luhmann[18] wrote in his theory of procedure. Initially, there is a situation of openness. In our example, Samuel may have committed suicide, he may have even planned to provoke Sandra to kill him as a warped form of getting back at her, similarly, he could have killed himself and left evidence to incriminate his wife. Or, simply, Sandra may have murdered him in cold blood or following a sudden impulse.[19] She may also be indeed innocent.

According to Luhmann,[20] in the "funnel of procedure", the parties are forced to react to the arguments presented by their opponent and in this way, they

---

14 Lieve Gies, 'Miscarriages of justice in the age of social media: The Amanda Knox and Raffaele Sollecito innocence campaign' (2017) 57 British Journal of Criminology 723, 725.

15 Stevie Simkin, '"Actually evil. Not high school evil": Amanda Knox, sex and celebrity crime' (2013) 4 Celebrity Studies 33, 40.

16 (n 5).

17 Ibid.

18 Niklas Luhmann, *Legitimation durch Verfahren* (10th edn, Suhrkamp 2017) 40.

19 "Irresistible impulse" is the defence conjured up by the accused's attorney in ANATOMY OF A MURDER. For discussion and legal background: Paul Bergman and Michael Asimow, *Reel justice. The courtroom goes to the movies* (n 7) 236–238; John Denvir, 'The ecstasy and the agony' (*Cap Press*) <https://cap-press.com/sites/pj/mytake-denvir.htm> accessed 22 August 2024.

20 (n 18) 4, 115.

narrow down possibilities until a point is reached in which they have worked out the key elements for a decision. And now the judge can decide. Lawyers and legal scholars know that "truth" in trial is a (re-)construction happening in the trial. A special variety of "truth", namely, the "identification of a fact that justifies the judgment and is generally accepted".[21]

"On high sea and in court, we are in God's hand" used to be a saying among German lawyers. There may be surprises, however well prepared one is, however well-crafted the story. In the trial, Sandra loses control. The prosecutor presents an audio-recording of an argument Sandra had with her husband 20 hours before his death. The tape suggests that, presumably, as we only hear the audio, provoked by Samuel, Sandra hits him hard repeatedly. The bruises on her arm now appear not so innocent after all. The couple's relation is revealed as rather broken and she is able of resorting to aggression and violence. Read from Samuel's gruesome end, it does not reflect well on her character and threatens to destroy her story in court. Earlier in the trial, another tape was played in court: the student's recording of Sandra's flirtatious tone in the interview. Sandra is forced to admit in the courtroom that the marriage was in crisis and she had a fling with a woman.

Both sides in court try to bolster their stories with expert witnesses who either support the prosecution or the defences' version. Crucially, Vincent's trusted expert for blood splatters shows a video of an experiment that would explain the suspicious pattern. The argument, though, is somewhat speculative: the sun has melted away ice and snow on the shed's roof and washed away blood splatters proving Samual's suicide. Still, the experts' appearances do not amount to much. Experts and other witnesses for the prosecution arguably cross the line, when they visibly to everyone start theorising about the events that took place. Samuel's psychiatrist also testifies but is undermined by Sandra's intervention that he only heard her husband's account of their relation and that Samuel in her view tried to ween himself off the psychiatrist's influence and his antidepressant drugs. The outcome of the trial is still completely open. It is now, that Vincent's point made earlier to Sandra: "what will really count is who you have around you" comes to bear.

21 Rüdiger Voigt, 'Thesen zum Thema „Rechtspolitische Kommunikation"' in Johannes W. Pichler (ed), *Rechtsakzeptanz und Handlungsorientierung* (Böhlau 1998) 131, as translated by the author of this contribution.

3 The Child Witness

Daniel is visually impaired to a degree that he relies on his guide dog. Impaired witnesses occur in classic courtroom dramas. For example, the hard-of-hearing. The housekeeper in WITNESS FOR THE PROSECUTION (USA, 1957) is exposed by barrister Sir Wilfrid Robarts as too deaf to distinguish between actual human voices and voices on TV. In 12 ANGRY MEN (USA, 1957) the jurors in their deliberation room reenact the behaviour of an elderly witness with mobility issues and rule out his testimony. Child witnesses are not unique to ANATOMY OF A FALL either, there is for example, the film WITNESS (USA, 1985) in which the life of a boy is threatened. The boy's testimony is key to solve a murder. Most definitely, stakes are raised in ANATOMY OF A FALL with the introduction of a blind child witness.

It is the son's, Daniel's, choice of story to tell in court, which decides the trial. A final, surprising witness statement is a staple device in courtroom dramas. In Preminger's ANATOMY OF A MURDER it is that of the "illegitimate daughter" of the killed man, as Kuzina[22] points out. In real life as on film, police, lawyers, courts and forensic psychologists grapple with witness reliability and credibility. Witnesses can come to believe in an unfounded version of events. Some of the problems are listed by Miller:[23]

> A high degree of stress or a person's expectations can taint memory encoding. … The second step of memory, retention, is corrupted by the passing of time. The longer a memory is stored, the greater the likelihood a person will embellish the memory or it will become flawed or lost. One common problem is the tendency for a witness to compromise memories when he learns of new information that contradicts the actual experience. … Suggestive questioning also can interfere with the accuracy of memories.

Many months have passed between the death of Samuel and the start of the trial. Interrogated by the police and the investigative judge, Daniel had already contradicted himself. Back then, Sandra had tried to comfort him: She does not want him to change his memories. He should tell exactly what he remembers. "It can never hurt me."

---

22 Matthias Kuzina, *Der amerikanische Gerichtsfilm: Justiz, Ideologie, Dramatik* (n 7) 78–79.

23 Monica K. Miller, 'Witness testimony, psychology of' in David S. Clark (ed), *Encyclopedia of law and society: American and international and global perspectives* (Sage Publications 2007) 1589.

In a murder case in France, an investigative judge (juge d'instruction) leads the investigation and prepares the dossier for the trial on which the court will "heavily" rely.[24] Furthermore, "the idea is that ... the accused person, along with the public prosecutor ... can feed into that investigation". The accused and her lawyer may "try to contribute to the investigation by suggesting lines of enquiry to the juge d'instruction." The latter decides "whether to pursue these or not".[25]

The investigative judge, Juge Janvier, is shown at work in Anatomy of a Fall and comes across as diligent and strong-minded.[26] He orders that a court monitor lives with the family to make sure the mother does not unduly influence her son's testimony. Sandra will have to speak in French with her son, further indicating how intrusive the measure is. Marge Berger, the young court monitor, clarifies her role to Daniel, who is initially seeking her friendship: "The law sent me, and the law can't be someone's friend. Otherwise, it couldn't be someone else's. And the law must be the same for everyone. So you're right, I can't be your friend." Daniel is left in a very difficult situation; it is as if he has to decide between his parents. The judge informs him that the court's role is to find the truth.

After his initial testimony in court, which was inconclusive, on his own request, Daniel is allowed to follow the trial in the audience. The topic of the protection of children in court comes up in a nonconventional way in Anatomy of a Fall. Normally, it is discussed as an imperative overriding other concerns. Initially, this is the position of the presiding judge Bollène. However, Daniel himself asks to forego this protection, arguing that he will hear about what was said in the court anyhow through the media.

---

24 (n 9).

25 Ibid.

26 French investigative judges are shown as less effective and determined in a TV miniseries from about the same time as Triet's film: Sambre (France, 2023), English title "Sambre—Anatomy of a Crime", director: Jean-Xavier de Lestrade. It deals with the historic case of a serial rapist who committed his crimes over four decades. Episode 2 Irène (La Juge), is about the actions of an inexperienced young investigative judge. Although she ends up concentrating completely on the case, to the point of neglecting one against organised criminals (where a witness comes to harm due to her inaction), she fails to force the recalcitrant local police to cooperate. In episode 5 Winckler (Le Commandant), another (female) investigative judge tasks the head of the cold cases unit with a final investigation with the aim of (prematurely) closing the case. A striking similarity between the miniseries and Anatomy of a Fall is the quasi-realistic acting and filming of the stories. In the film, however, the photography is more polished and less dark.

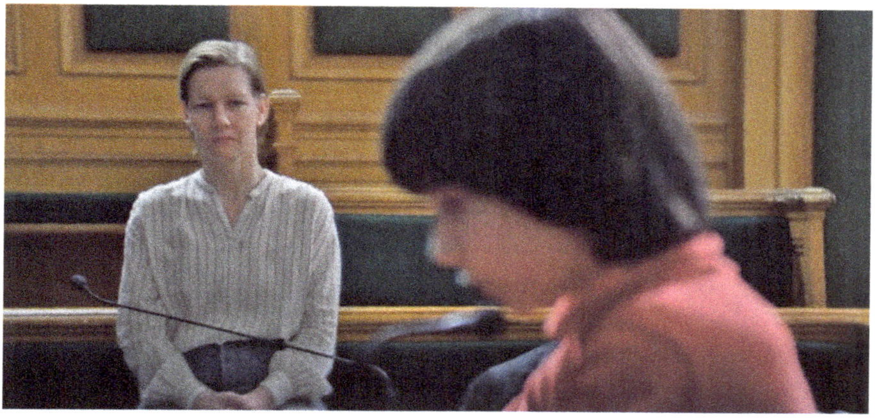

FIGURE 2.1 Sandra (played by Sandra Hüller) hears her son's testimony in court, suggesting that her husband contemplated suicide. Scene from "Anatomy of a Fall". (Picture source: "Anatomy of a Fall" Review' (*Spotlight on Film*, 17 December 2023) <https://spotlightonfilm.com/2023/12/17/anatomy-of-a-fall-review/> accessed 10 August 2024)

In court, he witnesses his mother reporting a previous suicide attempt by his father. Now Daniel remembers an incident when his dog got very ill from digesting something and had to be driven to the veterinary at about the same time. He conducts an experiment by feeding Snoop his father's sleeping pills. The effect is the same: the dog shows identical symptoms. His mother must have told the truth, Daniel concludes.

Before the experiment, Daniel had asked his mother to leave the house what she does, and makes the viewer wonder if he is about to turn against her. Both, she on her hotel bed, comfort-eating, he at home, watch a television show in which a literary critic quotes the mother, who once said: "My job is to cover the tracks, so fiction can destroy reality." In desperation, Daniel begs Marge for guidance, who finally tells him that sometimes, one has to decide what the truth is. In his final testimony in court (Figure 2.1), Daniel reports that at the drive to the veterinary, his father talked about the dog being extraordinary but old already and weary of life and that Daniel's will continue after the dog's death. Daniel in retrospect reads it as the father unveiling his decision to end his life: "He meant himself." Earlier, Daniel had stated in court, echoing Marge's advice about decisions: "I imagine my mother doing it, I don't understand. But if I imagine my father, I think, I can understand." It is suicide therefore and no murder to him. This proves to be the moment at which the case is decided. The audience does not see the deliberation of judges and jurors, or watches the presiding judge announcing the decision, but learns of the outcome when a reporter conveys it in front of the courthouse. Then, Vincent comes out and declares to the media representatives that the "jury"[27] has made the right decision.

This constellation makes Anatomy of a Fall a courtroom drama. Daniel's final testimony in front of the judges is pivotal. As he made it, the presiding judge's facial expression conveys that she took Daniel's message on board: "When we have looked everywhere and still don't understand how the thing happened, I think we have to ask why it happened."

4 Anatomy of a Fall within the Courtroom Drama Genre

Having established that the film is a veritable courtroom drama, what is its place within the genre? In some ways, Anatomy of a Fall is not a typical courtroom drama. This follows in part from the film trying to represent the French court system. There are some features of it which lend themselves well to dramatization and may appear intriguing to viewers from the anglosphere with its different traditions.

In a staple American courtroom drama, lawyers are the hero characters. Nicole Rafter[28] distinguished between "justice figure" and "injustice figure": one strives for justice and the opponent tries to stop this from happening. In a typical Hollywood production, the constellation is that of a duel between two lawyers. In Anatomy of a Fall, however, Vincent Renci's figure is too subdued to become a full-on, shiny hero character. The most that can be said is that he tries his best to support Sandra despite and even regardless of her "money problems". The banks seem reluctant to lend her money as deposit to avoid pretrial incarceration. Vincent understands that a client, Sandra in this case, is putting their life into someone's hands. For the upcoming trial,

27 What is referred to as "jury" in France, is actually a "mixed court" in which three professional judges and six lay judges deliberate and decide together on fact, law, guilt and sentence (Claire M. Germain, 'Trials by peers: The ebb and flow of the criminal jury in France and Belgium' in Sanja Kutnjak Ivković and others (eds), *Juries, lay judges and mixed courts: A global perspective* (Cambridge University Press 2021) 219). Vincent and the film are using a French expression correctly. An international audience may, however, think of the UK or US jury where the jurors alone decide on guilt and innocence of the defendant and the professional judge in a second step determines the sentence. It is this model of the jury which has been made familiar to international audiences by the global influence of the Hollywood courtroom drama (Stefan Machura and Stefan Ulbrich, 'Law in film: Globalising the Hollywood courtroom drama' (2001) 28 Journal of Law and Society 117).

28 Nicole Rafter, *Shots in the mirror: Crime films and society* (2nd edn, Oxford University Press 2006) 136.

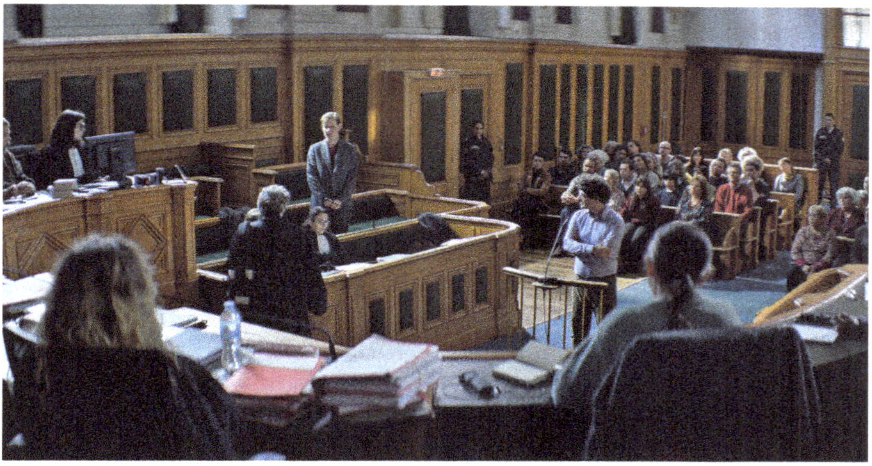

FIGURE 2.2 The courtroom architecture in the *court d'assises* symbolises a strict hierarchy: The judges' bench is high above the location of the defence attorney (on the left in black robes), the defendant (Sandra) and the witness stand. Scene from "Anatomy of a Fall". (Photo 12/Les Films Pelléas/Les Films de Pierre)

he has only one good card up his sleeve, his forensic expert's evidence, and is otherwise reduced to casting doubts on what the prosecution and its witnesses present as truth. The latter is the classic role of the defender, but a client might wish for more, even if the accused does not need to evidence their innocence. Vincent also shares his court appearances with a female colleague: Madame Boudaoud. Her part is even more limited. However, in Sandra's bail hearing, she successfully raises Daniel's best interests as a child who has lost a parent already and makes some points in the main hearing. The depiction of the key actors in court is true to the French system as suggested by an expert describing the hierarchy in the court (see also the layout of the court in Figure 2.2):

> "Really, the [presiding, SM] judge is running the show, and you wouldn't object to what the judge is saying. The judge might object to your [the lawyer's, SM] questions. And they have a lot of latitude. They make comments that are sometimes inappropriate and they ask questions that are maybe not relevant.
>
> Lawyers don't play such a massive role in the French criminal justice system at all. … The judge and advocate general [public prosecutor] are much more important. And the defense lawyer is sort of the poor relation."[29]

29 (n 9).

The public prosecutor is very keen to get Sandra convicted and labours his case hard. He lacks, though, in brilliance, and will certainly put off a modern audience with his anti-lesbian insinuations. Arthur Hariri, co-author of the script, declared having been influenced by the prosecutor in ANATOMY OF A MURDER, who, in Hariri's words, with his aggressiveness almost rapes the female defendant in court.[30] In the French film, however, the prosecutor does not come across this way as the film makers decided differently.[31] Until Daniel's experiment and final testimony, the case hangs in the balance, the audience is left in the dark as to the key question of guilt, and therefore, the prosecutor can hardly appear as justice or injustice figure. No private details are shown for the prosecutor. The main focus of the court scenes is not on the officers of the law but on Sandra and Daniel, on the appearances of mother and son.

In a way, the prosecutor himself is to blame for losing in court as his actions, drawing on the father's suicide attempt, particularly, trigger Daniel's thinking process and later statement which invalidates the prosecution case.[32] He also could not know how effective the boy will eventually be in court.

The presiding judge Bollène is, before the viewer sees her for the first time, characterised as a better option compared to another, more severe judge. During the prosecutor's interrogation of Sandra, she intervenes aggressively, pressuring her to answer. In France, it is normal that the presiding judge asks the defendant directly.[33] After all, the country has an investigative type of trial in which judges are more active than in the English and US adversarial trial type. The appearance of the middle-aged woman in the scenes when dealing with Daniel may remind German viewers of that of the decidedly calm and fair German youth judge Ruth Herz in the TV series DAS JUGENDGERICHT.[34] During the trial, Bollène is keen on efficient hearings and sympathetic to Daniel. Apart from in the courtroom she is filmed in a rather unglamourous judge's office. In no way she is a heroic judge, these are rare, anyhow, in courtroom dramas, but also not a conflicted, maybe prejudiced, or corrupt judge.

30 Oscars, 'Arthur Harari's "Words to Live By" | 'Anatomy of a Fall' | Oscars' (*YouTube*, 08 March 2024) <https://www.youtube.com/watch?v=HecyjmnikQU> accessed 12 August 2024.

31 Ibid.

32 This was suggested to me by Rosemary Nwimueyi, a student in my "Crime and the Media" class, in which I showed the film. Only 10 students out of maybe 25 indicated they were convinced after the screening that Sam has committed suicide.

33 (n 9).

34 The title translates as THE YOUTH COURT (Germany, 2001–2005), for the figure of the judge: Ruth Herz, *Recht persönlich: Eine Jugendrichterin erzählt* (C. H. Beck 2006); Stefan Machura, 'Television judges in Germany' in Peter Robson and Jessica Silbey (eds), *Law and justice on the small screen* (Hart Publishing 2012).

The court monitor Marge Berger forms an element unique to ANATOMY OF A FALL. The writer of these lines has not come across such a figure before. Marge grows closer to Daniel but never becomes a full-blown actor in her own rights, apart from when she plants the idea in his mind that it is correct sometimes to make a decision when caught between two alternatives for the "truth".

Pfau and others distinguished between "front stage" and "backstage" behaviour of lawyers in US popular culture. Lawyers are typically shown as competent in the former, comprising of the courtroom and their offices, but rather unhappy in their private life.[35] They have bad relations with their children and partners, that is, if they have a love life at all given their dedication to their professional calling. Sandra's defence attorney Vincent Renci is depicted in this mould. Though not heroic, he is effective and committed. In court, the presiding judge occasionally sees the need to reign him in. Privately, Renci has vices, but he never crosses the line. An obvious one is smoking. Summarising the American development, Goode[36] writes: "In a couple of generations, smoking moved from being mainstream and conventional to being wrongful and deviant." This may be different in France but is not far from the truth for countries like Germany and the UK. Tellingly, Renci is shown indulging in smoking while listening to Sandra but blows the smoke out through an open window. He walks a thin line as he very obviously fancies his former acquaintance, and it may even be part of why he took on the case. Still, he manages to comply to legal ethics. After all, a lawyer should not be in a romantic affair with a client. "[T]he roles of lover and lawyer potentially conflict".[37] Only after the verdict, at the celebration in a modest East Asian restaurant, Vincent shyly makes a move. Yet, Sandra is not open for a relation as her body language tells. Both recoil from getting closer. Again, Vincent appears to the viewer as a decent man.

In Preminger's ANATOMY OF A MURDER, the defence lawyer "probably violates the attorney's code of ethics" by creating "the story the client tells".[38] In ANATOMY OF A FALL, Lawyer Vincent's suggestion that a suicide is the only narrative that can be defended, comes close to such a behaviour. Especially as he emphasizes that truth won't be much relevant in the upcoming trial. At this

35 Michael Pfau and others, 'Television viewing and public perceptions of attorneys' (1995) 21 Human Communications Research 307, 326.

36 Erich Goode, *Celluloid mischief: Deviance and crime on the silver screen* (Routledge 2023) 113.

37 Linda Crowley-Cyr and Carol Caple, 'Sex with clients and the ethical lawyer' (2001) 8 James Cook University Law Review 67, 67.

38 Paul Bergman and Michael Asimow, *Reel justice. The courtroom goes to the movies* (n 7) 236.

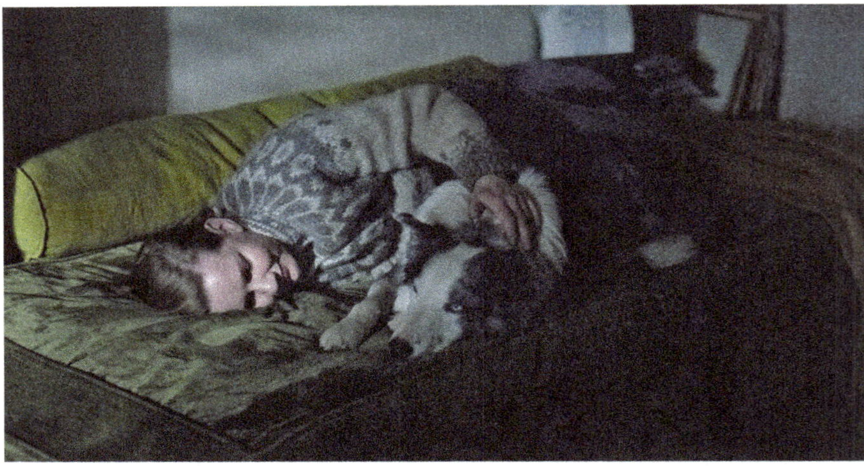

FIGURE 2.3 Final scene of "Anatomy of a Fall": Sandra, acquitted but completely exhausted, is comforted by her son's guide dog. (Film still by Landmark Media. Cf. Lindsey Dunn, 'Anatomy of a Fall & The Holdovers Double Feature Review' (*1 of my Stories*, 16 November 2023) <https://www.1ofmystories.com/2023/11/anatomy-of-fall-holdovers-double.html> accessed 4 March 2025)

point, some viewers may perceive Vincent as not at all an exemplary professional. Others may see it as nothing else but cynical realism.

As alluded to earlier, many courtroom dramas also have uncertain endings. In ANATOMY OF A FALL, mother and son are reunited, Marge leaves the house rather abruptly, and we see Sandra lying completely exhausted on the sofa, cuddling with Snoop, the dog (Figure 2.3). Solemn music is played, and the credits start rolling. This last shot may suggest to some readers that Sandra was a victim of the trial. The book title "The process is the punishment"[39] comes to mind. It marks the exhaustion, the grinding down of the parties involved in a procedure,[40] even if they are not the guilty ones.

Yet, uncertainty remains. The anti-climactic ending is foreshadowed earlier when Sandra and her legal team are celebrating the victory: Sandra states that in contrast to after a conviction, nothing is coming after an acquittal has been achieved. ANATOMY OF A FALL is a private drama, though dragged out into the forum of the trial, first and foremost.

This leaves one last question: Is the film in any way political, does it have a message? If politics is defined by influencing how people live together or

39 Malcom M. Feeley, *The process is the punishment: Handling cases in a lower criminal court* (Russell Sage Foundation 1992).

40 Niklas Luhmann, *Legitimation durch Verfahren* (n 18) 3–4.

how well state institutions function, that is, in the Aristotelian sense, the answer is not straightforward at all. ANATOMY OF A FALL does not suggest changes like many social issue dramas. "When it comes to problem-oriented courtroom dramas (social issue courtroom dramas), a single legal case is at the centre which is of general social significance".[41] The social issue at stake in ANATOMY OF A FALL is the challenging situation of a dual-career couple including the difficulty when the spouses cannot agree how to distribute the chores of every-day life.

Yet, ANATOMY OF A FALL does not criticize the abuse of political, economic, police, prosecutorial or judicial powers as in a long line of historic courtroom dramas. The most that can be said is that ANATOMY OF A FALL chimes in with the ground swell of law-related films which, as I have elsewhere argued,[42] favour a liberal, rule-of-law philosophy. ANATOMY OF A FALL vaguely points at the importance of who the decision-makers are and alerts the public to efforts to avoid undue influences during a trial. And, of course, both sides must be able to present their case as demanded by procedural justice.[43]

But more than peddling a political cause, ANATOMY OF A FALL is one of the courtroom dramas fuelled by artistic ambition. It answers to previous exemplars of the genre, plays with its building blocks creatively and consequentially, has been mainly received as a masterpiece of filmmaking and acting. Justine Triet as director and Sandra Hüller as actress have been emphatically celebrated for their achievement. ANATOMY OF THE FALL thereby has proven that the courtroom genre continues to be an important branch of the art of filmmaking.

References

'Anatomy of a Fall awards' (*IMDb*, 2025) <https://www.imdb.com/title/tt17009710/awards/?ref_=tt_awd> accessed 27 August 2025.

Asimow M. and Silbey J., *Law and popular culture. A course book* (3rd edn, Vandeplas Publishing 2020).

41 Matthias Kuzina, *Der amerikanische Gerichtsfilm: Justiz, Ideologie, Dramatik* (n 7) 217, as translated by the author of this contribution.

42 Stefan Machura, 'Representations of law, rights and criminal justice', *Oxford research encyclopedia of criminology* (2017) <https://doi.org/10.1093/acrefore/9780190264079.013.201> accessed 28 July 2024.

43 Gerhard Leventhal, 'What should be done with equity theory?' in Kenneth J. Gergen, Martin S. Greenberg and Richard H. Willis (eds), *Social exchange: Advances in theory and research* (Plenum Press 1980).

Bennett W.L., 'Storytelling in criminal trials: A model of social judgment' (1978) 64 Quarterly Journal of Speech 1.

Bergman P. and Asimow M., *Reel justice. The courtroom goes to the movies* (Andrews McMeel Publishing 1996).

Crowley-Cyr L. and Caple C., 'Sex with clients and the ethical lawyer' (2001) 8 James Cook University Law Review 67.

Denvir J., 'The ecstasy and the agony' (*Cap Press*) <https://cap-press.com/sites/pj/mytake-denvir.htm> accessed 22 August 2024.

'Die vielen Gesichter der Sandra Hüller. Dokumentation' (*ARD Mediathek*) <https://www.ardmediathek.de/video/dokus-und-reportagen-im-br/die-vielen-gesichter-der-sandra-hueller/br-fernsehen/Y3JpZDovL2JyLmRlL3ZpZGVvLzFhZjFjNWRhLWEwMzItNDBlOC04OTVjLTU2MzRlMWQzMzNkZg> accessed 28 July 2024.

Feeley M.M., *The process is the punishment: Handling cases in a lower criminal court* (Russell Sage Foundation 1992).

Film at Lincoln Centre, 'Justine Triet, Sandra Hüller & Arthur Harari on Anatomy of a Fall | NYFF61' (*YouTube*, 10 October 2023) <https://www.youtube.com/watch?v=IvEhmdPgCgM> accessed 10 August 2024.

Germain C.M., 'Trials by peers: The ebb and flow of the criminal jury in France and Belgium' in Sanja Kutnjak Ivković and others (eds), *Juries, lay judges and mixed courts: A global perspective* (Cambridge University Press 2021).

Gies L., 'Miscarriages of justice in the age of social media: The Amanda Knox and Raffaele Sollecito innocence campaign' (2017) 57 British Journal of Criminology 723.

Goldstein J.M., 'A French criminal justice expert answers all our questions about Anatomy of a Fall' (*Vulture*, March 2024) <https://www.vulture.com/article/anatomy-of-a-fall-trial-explained-by-a-french-law-expert.html> accessed 24 August 2024.

Goode E., *Celluloid mischief: Deviance and crime on the silver screen* (Routledge 2023).

Greenfield S., Osborn G. and Robson P., *Film and the law* (Cavendish 2001).

Herz R., *Recht persönlich: Eine Jugendrichterin erzählt* (C.H. Beck 2006).

Kuzina M., *Der amerikanische Gerichtsfilm: Justiz, Ideologie, Dramatik* (Vandenhoeck and Ruprecht 2000).

Kuzina M., 'The social issue courtroom drama as an expression of American popular culture' (2001) 28 Journal of Law and Society 79.

Leventhal G., 'What should be done with equity theory?' in Kenneth J. Gergen, Martin S. Greenberg and Richard H. Willis (eds), *Social exchange: Advances in theory and research* (Plenum Press 1980).

Luhmann N., *Legitimation durch Verfahren* (10th edn, Suhrkamp 2017).

Machura S., 'Television judges in Germany' in Peter Robson and Jessica Silbey (eds), *Law and justice on the small screen* (Hart Publishing 2012).

Machura S., 'Representations of law, rights and criminal justice', *Oxford Research Encyclopedia of Criminology* (2017) <https://doi.org/10.1093/acrefore/9780190264079.013.201> accessed 28 July 2024.

Machura S. and Davies L., '"Law is an odd thing"—Liberalism and law in the TV-series "The Good Wife"' (2013) 45 Kriminologisches Journal 279.

Machura S. and Ulbrich S., 'Law in film: Globalising the Hollywood courtroom drama' (2001) 28 Journal of Law and Society 117.

Meyer P.N., *Storytelling for lawyers* (Oxford University Press 2014).

Miller M.K., 'Witness testimony, psychology of' in David S. Clark (ed), *Encyclopedia of law and society: American and international and global perspectives* (Sage Publications 2007).

Oscars, 'Arthur Harari's "Words to Live By" | 'Anatomy of a Fall' | Oscars' (*YouTube*, 08 March 2024) <https://www.youtube.com/watch?v=HecyjmnikQU> accessed 12 August 2024.

Pfau M. and others, 'Television viewing and public perceptions of attorneys' (1995) 21 Human Communications Research 307.

Rafter N., *Shots in the mirror: Crime films and society* (2nd edn, Oxford University Press 2006).

Simkin S., '"Actually evil. Not high school evil': Amanda Knox, sex and celebrity crime' (2013) 4 Celebrity Studies 33.

Sykes G.M. and Matza D., 'Techniques of neutralization: A theory of delinquency' in Delos H. Kelly (ed), *Criminal behavior: Readings in Criminology* (St. Martin's Press 1980).

Vely Y., 'Justine Triet: "Pour 'Anatomie d'une chute', j'ai été fascinée par l'affaire Amanda Knox"' (*Paris Match*, 24 May 2023) <https://www.parismatch.com/culture/cinema/justine-triet-pour-anatomie-dune-chute-jai-ete-fascinee-par-laffaire-amanda-knox-225461> accessed 28 July 2024.

Voigt R., 'Thesen zum Thema "Rechtspolitische Kommunikation"' in Johannes W. Pichler (ed), *Rechtsakzeptanz und Handlungsorientierung* (Böhlau 1998).

CHAPTER 3

ANATOMY OF A FALL: Interpersonal Drama as a Courtroom Drama

Agata Fijalkowski

1 Introduction

This paper considers the French filmmaker Justine Triet's 2023 award-winning film, ANATOMY OF A FALL, through a screenwriter's lens. It challenges the assertion that the film is a courtroom drama. Using the work of one of the key thinkers in the field of film studies, Phil Parker,[1] this paper will demonstrate how and why ANATOMY OF A FALL is in essence an interpersonal drama. It will provide an overview of courtroom dramas before discussing the most popular template used in genre, the one based on the hero's journey. It will then set out the seven components of an interpersonal drama, as described in Parker's account, applying each in turn to Triet's film. This paper will evaluate how law is itself a protagonist in interpersonal drama. Although this film is not a legal movie, it is nonetheless an excellent comment about the law, because all social relations can be seen as legal relations and legal subjectivity.

2 Film and Law? Law and Film?

Film has everything to do with law. Films can be about the law overtly, and often they are re-enactments or adaptations of famous cases. Law films involve the audience, as pretend jurors, judges, prosecutors, or detectives. Law films frequently reconstruct the courtroom process and involve the audience in the adversarial or inquisitorial process. In other words, the law is a character and serves to launch a story, which could be a whodunnit or might not be about the law at all. Even so, films that are not about the law can provide insights into analytical methods, social values, societal aspirations—all of which are also at the core of legal culture and legal consciousness. In fact, the search for justice is never far away in a story, which can be played out as a quest to solve

1 Phil Parker, 'What is the Personal Drama Journey' (*BCre8iv Blog*, 02 October 2015) <https://blog.bcre8ive.net/dramas-personal-journey/> accessed 22 August 2025.

© 2026 THE AUTHOR(S) | HTTPS://DOI.ORG/10.1163/9789004761704-004

a mystery, or as a battle between good and evil. The notion of justice will be explored later in relation to the notion of cinematic jurisprudence. Law meets film is an encounter. These meetings, where law is understood as a cultural concept, occur "in and through the archaic, discreet, and arcane practices and institutions of law".[2] Where law and film converge and re(shape) concepts and relationships, the movie screen becomes the ideal site on which to show how these legal questions play out.[3]

3 Courtroom Dramas

As Ashley Merryman[4] observes, movies set in a law or court-based arena are the perfect venue for cinematic drama. After all, there is some sort of conflict—often an actual lawsuit—at their heart. But truly memorable films have more than that. First, there is the case at issue, and the stakes can often be very high: life-and-death. Next, the legal professionals are usually facing a personal crisis relating to the main case. Finally, the best legal films accurately portray the law and effectively use its actual twists to turn the story itself into something powerful.

Classic courtroom dramas include the 1957 film 12 ANGRY MEN. Almost the entire action takes place within a jury room, as the jurors argue about the case of a young man accused of murder. The lone juror to hold out against the others is played by Henry Fonda. This film never feels dated because it addresses the way that individuals' perceptions, racism, social class, and family history all affect a jury's decision. Then there is the 1959 film ANATOMY OF A MURDER, held by many to be the best legal movie ever made. Jimmy Stewart takes on the role of a disillusioned defence attorney representing a client accused of murder. With much of the action unfolding within the courtroom, the film is unsettling because it reveals that trials are more about lawyering than truth. Stewart's performance underscores the scepticism the audience is led to feel over the course of the trial. Indeed, there are similarities between this film and ANATOMY OF A FALL as regards the way facts are revealed and distorted during a trial. For example, Triet has said that she followed the 2007 Amanda

2 Leslie Moran and others, *Law's Moving Image* (Routledge 2004) 1.

3 Ibid 5.

4 Ashley Merryman, 'The Best Legal and Courtroom Dramas' (*RogerEbert.com*, 04 March 2024) <https://www.rogerebert.com/features/the-best-legal-and-courtroom-dramas> accessed 22 August 2025.

Knox murder trial very closely; Triet noted the negative treatment of Knox by the press and by the Italian authorities that would later lead to her mistrial.[5]

Kristian Klockars considers that law is best understood "as a form of perception and signification that allocates ways of sensing, feeling, being, moving, and thinking within a given society".[6] The manner in which law operates is, in fact, not confined to a box. Law has jurisgenerative action[7] that is found inside and outside its juridical sphere. This framing of law puts law on a stage on which to act, transforming it into an aesthetic frame such that law is more than simply a set of rules.[8] Klockars shifts our attention away from the compartmentalisation of the law, preferring rather to situate it within societal relations, so as to demonstrate how it actively constructs normative frameworks that individuals follow in their interactions. Desmond Manderson[9] for his part sees law as a way of thinking that binds society. He argues that "[t]he gaze of the law—its way of talking about problems and of dividing up the world—influences our interpretation of the world, and we find it revealed in the form and structure of laws and the metaphors and imagery to be found in legal texts".[10] In other words, law is in a reciprocal relationship with the world around it. The relationship exists in many different forms, not least in the connection between the viewer and the film: the world is seen as a sensory experience and the film portrays aspects of our dispositions in this complex world. At its heart ANATOMY OF A FALL is about a marriage, but as the cliché goes, anyone outside of a relationship cannot really know what is going on within it. This too becomes a profound comment about law, a point returned to later in this discussion. Viewed this way, for most Hollywood courtroom dramas, the courts, as articulated by Harper Lee's Atticus Finch in *To Kill a Mockingbird* (1962), are the "great levellers" because they represent and uphold ideas about personal and social justice.[11]

5 'Anatomy of a Fall' (*Forgetfulfilmcritic.com*, 01 March 2024) <https://www.forgetfulfilmcritic.com/home/2024/03/01/anatomy-of-a-fall> accessed 22 August 2025.

6 Kristian Klockars, 'Book Review Mónica López Lerma & Julen Etxabe (eds): *Rancière and Law*, Routledge, London 2018' (2023) 15 Nofu 147, 151.

7 Ibid 149.

8 Ibid 151.

9 Desmond Manderson, *Song Without Music: Aesthetic Dimensions of Law and Justice* (University of California Press 2000).

10 Ibid 28.

11 Stella Bruzzi, 'Imperfect Justice: Fritz Lang's Fury (1936) and Cinema's Use of the Trial Form' (2015) 4 *Law and Humanities* 1.

4 Genre and the Hero's Journey

Academic accounts of the nature of film genre usually discuss the hero's quest or journey, also known as the monomyth. This quest is the common template of stories that involve a hero. Having embarked on an adventure, the protagonist, after many trials, survives a major crisis to return home a changed person. Consider, for example, John Campbell's hero's quest, or monomyth[12] is depicted here.

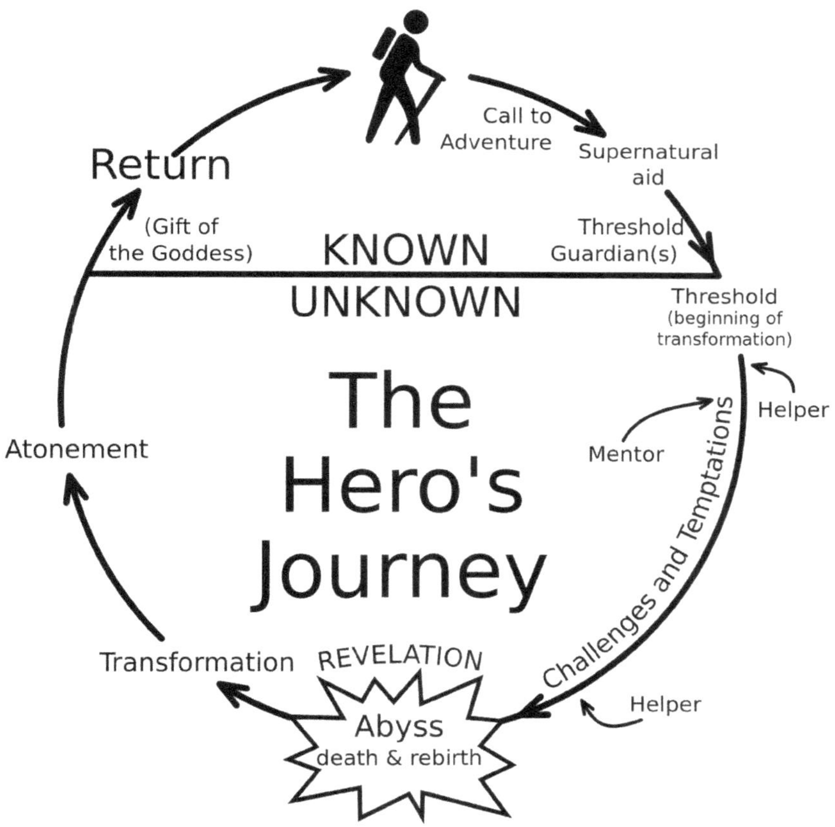

FIGURE 3.1 The Hero's Journey ('The Hero's Journey' (*Wikimedia Commons*) <https://commons.wikimedia.org/wiki/File:Heroesjourney.svg> accessed 27 October 2025)

12 John Campbell, *The Hero with a Thousand Faces* (Princeton University Press 1949).

Other works in genre, such as Robert McKee's *Story*[13] or Blake Snyder's *Save the Cat!*,[14] show how the most important scene in all stories is the climax: the final, most extreme, and irreversible change the hero undergoes.

5 Phil Parker's Idea of the (Inter-)personal Drama

Phil Parker's *The Art and Science of Screenwriting*[15] outlines his initial ideas about genre. Parker has subsequently written more extensively about genre and has defined the components of personal drama, a powerful and popular genre. The personal drama journey has a structure well-suited to cinema but is based upon the framework of the personal drama in television, where the genre dominates. It is, however, easier to look at its manifestation in a one-off linear form first, i.e. film, rather than in the television series form. Parker's writing on genre, particularly the interpersonal/personal drama,[16] provides a good foundation for a more meaningful analysis of the topic.

This paper will now look at Parker's key elements in relation to Triet's film, and particularly to Sandra Voyter, the main character in ANATOMY OF A FALL. There will be reference to some key dialogue as the paper goes through the components identified by Parker.[17] Given the fact that the film is mostly dialogue, it needs big, episodic scenes. The primary elements will then be related back to the wider questions of law and film noted at the start.

6 First Element: the Single, Isolated Protagonist

The first defining quality of the (inter-)personal drama is a single, isolated protagonist. The protagonist undergoes or attempts a major transformation of themselves or their world. In fact, the nature of this isolation is dependent on the type of genre in question.

Sandra Voyter is a writer. We catch glimpses of her life as a child, teenager, young woman, partner, wife, mother, writer, and somehow her trajectory has led her to this isolated, cold place, surrounded by snow, ice, and snow-capped peaks. As viewers, we are confronted with a vast, cold, snowy, mountainous landscape and we wonder why she is there, of all places? The audience can almost

13 Robert McKee, *Story* (Methuen Publishing 1997).
14 Blake Snyder, *Save the Cat! The Last Book on Screenwriting You'll Ever Need* (Michael Wiese Productions 2005).
15 Phil Parker, *The Art and Science of Screenwriting* (Intellect Books 1998).
16 (n 1).
17 The dialogue in this paper is taken from the screenplay ANATOMY OF A FALL, written by Justine Triet and Arthur Harari. On file with the author.

feel the visible cold breath inside and outside the house. Windows are open and people wear thick turtleneck sweaters. In fact, it is very hard to perceive anything warm. Even the sunshine is cold. In the initial scene, where the student Zoe is interviewing Sandra about her book, viewers wonder what exactly Sandra is trying to achieve, whether she is trying to fill this cold space, through conversation and flirtation. Sandra admits this herself, to Zoe. Suddenly we see that Sandra, the writer, is driving the story. Her dialogue here is telling.

> Sandra Voyter: I left my shithole in Germany and ended up stuck here … in this shithole.

Sandra too is wondering why she is here.

Writers make great characters. And there are great movies with characters who are writers, such as IN A LONELY PLACE (1950), SUNSET BOULEVARD (1950), THE SHINING (1980), BARTON FINK (1991), MISERY (1990), ADAPTATION (2002), or LITTLE WOMEN (2019). While people may aspire to be artists, writers, or poets, these films show that there is a stigma attached to being creative. There is a particular interest in those who see the world a bit differently. And, perhaps, this is the reason that screenwriters often bring writers into their stories, being aware that they make compelling protagonists. Not only do writers tell a story, but they can also rewrite it before the viewer's eyes. Having a writer as one of the main protagonists changes the tone and plot of a film. Having characters who are writers makes for the best movies.

Triet wrote ANATOMY OF A FALL for the German actor Sandra Hüller. In fact, the similarities between Triet and Hüller are such that at moments the two seem all but indistinguishable. The character is credible because Triet is drawing on personal experience.[18] Moreover, Triet will know that a writer is a great character but a woman writer a still greater one.[19] In fact, when screenwriters choose to have a female protagonist, they inevitably are confronted with a whole range of choices that require them to confront their own beliefs about the situation of women in society, and to what extent they want their chosen character and their screenplay to reflect these.[20] Ever since moving

18 'Anatomy of a Fall' (*Fandom.com*) <https://movies.fandom.com/wiki/Anatomy_of_a_Fall> accessed 22 August 2025.

19 Rebecca Leffler, 'Justine Triet breaks down four key scenes from 'Anatomy Of A Fall': "'P.I.M.P.' wasn't our first choice for the song' (*ScreenDaily*, 12 February 2024) <https://www.screendaily.com/features/justine-triet-breaks-down-four-key-scenes-from-anatomy-of-a-fall-pimp-wasnt-our-first-choice-for-the-song/5190406.article> accessed 22 August 2025.

20 Helen Jacey, 'Heroines in Flux: Gender and Screenwriting' (*Viewfinder Magazine*, 2021) <https://learningonscreen.ac.uk/viewfinder/articles/heroines-in-flux-gender-and-screenwriting/> accessed 22 August 2025.

images began, female characters and their representation have been subject to changes, reflecting what is occurring in women's lives, changes that are culturally, socially, politically, and economically specific. In addition to this evolving female character representation, the gender of the screenwriter has also been scrutinised.[21] Countless studies have revealed that when women are behind the camera as writer, director and producer, very different stories are told.[22] Accompanying this is the question: why are these women writers so problematic?[23] And, what does the law have to say about women writers? In other words, in film, in general, law is not their friend. What do we see when we look at these women? What does the law see? In 'ANATOMY OF A FALL' it is clear to viewers that Sandra is very aware of being watched by everyone around her and conscious of being judged. Sandra is an outsider, but she is not cowed. She shows as much in her discussion with her lawyer, Vincent Renzi.

> Sandra Voyter: But I'm innocent. You know that, right?
> Maître Vincent Renzi: Yes.
> Sandra Voyter: I mean, really.
> Maître Vincent Renzi: Yes.
> Sandra Voyter: I don't know what you're thinking really.
> Maître Vincent Renzi: I think a lot of things I don't tell you. Otherwise, you'd fire me right now.
> Sandra Voyter: No, no, no, Vincent. In your head, you're thinking, aren't you, because sometimes, when you look at me, just like right now, I can feel that you are judging me. I don't know what you think.

The key issue in this conversation is judgement, which also becomes the bridge where law and film meet, and where it becomes clearer that film is an excellent commentator on, and observer of the law.

7 Second Element: a World with which the Protagonist is At Odds

The second element is a distinct world with which the protagonist is at odds. The length of the film (2 hours, 32 minutes) allows viewers to really feel the cold in the family home, the outside, and in the courtroom. Significantly, in this world language is the gatekeeper. Triet told Hüller that language would

21 Ibid.
22 Ibid.
23 Ibid.

itself be an important subject in the film, as the couple did not speak the same language and communicated through English:

> There was also this idea of what it means to be a foreigner on trial in France. To be tried in a country that is not your own can be tough because you're judged for how you express yourself but as you're not speaking in your mother tongue and there are lots of filters between you and your reality.[24]

As a German person speaking English and trying to speak French it is difficult to know who the real Sandra is. Importantly, these filters that the filmmaker refers to are very real. Viewers watch this courtroom scene with different sets of lenses, whether it is common law, or the civil law, and these filters lead the viewer in different directions and to different thoughts about Sandra and her guilt. Sandra's lawyer Vincent addresses this with Sandra.

> Maître Vincent Renzi: I don't give a fuck about what is reality, okay? You … you need to start seeing yourself the way others are going to perceive you. A trial is not about 'the truth,' it's … it's about …

As does the prosecutor.

> Avocat général: Wait, are you implying you're the victim of a twisted man?
> Maître Nour Boudaoud: Seriously? He recorded her in secret. It's a valid question. You forget the situation is perverse.
> Avocat général: Now the victim is on trial!

Not only are the viewers confused, the prosecutor and defence lawyers understand how the defendant can be judged because language is the gatekeeper of this world.

8 Third Element: Character Cannot Be Put Down

The third element is the fact that a character cannot be defeated. Sandra will not be subdued by settling down with her husband Samuel Maleski in his hometown.

24 Melanie Goodfellow, "'Anatomy Of A Fall' Director Justine Triet Talks Love Of Cannes Competition: "It Can Be Violent"—Deadline Q & A.' (*Deadline*, 24 May 2023) <https://deadline.com/2023/05/anatomy-of-a-fall-director-justine-triet-cannes-1235376653/> accessed 22 August 2025.

> Samuel Maleski: Why do you refuse to talk about it? Why can't you just admit that it has to do with how things are divided between us?
> Sandra Voyter: Because you are wrong. I don't owe you any time, I do my part. C'mon, let's not start taking an inventory here, please. Let's relax. I love you.
> Samuel Maleski: I've given you too much … too much time, too many concessions. I want this time back, and you owe it to me, be fair!
> Sandra Voyter: [laughing] I'm sorry, but no, are you insane? I don't owe you anything, really.
> Sandra Voyter: You should be flattered that I was inspired by you. This is life, things circulate, you know.
> Samuel Maleski: Yes.
> Sandra Voyter: Yes? And frankly, I wish you'd be inspired to 'plunder' me someday.
> Samuel Maleski: You really have no shame. That's your superpower, it allows you to see no one but yourself.
> Sandra Voyter: I see you very clearly. I just don't see you as a victim.

In this complex scene, the viewer learns a bit more about Sandra, without really knowing her. This dialogue also points to the filmmaker's attention to the evolving female character representation noted above. Equally, Sandra will not let her son's visual impairment hold him back.

9 Fourth Element: Dramatic, Linear Structure

The fourth element relates to the dramatic, linear structure that often has an episodic form. Here the paper will look at the key scene concerning Sandra's preparation of answers to possible questions posed at her trial. The scene has Sandra prepare for her trial with her lawyer Vincent, who is filming her with a video camera. She talks about her husband Samuel, and how things changed between them when their son Daniel had an accident that left him partially visually impaired.

According to Triet, the scene is of pivotal importance owing to the way that viewers are introduced to Sandra.[25] They see Sandra discuss her marriage at some length for the first time, almost as a monologue. Prior to this Sandra has not revealed very much about herself. As a writer her reference points are abstract and it is not clear who she really is. This scene sets up what will later

25 (n 19).

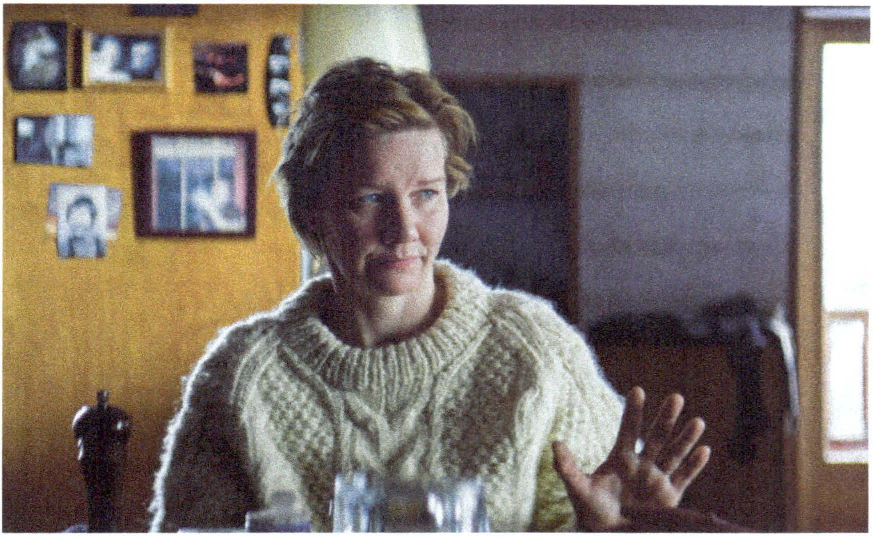

FIGURE 3.2 Sandra speaks to her husband (Film still by Lionsgate/Picturehouse Entertainment)

be disclosed in the courtroom and judged in court, in the community, and by the viewers. Of course, the viewers have already started to judge. Triet explains that it is at this precise moment that the viewer grasps that it is indeed because she is a writer that it will be hard to judge this woman. She is speaking in a language which is not her native language. And as a writer she is perhaps manipulating her life story to her own advantage. She is also emotional.

10 Fifth Element: Desire for Validation

The fifth element shows thematically a desire for order or for validation. As noted above, Samuel seeks to have his feelings validated. Sandra for her part seeks validation from her lawyer and from the legal process itself, upon seeing her marriage under scrutiny. Actually, it is Samuel's recording that brings to the fore the couple's rivalry, jealousy, resentment. Sandra walks a thin line between her own professional aspirations and those of her husband. Her feelings of being misunderstood come to a head when the court turns its attention to her marriage, which is depicted as toxic. In the one flashback of Sandra and Samuel viewers see a confrontation during which long-held resentments erupt. Samuel's raw anguish and Sandra's desperation and anger render the scene deeply distressing.

11 Sixth Element: Central Character's Dramatic Arc

The sixth element, the central character's dramatic arc, compared with the changes within the characters featuring in other genres, is a matter for debate.[26] This paper contends that Sandra does have a dramatic arc, and it is this that makes the film so compelling. Particular emphasis should be placed on how the filmmaker has set up the dramatic arc, and the attention she pays to evolving female character representations. There are clues that point to this arc when Sandra's son Daniel delivers crucial testimony. When Daniel testifies for the second time in the courtroom, he describes a conversation he had with his father that features a flashback scene in a car; we see his father speaking to him but hear Daniel's voice.

According to Triet, the scene was among the most difficult to film.[27] What was paramount for her was the need to make the courtroom scenes realistic, in contrast to US courtroom dramas. Apparently, when she was in her mid-20s, Triet spent a great deal of time in courtrooms. She made documentaries in order to be close to this world and watch cases unfold in real time. Triet contends that what people are accustomed to seeing in fictional courtrooms is very different from the reality.[28] In ANATOMY OF A FALL, she wanted to show

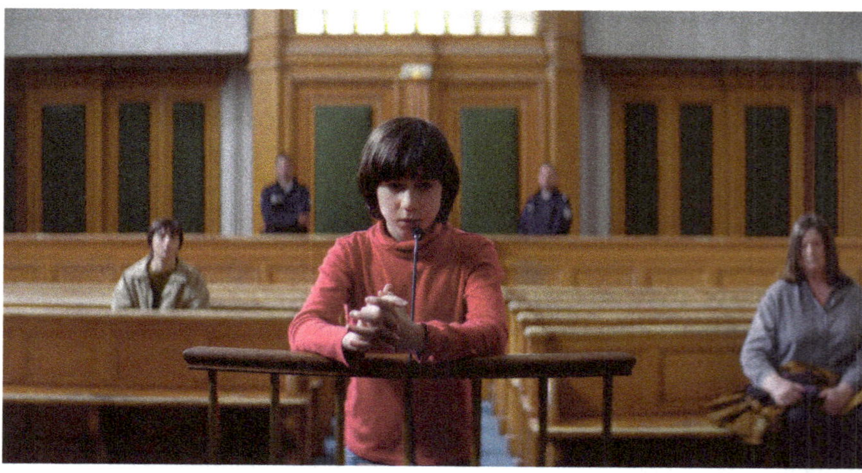

FIGURE 3.3 Daniel delivers his testimony (Film still by Les Film Pélleas/Les Films de Pierre)

26 See Stefan Machura's contribution in this special series.
27 (n 19).
28 Ibid.

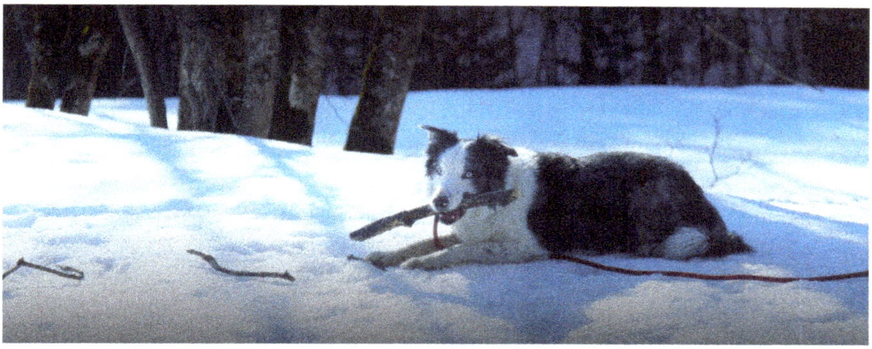

FIGURE 3.4 Snoop, the dog (Film still by Les Film Pélleas/Les Films de Pierre/album)

something that was not so clearcut and that depicted the French legal system accurately. She put a great deal of thought into the way the lawyers looked and were portrayed, the prosecutor being less old-fashioned and the defence lawyer more androgynous. And of course she took the crucial decision to make the defendant a woman and a writer.

The film is as much about this woman on trial as it is about her son—who will have to learn to live with doubt for the rest of his life. We do not know precisely what Daniel has to endure, but we do need to decide what it was, or at least form an opinion. In other words, growing up means accepting what we do not know to be certain. It is in any case a way of moving forward. This is evident not only in Daniel but in Sandra's realisation of this same point. It is this acknowledgement on Sandra's part that is a crucial aspect of her character arc. It is depicted in the final scene when the family dog Snoop curls up next to her. In fact, dogs themselves represent justice. As sentient beings, dogs have been valued for their loyalty and protection by ancient civilisations and more recently for their emotional intelligence.[29] Dogs symbolise justice in certain myths and traditional stories and are the decisionmaker as to whether the individual acted accordance with their inner ethical and moral standards.[30] Triet points to the uncomfortable necessity of being able to live in, and with, this grey area. This is real for her characters and viewers alike.

29 Jessica Torrance, 'Exploring the Recognition of Dogs as Sentient Beings: Understanding the Evolution of Dog Psychology' (2023) 10 Open Access Library Journal 1.

30 Joseph Lee, 'Dog Symbolism in Dreams: Companions, Protectors and Guides of Souls' (*ThisJungianLife.com*, 10 October 2024) <https://thisjungianlife.com/dog-symbolism-in-dreams/> accessed 22 August 2025.

12 Final Element: Dominant Style of Expressionism

The final element is the dominant style of film as expressionist, alongside naturalism, which is common as well. This is demonstrated in the film in dialogue. Here are some excerpts from Sandra's dialogue.

> Sandra Voyter: You made us live here among the goats! You complain about the life that you chose! You're not a victim! Not at all!

This dialogue is part of the scene in which the courtroom is listening to an audio recording of a quarrel turned violent confrontation and fight between Sandra and Samuel. According to Triet, the biggest challenge was to make a deeply personal film about a family and a couple. The filmmaker asks what it means to live together in reciprocity and whether it is possible for a couple to live together and for both to feel fulfilled.

> Sandra Voyter: Me, personally, I refuse to rot inside, so I find solutions, and at this point, sex was just a question of personal hygiene.

In the quest to find an answer, the film eventually offers little hope, and Triet was not sure if the audience would empathise or even relate to the couple.[31]

> Samuel Maleski: I'm saying maybe, just maybe, things are a little out of balance between us, and I want you to take a look at that. Why is this so hard to discuss?
> Sandra Voyter: First of all, I don't believe in the notion of reciprocity in a couple. It's naive and frankly it's depressing. Yes. And I think discussing it is a waste of time, considering the state you're in, seriously. All this blah, blah, blah here and more time is gone, all this time spent chitchatting could be spent in silence, doing whatever you want to do, if only you knew what it is that …

The scene lasts for 10 minutes, which is very long. It ends quite violently in terms of the soundbites the courtroom hears. In addition to the dialogue, Triet spent hours considering the placing of the actors' bodies. Sandra and Samuel are shown apart. He is at the kitchen counter and she is at the table eating spaghetti. As the scene unfolds, the action brings them closer together. The scene was incredibly complex physically and emotionally.

31 (n 19).

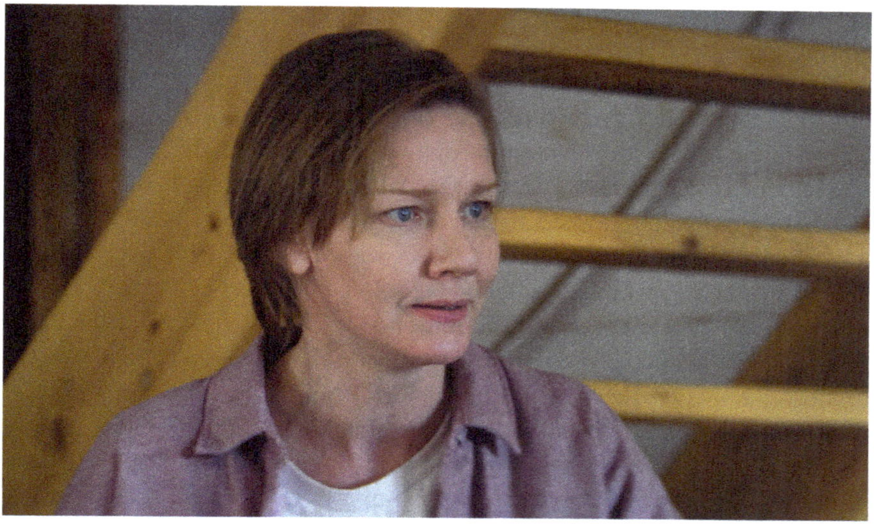

FIGURE 3.5 Sandra fighting with Samuel (Source: Landmark Media/Alamy)

13 Concluding Remarks

This contribution has argued that while ANATOMY OF A FALL is not a legal movie, it is nonetheless an excellent comment about the law, because all social relations can be seen as legal relations and legal subjectivity. The film starts with a traditional mystery but becomes an analysis of a kind of "fall" that differs from the literal one at its heart. What is anatomised is the decline of a marriage. A marriage is scrutinised from all angles while the notion is maintained that we can never fully comprehend anyone but ourselves. The filmmaker is exploring how couples communicate or fail to do so and what that failure can lead to in the end. It is of vital importance that neither Sandra nor Samuel speak in their native tongue. Their common ground is English. Daniel suffers from reduced eyesight from an accident. The film asks profound questions about its characters but the greater part of its power derives from its recognising that it does not have all the answers. Triet is more interested in the lack of answers than in certainty. In fact, this film is about judgement, its place in law, and the fact that it is a feature of our societal relations and lives.

The theme of judgement recalls the topics of law and justice that constantly appear in the late Polish director Krzysztof Kieślowski's films.[32] In his

32 Alex Boguniewicz, 'Restoration Versus Retribution: Justice in Krzysztof Kieślowski's Dekalog' (Undergraduate thesis, University of Colorado Boulder 2011).

movies, Kieślowski reveals his interpretations of justice and yet in them the notion of justice never takes on an absolute definition. This is most evident in his DEKALOG series (1988). The Polish filmmaker acknowledges the many different approaches there can be to amending wrongs. Kieślowski depicts those concepts of justice that are most effective in creating harmony after an offence. In particular, restorative justice, which rejects punishment and tries to create a dialogue between the victim and the offender.[33] And, by entering into a dialogue, the offender may recognise their wrongdoing and make amends, thereby becoming an indispensable part of society.[34] Furthermore, in restorative justice the legal system is encouraged to understand the background of the offender, when seeking to address the mitigating circumstances that could have provoked the crime.[35] To further amplify this point, Kieślowski uses retributive justice to call for a proportionate punishment, in the hope of deterring future crime.[36] Yet emotional connections, in the form of interactions between individuals, prove far more important than punishment.

Here is where film meets law. Laws are meant to govern relationships between individuals, dictating what behaviour is acceptable and what behaviour is not. Courts act as the mediation between individuals when a crime has occurred, with the intention of restoring balance. As in each film in the DEKALOG series, ANATOMY OF A FALL also acts as a court proceeding, with the crime taking place, followed by a mediation and an eventual resolution. On the surface, justice carries the popular connotation of fairness and maintenance of some kind of societal balance. The idea of communication and interaction remains key to this process. At the same time, the motivations of the offenders obscure the boundaries between right and wrong. In ANATOMY OF A FALL, the dialogue also plays a similar role. The victim is heard (albeit in a recording, and through flashbacks), but so is the defendant and various others. Kieślowski's emphasis on dialogue in his films is quite deliberate, and he also never fully condemns his characters, granting the "villains" a great deal of humanity because of the mitigating circumstances.[37] In fact, the perpetrator, rather than being punished, plays a significant role in the ultimate, just outcome of a case.[38] As seen in ANATOMY OF A FALL, the supposed murder proves to be far more complex than one might expect. Triet's film, through the depiction of Sandra, eloquently shows that the way for us to follow is to work

33 Ibid 23.
34 Ibid 2.
35 Ibid 2, 43.
36 Ibid 45.
37 (n 32).
38 Ibid 23.

through, by working with, our current cultural circumstances,[39] making this very much an interpersonal film that is also very much a film about the law.

This paper considered the French filmmaker Justine Triet's 2023 award-winning film, Anatomy of a Fall, through a screenwriter's lens. Using the work of one of the key thinkers in the field of film studies,[40] this paper demonstrated how and why Anatomy of a Fall is an interpersonal drama at its core. It is still, however, a movie about the law, in its portrayal of a breakdown of a marriage and the criminal investigation of the husband's death and alleged murder and the role of the wife—who is a woman, a writer, and not a local—in the foul play. Triet's film challenges the viewers to think about the manner in which we judge ourselves, and how others judge us, in particular when a woman, who happens to be a writer, is at the heart of and driving the story.

References

'Anatomy of a Fall' (*Fandom.com*) <https://movies.fandom.com/wiki/Anatomy_of_a_Fall> accessed 22 August 2025.

'Anatomy of a Fall' (*Forgetfulfilmcritic.com*, 01 March 2024) <https://www.forgetfulfilmcritic.com/home/2024/03/01/anatomy-of-a-fall> accessed 22 August 2025.

'Anatomy of a Fall: Sandra Hüller: Sandra Voyter' (*IMDb*) <https://www.imdb.com/title/tt17009710/characters/nm1197689?ref_=tt_mv_close> accessed 22 August 2025.

Boguniewicz A., 'Restoration Versus Retribution: Justice in Krzysztof Kieslowski's Dekalog' (Undergraduate thesis, University of Colorado Boulder 2011).

Bruzzi S., 'Imperfect Justice: Fritz Lang's Fury (1936) and Cinema's Use of the Trial Form' (2015) 4 Law and Humanities 1.

Campbell J., *The Hero with a Thousand Faces* (Princeton University Press 1949).

Frosch J., "Anatomy of a Fall' Review: Sandra Hüller Is Brilliant as a Writer Accused of Murder in Justine Triet's Rivetingly Complex Drama' (*The Hollywood Reporter*, 21 May 2023) <https://www.hollywoodreporter.com/movies/movie-reviews/anatomy-of-a-fall-review-sandra-huller-justine-triet-1235496751/> accessed 22 August 2025.

Goodfellow M., "Anatomy Of A Fall' Director Justine Triet Talks Love Of Cannes Competition: "It Can Be Violent"—Deadline Q & A.' (*Deadline*, 24 May 2023) <https://deadline.com/2023/05/anatomy-of-a-fall-director-justine-triet-cannes-1235376653/> accessed 22 August 2025.

39 Richard K. Sherwin, 'Law's Enchantment: The Cinematic Jurisprudence of Krzysztof Kieslowski' in Michael Freeman (ed), *Law and Popular Culture* (Oxford University Press 2005).

40 (n 1).

Hajimirsadeghi A. and Jones C., '13 Best Movies With Characters Who Are Writers' (*Movieweb*, 15 September 2023) <https://movieweb.com/best-movies-characters-writers/> accessed 22 August 2025.

Jacey H., 'Heroines in Flux: Gender and Screenwriting' (*Viewfinder Magazine*, 2021) <https://learningonscreen.ac.uk/viewfinder/articles/heroines-in-flux-gender-and-screenwriting/> accessed 22 August 2025.

Klockars K., 'Book Review Mónica López Lerma & Julen Etxabe (eds): *Rancière and Law*, Routledge, London 2018' (2023) 15 Nofu 147.

Krauel J., 'Book review of Sensing justice through contemporary Spanish cinema: aesthetics, politics, law' (2024) 18 Law and Humanities 132.

Lee J., 'Dog Symbolism in Dreams: Companions, Protectors and Guides of Souls' (*ThisJungianLife.com*, 10 October 2024) <https://thisjungianlife.com/dog-symbolism-in-dreams/> accessed 22 August 2025.

Leffler R., 'Justine Triet breaks down four key scenes from 'Anatomy Of A Fall': "'P.I.M.P.' wasn't our first choice for the song' (*ScreenDaily*, 12 February 2024) <https://www.screendaily.com/features/justine-triet-breaks-down-four-key-scenes-from-anatomy-of-a-fall-pimp-wasnt-our-first-choice-for-the-song/5190406.article> accessed 22 August 2025.

López Lerma M., *Sensing Justice through Contemporary Spanish Cinema: Aesthetics, Politics, Law* (Edinburgh University Press 2022).

Manderson D., *Song Without Music: Aesthetic Dimensions of Law and Justice* (University of California Press 2000).

McKee R., *Story* (Methuen Publishing 1997).

Merryman A., 'The Best Legal and Courtroom Dramas' (*RogerEbert.com*, 04 March 2024) <https://www.rogerebert.com/features/the-best-legal-and-courtroom-dramas> accessed 22 August 2025.

Moran L. and others, *Law's Moving Image* (Routledge 2004).

Parker P., *The Art and Science of Screenwriting* (Intellect Books 1998).

Parker P., 'What is the Personal Drama Journey' (*BCre8iv Blog*, 02 October 2015) <https://blog.bcre8ive.net/dramas-personal-journey/> accessed 22 August 2025.

Sherwin R.K., 'Law's Enchantment: The Cinematic Jurisprudence of Krzystof Kieslowski' in Michael Freeman (ed), *Law and Popular Culture* (Oxford University Press 2005).

Snyder B., *Save the Cat!: The Last Book on Screenwriting You'll Ever Need* (Michael Wiese Productions 2005).

Tallerico B., 'Anatomy of a Fall' (*RogerEbert.com*, 12 October 2023) <https://www.rogerebert.com/reviews/anatomy-of-a-fall-movie-review-2023> accessed 22 August 2025.

Torrance J., 'Exploring the Recognition of Dogs as Sentient Beings: Understanding the Evolution of Dog Psychology' (2023) 10 Open Access Library Journal 1.

PART 2

Films on Legal Problems

CHAPTER 4

OPPENHEIMER: the Cold War on Trial

Elisabeth Bronfen

1 Genre Conventions of Courtroom Drama

To discuss Christopher Nolan's biopic OPPENHEIMER in terms of a courtroom drama, it is fruitful to recall what is specific about this film genre. As some critics have noted, it is a quintessentially American genre because of the importance of jury duty. As Alexis de Tocqueville notes in Democracy in America, because all citizens of the US can be called to jury duty, chosen at random, yet temporarily invested with the right to judge, people of all classes become familiar with legal ways and the language of the judiciary becomes common language. "There is virtually no political question in the United States that does not sooner or later resolve itself into a judicial question," he claims. The legal spirit spreads beyond the walls of the law schools and courtrooms, he adds, "and infiltrates all of society, as it were, filtering down to the lowest ranks, with the result that in the end all the people acquire some of the habits and tastes of the magistrate".[1] Picking up on this claim, the film scholar Carol Clover looks at how the fundamental role of the jury in American law translates into the dramatic rules of the courtroom drama. While, with very few exceptions, the jury itself remains fairly anonymous, these films often turn the courtroom into a movie theater and the audience into a film audience: "The reason that juries are largely unseen in trial movies and the jury system largely uncontested within the regime of cinema is surely that we understand the jury to constitute a kind of necessary blank space in the text, one reserved for us".[2]

We, the spectators, are the actual jury, albeit on the extradiegetic level of the film. The additional information we get about the defense, the prosecution as well as about the defendant and the witnesses, be it in form of flashbacks or scenes that take place outside the courtroom, supplies us with evidence the actual jury does not have. The camera work, moving between establishing shots and medium shots to position us in relation to the interrogations taking

1 Alexis de Tocqueville, *Democracy in America (1835–1840)* (Translated by Arthur Goldhammer, Library of America 2004) 310–311.

2 Carol J. Clover, 'God Bless Juries!' in Nick Browne (ed), *Refiguring American Film Genres: Theory and History* (University of California Press 1998) 265.

© 2026 THE AUTHOR(S) | HTTPS://DOI.ORG/10.1163/9789004761704-005

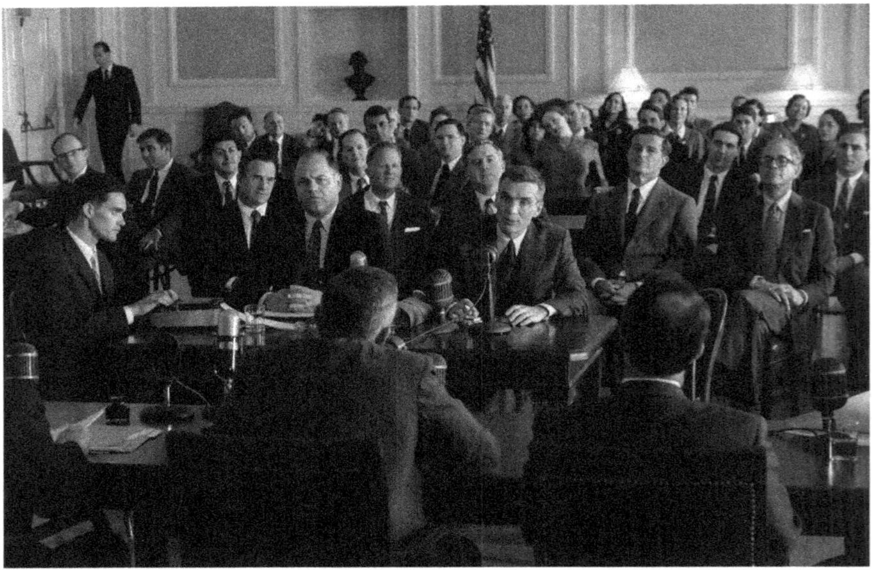

FIGURE 4.1 Oppenheimer at the hearing (Film still by Moviestore Collection)

place, the close-ups that allow us to partake in emotions on the faces of certain characters which the jury can't see, indeed all the theatrical display serves to position us as the active viewers whose judgement is the only one that counts. We not only know more, but we are also privy to the ambivalences and contradictions at stake.

This dramatic genre rule has to do with two aspects that are key to the courtroom genre. On the one hand, part and parcel of Hollywood's fascination with the courtroom drama "is the distinctive adversarial structure of the American legal process".[3] The examination and cross-examination are presented as a contest between the prosecution and the defense, with each side vying to convince the judge and the jurors. The opening and closing statements offer up competing narratives, supporting the sentence each side hopes to achieve. At issue is a battle for the truth, in which the side that has the better narrative wins. On the other hand, this legal battle involves theatricality. Key to the way both the audience, the jury and the judge are meant to respond to the arguments is the way the lawyers for the prosecution and the defense present their side of the case—the gestures, the delivery, the rhetorical tactics they deploy, the way they cross-examine, the way they seek to manipulate the evidence in

3 Elisabeth Bronfen, 'Court Martial Drama' in Elisabeth Bronfen (ed), *Specters of War: Hollywood's Engagement with Military Conflict* (Rutgers University Press 2012) 170.

their favor. In so doing, they, however, draw not just the film jury, but, more importantly, the film spectators into their confidence. They play with our sympathies, our outrage, our preconceptions even while debunking those of their adversaries. As a result, a "double-trial structure"[4] is, as Clover notes, fundamental to the courtroom drama, mounting a second, unofficial trial not on the actual case, but on the legal system's ability to pass the correct sentence, to find justice.

Significant for the courtroom genre is, thus, the tension between the diegetic audience (the jury, the judge, the people sitting in the courtroom) and the extradiegetic audience, the film spectators. At the end of the film, an ironic distance has been created between the decision to which those passing judgement came and the interpretation of both the case and the way the court handled it, which we are meant to forge for ourselves. At stake, however, isn't only the possible fallibility of the individuals, who have, if only temporarily, been invested with the right to judge, but also the distinction between legal and ethical judgement. The jury, or in the case of OPPENHEIMER, the members of the Personnel Security Board, have to make a simple choice between guilty or not guilty. The film spectators, in turn, are called upon the pass what one might call an "aesthetic judgement"; not, however, in the sense of whether the film is aesthetically accomplished or not. Rather, at issue is the immense gray zone between guilt and innocence.[5] A defendant may, in strict legal terms, be guilty of the crime she or he is accused of. If, however, one takes external circumstances into considerations—be they moral, psychological or cultural—this distinction may become fuzzy. The cultural values prevalent at the given historical moments, the political preferences (and prejudices) of the legal system at the time, may also need to be factored in to gain a more nuanced, more complicated view of the case.

What further distinguishes the genre is the fact that the evidence being presented at the trial in a courtroom drama involves various aspects. First, we have the facts of the case. Second, the manner in which these facts are presented by both sides, bringing subjective positions, prejudices as well as theatrical showmanship into play. Third, the verdict the jury reaches and the sentence that is passed by the judge. Fourth, the way the spectators judge the case. Finally, the question of whether justice has been served or not. Can the legal system, can a group of twelve people, get at the truth or not? Is the law, and the legal

4 (n 2) 264.

5 For a discussion of the difference between legal language and aesthetic language see Shoshana Felman, *The Juridical Unconscious: Trials and Traumas in the Twentieth Century* (Harvard University Press 2002).

system embodying it, reliable? Does the film support our trust in the system or our suspicion that the American courts are not the place where justice can be found? Are we, in hindsight, in a better position to find the truth? This ambiguity also explains the "double-trial structure" so seminal to the genre. There is always more than one case being negotiated. In the case of OPPENHEIMER, the film narrative presents us with both a secret hearing on the part of the Personnel Security Board, and a public hearing during the Senate confirmation process at the beginning of the Eisenhower administration, interweaving the two. One is official but secret, the other official but out in the open. On the extradiegetic level we have a third trial, namely the case the film is making implicitly regarding both of these hearings. On this level, the question of judging involves the way both legal proceedings were conducted; it involves a critical distance and a commentary on what was being deliberated and negotiated in the process of the courtroom proceedings. While one, or both of the hearings staged in the film are debunked, the one presented by the film itself holds strong emotional weight.

Given these genre rules, it is fruitful to first distinguish the various cases that are being put on trial in the film OPPENHEIMER, so as to analyze how—and why—our evaluation, our judgement might differ from those passed by the board and by the Senate committee, but also the one passed by the director and screenplay writer Christopher Nolan. Furthermore, given that we are dealing with a historical case that is being re-enacted on screen, we also want to ask ourselves, why it makes sense to re-enact these hearings on screen? What temporalities are at issue? At issue isn't only a revisitation of a past historical event, judging it again, only now through the lens of the consequences it has had. Rather, we are also called upon to ask, why it is timely and urgent to return to these cases now. What does reopening the case against—or for—Oppenheimer tell us about our current moment?

2 OPPENHEIMER—Two Parallel Court Cases

In OPPENHEIMER, the narrative moves back and forth between the two court cases, and, in so doing, splices together different historical moments, so that the parallel cases serve to comment on each other. Indeed, the adversarial nature of the American courtroom turns into a confrontation between the two hearings, with the latter indicting the secret adversary who was in charge of the indictment in the former case. As already noted, the double-trial structure on the level of the film's diegesis involves, on the one hand, the Personnel Security Hearings that took place in 1954. As a result, Robert Oppenheimer

(Cillian Murphy) was ultimately denied his Q clearance. It was an attempt to discredit his political influence after WWII by recalling his alliance with the American communist party before the war. Oppenheimer defends himself, though unsuccessfully, by explaining that his conviction not to continue developing an H-bomb can only be understood in the context of his previous life and work. The film takes him up on his claim and offers us flashback scenes, illustrating the events that led up to the politically precarious situation he now finds himself in. The adversarial nature of American legal proceedings pits the aggressive prosecutor and his team against a defense lawyer, who, because he has not had access to the files on Oppenheimer, can do very little for him. The man presiding over the Gray commission, in turn, points out that they are not judges and, thus, do not have the power to convict him of a crime, but simply to deny his security clearance. They will ultimately decide two to one that he is guilty only in the sense that he is a threat to American national security. The secret proceedings take place within the context of the public McCarthy hearings on Un-American activities.

On the other hand, a parallel narrative strand revolves around the businessman and politician Lewis Strauss (Robert Downey Jr.), a high-ranking member of the AEC (US Atomic Energy Commission), who had clandestinely staged this Kangaroo court against his political adversary. It takes place several years later, during the 1959 Senate Hearings for Secretary of Commerce. President Eisenhower wants Strauss to be part of his cabinet. Though this would be a supreme triumph for him, there is the thorny issue of his previous relation with Oppenheimer. This, in turn, brings back into play what had been at issue in the secret hearings, namely the security clearing Oppenheimer had been granted for the Manhattan project and the fact that this was later revoked. Strauss ultimately loses by a narrow margin, and he does so precisely because what he had hoped would remain a clandestine affair is brought into the open. Nolan thus draws into focus how the past (both the Manhattan project and the clandestine case against Oppenheimer) haunts the present. At the same time, at issue is also how the previous hearing offers a commentary and a reflection on the subsequent one, contesting it. What explicitly links the two is the moment, at the end of the Security hearing, when Oppenheimer asks his lawyer in despair, "is anyone ever going to tell the truth of what is happening here". That is exactly what the scientist, Dr. David Hill, does almost a decade later, signally that something has changed significantly in the past six years for this to be possible in the American political culture of the Eisenhower presidency.

Given the adversarial structure of the film narrative, it is worth delving more closely into what it entails. The trouble begins when Strauss asks Oppenheimer to join him at the Princeton Institute of Advanced Studies. The opposition between these two Jewish men can be seen in terms of class. Oppenheimer is wealthy, has studied at different European universities, is fluent in many languages, but doesn't speak Yiddish. To the self-made man, who started out as a shoe salesman, he comes across as arrogant. The film script itself is ambivalent about its eponymous hero. We get CGI visualizations of the way Oppenheimer is able to see beyond the world normal people live in and thus understand why he feels he stands above his fellow men. At the same time, his self-confidence not only makes him blind to the political machinations taking place around him. He also self-consciously cultivates a genius persona; and, given the way Cillian Murphy performs the role, he appears as a solitary person, tortured by his extraordinary gift while also basking in his charismatic power. We understand why others might describe him as "unstable, theatrical, egotistical, and neurotic".

The key scene in the battle between the two men is nominally the one in which Oppenheimer publicly humiliates Strauss over the sale of isotopes to Norway; a scene that is referred to more than once in the course of the film narrative by diverse characters. Yet there is a more seminal, albeit more private scene, which takes place at a pond on the Princeton campus, and this is a scene the film also keeps returning to. The fact that it is a clandestine moment corresponds to the obsession with secrecy during WWII and post-war American culture. Only late in the film do we learn that Oppenheimer is talking to Einstein about the consequences of his discovery of the atom bomb. At the time of this conversation, Strauss did not hear what the two men were saying but was looking on from afar. When Einstein, upset by what he has been told by his younger colleague, doesn't greet Strauss, who has approached the two men, he assumes that Oppenheimer has turned the scientist sour against him. His paranoia, which is to say his sense that the people around him are working against him, is the counterpart to Oppenheimer's arrogance.

It is also important to note that Oppenheimer's subsequent moral qualms about having started a nuclear war race between the USA and Russia involves several separate historical moments. In the 1930s and then, once the Americans join WWII, at issue for him is antisemitism. He defends his passion for developing the atomic bomb by pointing out to others that it is the Jewish people whom the Nazis are killing in the camps. This is, however, also a period in which anti-communist sentiment was prevalent in American politics, and, once the Soviet Union is no longer an ally, this again becomes widespread among members of the government, while Holocaust commemoration replaces antisemitism. During the war, Oppenheimer distances himself from his communist friends, insisting that he is a New Deal Democrat. He assures the military officers in charge of the Manhattan project "my involvement in

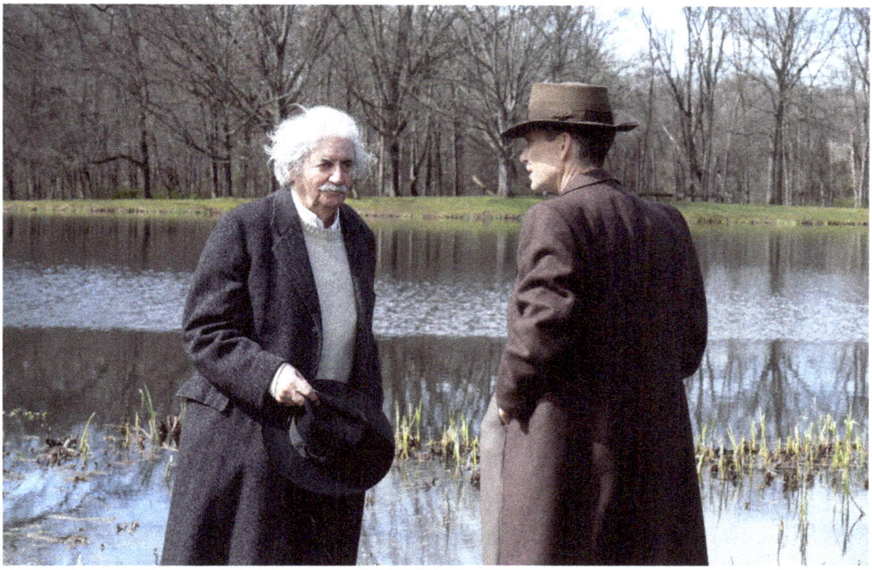

FIGURE 4.2 Einstein and Oppenheimer are talking (Film still by Photo 2, Universal Pictures, Melinda Su Gordon)

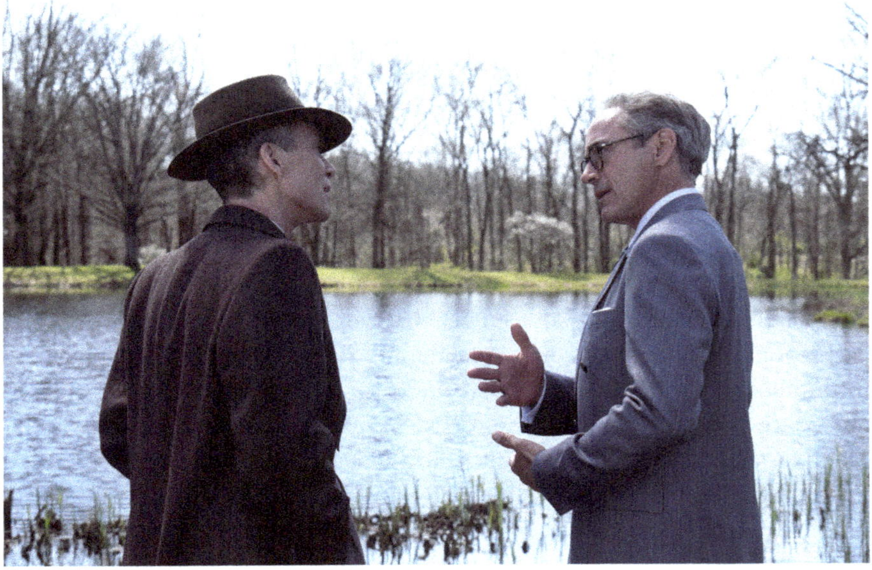

FIGURE 4.3 Strauss approaches Oppenheimer after Einstein left without greeting. (Film still by Photo 2, Universal Pictures, Melinda Su Gordon)

left-wing groups would not prove a bar to my working on the atomic program". The secret hearings that take place in 1954 are subsequently also about whether this former claim is true or not.

So key for the "aesthetic judgement" (rather than a purely legal one) which we are meant to pass concerns how we judge Strauss's attitude towards Oppenheimer, both during WWII and during the Cold War that followed. But equally key is how we judge the entanglement between their personal and their political rivalry in each of these historic moments. The paramount question during the Senate hearings has to do with what happened between 1947 and 1954 to convince Strauss, who was a major figure in the development of nuclear weapons, to first grant and then deny security clearance to the star physicist he had called to Princeton. As the title of my essay suggests, the cultural transformation that explains this change of heart involves the shift from a situation of emergency during and right after WWII to the Cold War paranoia of the 1950s, and the culture of suspicion, surveillance and interrogation this brought with it. Strauss is able to follow through on his personal feud because he knows that by giving Oppenheimer's file to a man in the FBI, this will set a clandestine chain of events in motion, which will culminate in the secret hearings against his rival. The adversarial nature so seminal to the courtroom proceedings exceeds these in its political spirit. The prosecutor and the defense lawyers are proxies for the actual "prosecutor", Strauss, who has made sure to be absent from the actual investigation. For the defendant, in turn, far more is on trial than simply the issue of his Q-clearance; namely his reputation, his political power as a scientist, and his public standing.

The double-trial structure of the courtroom drama, pitting diegetic narration against extradiegetic argument, however, brings a further question into play, that transforms the Security hearings into a proxy investigation for a larger political issue. Did the scientist at the Manhattan project really have no choice but to produce weapons of mass destruction because the Nazis couldn't be trusted with them? The advice Einstein gives to Oppenheimer in the scene at the pond, advice Strauss doesn't hear and which we are presented only late in the film as a flashback, is that "if the truth is catastrophic, then you stop and share your findings with the Nazis. So neither side destroys the world". The question that the film rephrases for the early 1950s, and which is key to the moral conundrum Nolan as a scriptwriter draws into focus, is whether the US government subsequently had no other choice than to continue the arms race. It is worth recalling that it was Eisenhower, who, in his farewell address, warned,

> in the councils of government, we must guard against the acquisition of unwarranted influence, whether sought or unsought, by the military-industrial

> complex. The potential for the disastrous rise of misplaced power exists and will persist. We must never let the weight of this combination endanger our liberties or democratic processes.[6]

The women around Oppenheimer play a subordinate role in the rivalry between the two Jewish men. Jean Tatlock (Florence Pugh), is a psychiatrist and communist, with whom he continues to have an affair, even after he marries, sees herself in rivalry with his wife. Yet Kitty Pueng (Emily Blunt), a biologist and former communist, not only forgives her husband this extramarital affair. After Tatlock has committed suicide and Oppenheimer accuses himself of having abandoned her, she tells him to pull himself together. She is also the one who quickly realizes that Straus was the one to give her husband's file to the FBI. During the secret hearings she is again the feisty one, telling her husband that he should fight and stop playing the role of the martyr. Her testimony is, furthermore, seminal for the decision the Gray commission reaches, declaring Oppenheimer to be a loyal citizen even though they revoke his Q-clearance. Finally, she is the one who, in the final scene of the film, continues to bear a grudge against the businessman who spoke out against her husband. In other words, on the extradiegetic level of the film, she emerges as the most forceful figure of moral judgment.

3 The Extradiegetic Case

Let us, therefore, return once more to the tension between the diegetic investigative proceedings—first against Oppenheimer and then against Strauss—and the way the film OPPENHEIMER makes its own case regarding both with an ironic distance and from the position of our current moment. If this case appeals only to us, the spectators, we are the ones to decide on who is guilty and who is not guilty. If, furthermore, we are asked to base our judgment on information that is never brought into either of the hearings (in the form of flashbacks and of scene that take place in private), this extra-legal material not only provides us with different points of view but also, and perhaps more importantly, brings ambivalences into play. The witness reports, the evidence, and the testimony they offer up, all this serves to pit the legal justice at play in the hearings against the aesthetic justice which the film brings into play; along

6 See Dwight D. Eisenhower, 'Military-Industrial Complex Speech, Dwight D. Eisenhower, 1961' (*The Avalon Project*) <https://avalon.law.yale.edu/20th_century/eisenhower001.asp> accessed 17 February 2025.

with the retrospective commentary and critique of all the historical moments that come to be revisited on screen.

Strauss, indeed, embodies an obsession with clandestinity, in line with what Richard Hofstadter called "the paranoid style in American politics" in his seminal essay for Harper's Magazine (November 1964).[7] Strauss is not only underhanded in getting Oppenheimer to be examined by the Atomic Energy Commission but also wants a closed hearing so he can discredit his opponent, and, indeed, destroy his credibility completely. A public hearing would have given Oppenheimer a platform for his political position on atomic weapons, while his opponent's goal is that he never be able to speak on matters of national security again. The choice of scene—a small room, far from the limelight, an unofficial trial presenting itself as a bureaucratic procedure—is the perfect equivalent of the Cold War climate in general. As Strauss explains, he wants "no audience, no reporters, no burden of proof". Yet there are reporters present, namely the director Christopher Nolan and his film team, and there is an audience, namely us, the spectators, who have taken on the role of the absent jury. What evolves is a systemic rehabilitation of Oppenheimer, both through the back story the narration includes in the form of memory flashbacks, and through the re-enactment of what was an unofficial hearing. On screen it becomes public, bringing what was a secret theatrical performance out into the open. Furthermore, Strauss' claim that they are not prosecuting, not convicting, but merely denying, meant to justify his clandestine actions, will be turned against him in his own hearing before the Senate.

The dual trial structure prevalent throughout OPPENHEIMER uses the final sequence to once again draw out the analogy between the two hearings, and it is worth recalling that at the beginning of the film we are told that both aren't trials in the ordinary sense of the word. For Oppenheimer that means that his defense lawyer has little power because, as already stated, most of the evidence against him has been defined as classified. For Strauss this means he has no power to cross-examine any of the witnesses speaking out against his nomination. To draw out the correspondence, the film culminates in a montage sequence deploying parallel editing, that shifts back and forth between the two hearings, both of which do not end in a juridical conviction but rather in something being denied—Oppenheimer's security clearance on the one hand, and, on the other, Strauss' position in the Eisenhower cabinet. The official hearing in 1959 and the closed hearing in 1954 mirror each other. In both cases, witnesses bring in testimony that is detrimental for the defendant.

7 Reprinted in Richard Hofstadter, *The Paranoid Style in American Politics* (Alfred A. Knopf 1965).

In the secret hearing, men who worked on the Manhattan project are compelled to assert that, in the changed political atmosphere, security clearance to Oppenheimer would be dangerous. In the Senate hearing Dr. Hill asserts that his fellow scientists not only didn't want to see Strauss involved in their research. He also brings up the case against Oppenheimer, asserting that it had to do with personal vindictiveness on the part of the man about to be appointed to a cabinet position.

As Strauss notes after the witness has been dismissed, "this is no longer a confirmation hearing but a trial about a trial". He proceeds to admit wryly that in his case, too, it is not about convicting him, but denying him something. As Oppenheimer did in the previous hearing, he, too, realizes that he has been publicly denigrated. Significant for the parallel representation of the two hearings is also the way he responds. While, in the prior scene, once more recalling the unofficial hearing, we see the prosecuting officer shout down any testimony arguing for Oppenheimer, Strauss now rails against the scientist who testified against his suitability for a cabinet post. He has become his own prosecutor, and in his case, this also plays itself out in a non-public setting. Only his helpers hear his rant. Once he steps out to greet the journalists, Strauss is again smiling. Noteworthy is the small ironic comment the script offers, when, having heard that he has lost, Strauss defiantly leaves the scene. The man who spearheaded the small group of Senators against Strauss was a young politician from Massachusetts called John F. Kennedy.

In more than one sense, the final verdict is up to us. At the end of the film, the decision of the Gray commission has been debunked. Judgement has been passed against both the men who conducted it as well as the political culture they represented. The Senate decision is more complicated, given that while we don't know what consequences Strauss's membership in the Eisenhower cabinet would have had we do know those of John F. Kennedy's rise to power. His support for US military engagement in Southeast Asia will culminate in the Vietnam War. At the same time, the film not only offers an indictment of the McCarthy era but also exonerates self-critical scientists, who are able to reflect on the responsibility they bear regarding the consequences that their research might have. For this reason it is dramatically so powerful that in its final sequence, the film returns once more to the scene at the pond in Princeton. Only then do we hear what Einstein actually said to Oppenheimer and discover that they never talked about Strauss at all. This is not only important because the advice Einstein gives, is an argument against an arms race, but because it implicitly reveals something that further indicts Strauss, over and beyond his clandestine involvement with the Gray commission. Thinking that Oppenheimer had soured the other scientist against him was part of his deluded fantasy. His personal paranoia is shown to have been unfounded and, by virtue of analogy, this also exposes the illegitimacy of the secret hearings he orchestrated to discredit the political influence of his opponent by questioning his loyalty. In retrospect the panel, too, can be judged to have been an expression of collective political paranoia. As a counterpoint—and that is dramatically significant for the multiple court cases that reflect each other in OPPENHEIMER as well—the conversation between Einstein and his young colleague revolved around a different form of judgement. They discussed the punishment that will be the consequence of their achievements. Oppenheimer suggests that he may have started a chain reaction to destroy the world. The final shot of the film offers us a close-up of his anguished face. He has passed judgement on himself.

There is, however, another form of judgment that is passed by the film. Kitty Pueng, has the last word, even if she doesn't have the last shot in the film. In the penultimate scene, she meets her husband in front of their house, looks at his grief struck face, and exclaims, "the world won't forgive you". In a prior scene she had, as already mentioned, refused to shake hands with Strauss because of his involvement in the dishonoring of her husband. As such, she is the character who not only predicts the future but who also won't forget past grievances. That, one might say, is also the position of this film, if we, picking up on the point her adversary made, understand it to be a trial about a trial about a trial. Christopher Nolan also wants us not to forget.

References

Bronfen E., 'Court Martial Drama' in Elisabeth Bronfen (ed), *Specters of War: Hollywood's Engagement with Military Conflict* (Rutgers University Press 2012).

Clover C.J., 'God Bless Juries!' in Nick Browne (ed), *Refiguring American Film Genres: Theory and History* (University of California Press 1998).

Eisenhower D.D., 'Military-Industrial Complex Speech, Dwight D. Eisenhower, 1961' (*The Avalon Project*) <https://avalon.law.yale.edu/20th_century/eisenhower001.asp> accessed 17 February 2025.

Felman S., *The Juridical Unconscious: Trials and Traumas in the Twentieth Century* (Harvard University Press 2002).

Hofstadter R., *The Paranoid Style in American Politics* (Alfred A. Knopf 1965).

de Tocqueville A., *Democracy in America (1835–1840)* (Translated by Arthur Goldhammer, Library of America 2004).

CHAPTER 5

The Fragility of Law and the Politics of Public Memory in Oppenheimer

Naomi Mezey

1 Introduction

This essay argues that Christopher Nolan's film Oppenheimer is an example of visual jurisprudence. It tells the story of Robert Oppenheimer and his legacy through the juxtaposed portrayals of two governmental hearings. Each hearing repeatedly disavows its relationship to law and legal processes, and each is presented as a moment of raw politics. The film, I argue, presents a space of alternative legality by functioning as a hearing in its own right; it is a hearing on the public memory of Robert Oppenheimer, on postwar paranoia and McCarthyism, on the uncertainty of a nuclear future, and the fragility of law in times of crisis. Nolan's film uses all the powers of visual proof and persuasion to revisit a national moment of rupture, when formal law was at its most fragile in the face of intense political power and global realignment.

In thinking about and revisiting the film, it became clear that the movie is about—among other things—what it means for something to be law or not law, and how law can recede and be displaced by power, particularly during periods of national stress, crisis, or paradigm shifts. It is a movie that is its own visual and narrative brief (a hearing, if you will) about the rules of the game, proof, persuasion, and power of many kinds. It is also a movie about how we remember and narrate the past, and what rules apply when legal rules are indeterminate and especially fragile.

Oppenheimer is ostensibly a biopic but as a film it is narratively structured around two government hearings of two different men—one a hearing in 1954 by the personnel security board of the Atomic Energy Commission (the AEC Hearing) to decide whether to revoke Robert Oppenheimer's security clearance and the other a Senate hearing in 1959 on whether to confirm Lewis Strauss as President Eisenhower's Secretary of Commerce (the Confirmation Hearing). The film's internal present is 1959 at the Confirmation Hearing, but almost all the action is in layers of flashbacks. The 1954 AEC Hearing is itself a flashback, but the narration of it is unstable, and there are flashbacks within the AEC Hearing flashback to other episodes. The flashbacks tell the story of

© 2026 THE AUTHOR(S) | HTTPS://DOI.ORG/10.1163/9789004761704-006

Oppenheimer's scientific career, his personal life, his role as Director of Los Alamos during the building of the atomic bomb, and the evolution of his public reputation after the war. It is, however, a strange kind of biopic in that it displaces its protagonist by giving the antagonist, Strauss, tremendous narrative power. Indeed, the movie becomes as much the story of two very different Jewish men navigating power in two very different but intersecting milieu, one operating according to the laws of physics and one according to the laws of politics at a moment when those endeavors overlapped significantly, and their rules were changing. It is also the story of two consequential mid-century government hearings at a moment of national crisis and legal fragility.

As an exercise of visual jurisprudence, Nolan's film is not presented in a traditionally persuasive way, in the manner of most trial films. It is visually distinctive, chaotic, nonchronological, and repetitive. Flashbacks tell a story that is constantly interrupting itself, jumping between temporalities, revisiting the same scene from different characters' perspectives, and sometimes even de-synchronizing the visual and the auditory aspects of the story. It is a film that mirrors the ruptures of its time—the destructive power of nuclear weapons, the international realignment after World War II, the ruthlessness of McCarthyism, and the fragmentation of modernism. It tells the story of a complex man in a complex way, by making the movie into a hearing on a morally fraught past and on a future beholden to the power of nuclear weapons, a future that is the audience's present. It is in this sense that the film has a jurisprudence of its own; it presents an alternative legality by visually creating its own hearing on how we should judge and remember Robert Oppenheimer and how the audience might take moral ownership of a future shadowed by nuclear weapons. Nolan's film uses all the powers of visual proof, persuasion, and collective memory to show us what it looks like when the politics of crisis displaces law, and the formal law is at its most uncertain and fragile, as it is in the hearings it portrays.

2 Law in Times of Crisis

2.1 Modernism and McCarthyism

Much of the film portrays events that occur during the inter-War period, a period when internationally there were major paradigm shifts in the arts, sciences, culture and politics. Encompassed most broadly by modernism, many areas of human inquiry and expression were undergoing their own revolutions.[1] In this sense, theoretical physics was to science what Picasso was to art, Stravinsky to music, Marx to political theory, and Freud to psychology. Viewers see and hear these references in the movie in a montage that mixes shots of OPPENHEIMER engaging with modernist classics: looking at Picasso's "Femme assise aux bras croisés," listening to Stravinsky's "Rite of Spring," and reading T.S Eliot's "The Waste Land." Marx is baked into the anti-communist plot and references to Freud appear explicitly and implicitly throughout the film. For example, Oppenheimer confesses to his lover Jean Tatlock that he has done two years of psychoanalysis. We understand that Oppenheimer sees all these paradigm shifts as linked. He references Picasso, Stravinsky, Freud, and Marx when he comments to a colleague, once "you accept the revolution in physics, can't you see it everywhere else?" And the movie doesn't just reference modernism, it mimics it.

Domestically, and closer to the film's present, the late 1940s and early 1950s in the United States were a period of political anxiety and Cold War suspicion. The House Un-American Activities Committee and Senator Joseph McCarthy were on a very public hunt for communists and Soviet agents, using federal power to root out subversion and disloyalty within and outside the government; prosecuting leftists, creatives, and academics; and fueling a second Red Scare not long after the first had subsided. In 1953, Senator McCarthy met with J. Edgar Hoover, the FBI Director, to suggest that his Senate Committee investigate Oppenheimer.[2] But the FBI was already investigating Oppenheimer, and in late 1953 the agent in charge of that investigation, William Borden, would inform Hoover that "based upon years of study, of the available classified evidence that more probably than not J. Robert Oppenheimer is an agent of the Soviet Union."[3] The FBI conclusion led the Atomic Energy Commission, now chaired by Strauss, to suspend Oppenheimer's top secret "Q clearance," his access to restricted data, and effectively his work for the Commission.[4] The

1 Richard Ellmann and Charles Feidelson Jr., *The Modern Tradition: Backgrounds of Modern Literature* (Oxford University Press 1965) vi: "Modernism strongly implies some sort of historical discontinuity, either a liberation from inherited patterns or, at another extreme, deprivation and disinheritance."

2 Douglas O. Linder, 'The Oppenheimer Security Hearing: A Chronology' (*Famous Trials*) <https://famous-trials.com/oppenheimer/2690-the-oppenheimer-security-hearing-a-chronology> accessed 03 March 2025.

3 Letter from William Borden to J. Edgar Hoover (7 November 1953) in (*Famous Trials*) <https://famous-trials.com/oppenheimer/2711-borden-letter-to-hoover-regarding-oppenheimer> accessed 03 March 2025.

4 Letter from K. D. Nichols, General Manager, AEC, to Robert Oppenheimer (23 December 1953) (hereinafter Nichols Letter) in (*Famous Trials*) <https://famous-trials.com/oppenheimer/2691-charges-against-oppenheimer-dec-23-1953> accessed 03 March 2025: "the

AEC Hearing, led by the personnel security board (the Board) of the AEC, was Oppenheimer's only opportunity to contest the charge of espionage, the suspension of his security clearance, and to clear his name.

2.2 The Hearings as Disavowals of Law

Both the hearings that form the core of the film belong at least as much to politics as they do to law.[5] Congressional and agency decision making generally has the force of law if the decision is within the authorized power of the committee or adjudicator. Congressional confirmation hearings, like the one in which Strauss was considered for a cabinet appointment, are assumed to be authorized by the Senate's power to confirm executive officers.[6] Formal hearings (falling under "adjudications") by federal agencies are normally governed by the Administrative Procedure Act, which establishes detailed processes for trial-type proceedings in which parties may present evidence and cross-examine witnesses.[7] Even informal agency hearings are usually procedurally robust and trial-like.[8] In contrast, adjudications of the Atomic Energy Commission were governed directly by the Atomic Energy Act (AEA) of 1946.[9] The letter notifying Oppenheimer of the hearing to adjudicate his security clearance references the Committee's authority under the AEA to ensure that employment by the AEC does not "endanger the common defense and

---

Commission has no other recourse, in discharge of its obligations to protect the common defense and security, but to suspend your clearance until the matter has been resolved. Accordingly, your employment on Atomic Energy Commission work and your eligibility for access to restricted data are hereby suspended, effective immediately, pending final determination of this matter."

5 I do not assume that law is formally distinct from politics or other major social endeavors. See eg David Kairys, *The Politics of Law: A Progressive Critique* (3rd edn, Basic Books 1998).

6 Josh Chafetz, 'Congressional Overspeech' (2020) 89 Fordham Law Review 529 citing US Const art II, § 2, cl 2.

7 Ben Harrington and Daniel J. Sneffer, 'Informal Administrative Adjudication: An Overview' (*Congress.Gov*, 10 October 2021) <https://www.congress.gov/crs-product/R46930> accessed 03 March 2025: "The formal hearing provisions establish detailed specifications for oral, trial-type proceedings. Parties may present evidence and cross-examine witnesses, and the adjudicator must issue a decision with findings and conclusions."

8 Emily S. Bremer, 'Designing the Decider' (2018) 16 Geo. J.L. & Pub. Pol'y 67 observing that "so-called informal adjudication is often conducted according to procedures that are as or more formal (in the colloquial sense of 'trial-like') than the procedures specified by the APA's 'formal' adjudication provisions".

9 Atomic Energy Act of 1946, 42 USC Chapter 23 (1946).

security."[10] Beyond giving the Commission the ability to notify relevant parties, administer oaths and subpoena people and documents, the AEA does not set out a specific procedure that must be followed in such a hearing. In other words, the procedural requirements for both hearings were vague at best and both were—unsurprisingly for highly political decisions—shot through with politics. In the portrayal of these hearings, the movie goes to great lengths to insist that what we see are moments of consequential judgment, but certainly not trials, and only remotely related to law.

The first spoken words of the film are a disavowal of law. But the movie begins without words; a series of images provide the bookends of the biopic version of the film: a young Robert Oppenheimer looks at the abstract ripples of raindrops, like so many shots that symbolize his mental interior, they are the geometries of his tortured imagination and the symbolic abstractions of modernism. Those images turn violent as swirling gases, imploding stars, and explosions of fire convey the contradictions, moral conflicts, and troubled visions of the man and the troubled era. Words appear on the screen from the Greek myth of Prometheus, who "stole fire from the gods and gave it to man. For this he was chained to a rock and tortured for eternity." We have the first framing of the film—a tortured hero experimenting with a power far beyond his control.

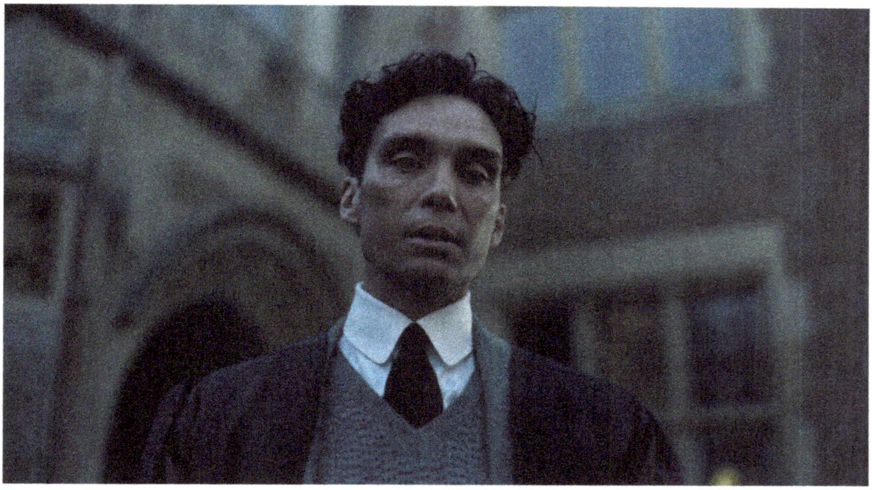

FIGURE 5.1 Young Robert Oppenheimer (Film still by TDC/PROD.DB)

10 See (n 4); Ibid. The AEA further provides for "such hearings as the Commission may deem necessary or proper to assist it in exercising any authority provided in this Act."

Moments later, Oppenheimer, now older, is being called back into the present of the AEC Hearing, being invited by the Board Chair to present his opening statement. His first words are a mumbled acknowledgment as he emerges from these visions and memories. He says, "Your Honor." The Chair responds: "We're not judges Doctor." The first dialogue establishes this moment as not quite law, at least not a trial, but something else. A moment of judgment, but in a different register.

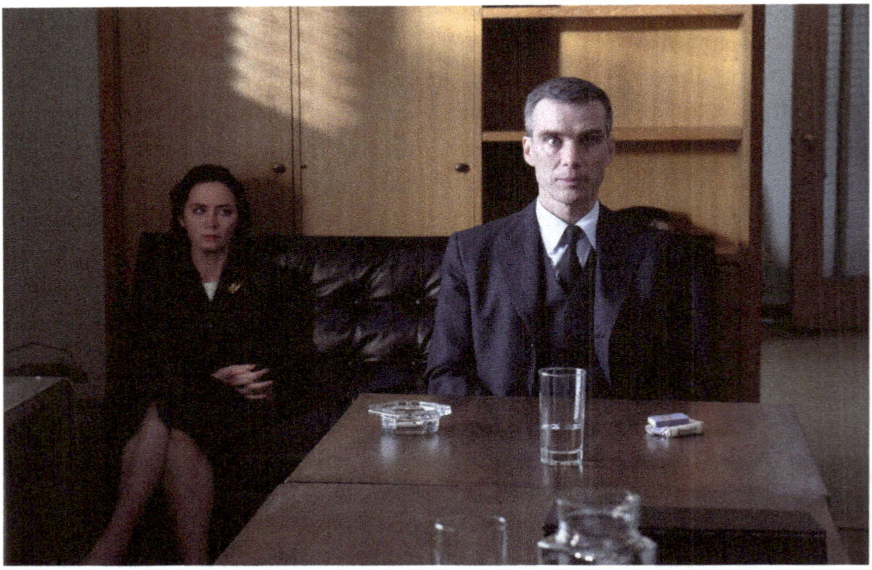

FIGURE 5.2 Oppenheimer at the Atomic Energy Commission (AEC) Hearing, in the background sits his wife Kitty (Film still by Landmark Media)

Within minutes, there is a cut to the film's present, the Confirmation Hearing of Lewis Strauss. He is walking to the hearing room with the Senate Aide, who is his handler for the hearing as well as Strauss' interlocutor to whom the Oppenheimer story is told. The Aide says, "Senator Thurmond asked me to say not to feel like you're on trial." Strauss responds, "Funny, I didn't until you just said that."

Our introductions to these men are in moments of national judgment, and yet our introduction to the hearings in which they are judged begin with the insistence that they are not on trial, and the implication that trials are a stand-in for law and legal processes. Strauss' role as the main narrator develops gradually and emerges almost entirely through his conversations with the Senate Aide during breaks in the Confirmation Hearing (off stage, so to speak).

Indeed, the drama of Strauss' potential confirmation does not truly enter the plot of the movie until 30 minutes or so in, once it has established the biopic narrative: Oppenheimer's education, his early days at Berkeley, his romantic relationships and leftist leanings. That is when Senators begin to question Strauss' role in the revocation of Oppenheimer's security clearance after the war, which invites Strauss to more fully inhabit the narration as he explains to the Aide (and to viewers) the backstory of his relationship to Oppenheimer.

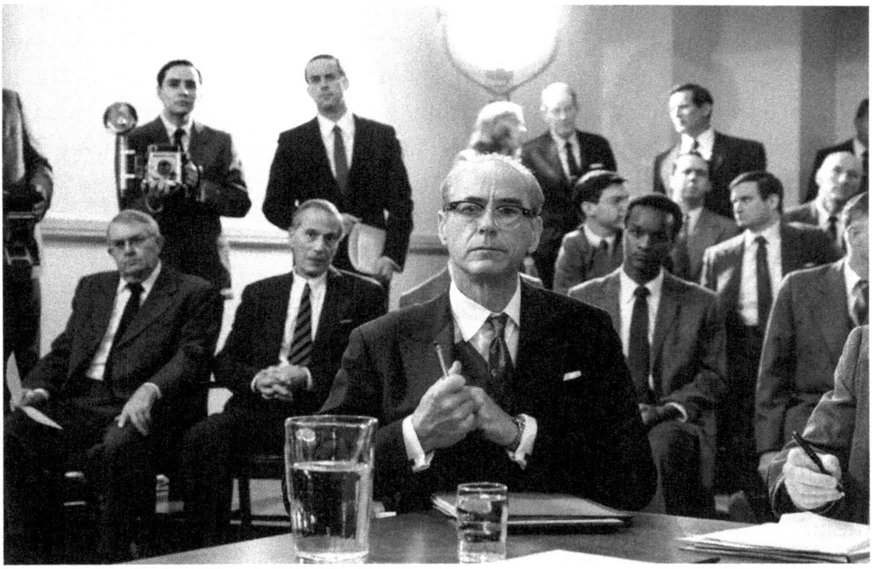

FIGURE 5.3 Lewis Strauss at the Confirmation hearing (Film still by Photo 2, Universal Pictures, Melinda Su Gordon)

It is at this point, the movie's present, that Strauss comes out of the shadows of the film and fully assumes the role of narrator as well as the role of personal and political antagonist to both Oppenheimer the man and to Oppenheimer's public memory. Strauss wants this nomination, and he senses the balance of power and public judgment shifting. When the Senators decide to invite scientists to testify at the confirmation hearing, Strauss says, "I'd like to know the name of the scientists testifying; I'd like the chance to cross-examine." The Chair responds, "This is not a court," as he stands and drops his folder heavily on the desk like a gavel. The architecture of legal power is evident in the hearing room, which has the marble formality of a courtroom, but the dialogue keeps announcing that it is not law; it is pure politics. Strauss, self-made and politically aligned with his time, thinks in terms of power. He is worried that they will call scientists who worked at Los Alamos, where Oppenheimer had all the authority and respect. Strauss says to the Aide, "Robert built that damned place. He was founder, mayor, sheriff all rolled into one." The antagonism, resentment, and power dynamic between Strauss and Oppenheimer has taken shape.

The same procedural protection Strauss seeks at the Confirmation Hearing—information about witnesses and the opportunity to cross-examine—is mirrored in a scene at the earlier AEC Hearing, a hearing we learn later that Strauss himself designed. Oppenheimer's lawyer, Lloyd Garrison, has been denied access to some of the evidence the Board has against Oppenheimer because it is classified. He demands, "Is this proceeding interested in entrapment or truth? If it's truth, where's the disclosure? Where's the witness list?" The Chair of the Board replies, "This is not a trial, as you are well aware. Evidentiary rules do not apply. We are dealing with national security." A theme has emerged—the disavowal of core legal procedures, especially those associated with public trials, and especially in the face of security or national crisis.

The revelation later that Strauss himself not only orchestrated the AEC Hearing but designed it to be an anti-trial is the most explicit insistence within the film that these moments of judgment are "not law." The point is emphasized because the revelation comes at a moment of cinematic climax when Strauss' own confirmation appears imperiled, and Strauss admits to manipulating Oppenheimer's legacy. It is here that Strauss assumes power within the movie as both antagonist and anti-hero, at the same moment that he is explaining how he values power at the expense of legal procedure. Strauss recounts to the Aide his strategy for changing the public perception of the charismatic Oppenheimer: "No trial—can't give Oppenheimer a platform. We need a systematic destruction of his credibility." Strauss explains how the hearing needed to occur in a shabby little room far from the limelight. A simple bureaucratic procedure because the only question was whether his "Q clearance" should be denied. The Aide asks whether there would be a prosecutor. Strauss replies, "In all but name. A closed hearing. No evidence. No reporters. No burden of proof. We're not convicting, just denying."

The status of both hearings as inadequately legal is made evident to viewers as Strauss' confirmation becomes more controversial and more in doubt. One of the scientists testifies against Strauss, describing his resentment of Oppenheimer, emphasizing his role as AEC Commissioner in initiating the investigation of Oppenheimer, and suggesting that Strauss prompted the FBI to spy on Oppenheimer. During a break, Strauss yells in frustration to the Aide,

"This is no longer a confirmation hearing but a trial. He can't prove I gave the file to Borden. He can't prove a god-damn thing." The Aide responds by echoing Strauss' description of how he designed the AEC Hearing. "We're not in court Sir. There's no burden of proof." Strauss recognizes the reference and repeats his own words bitterly, "Right, they're not convicting, they're just denying." The same failure of legal procedure, in other words, is evident in the Confirmation Hearing, but this time it registers as poetic justice rather than procedural injustice.

3 The Cinematic Jurisprudence of OPPENHEIMER: Persuasion and Public Memory

3.1 Cinematic Jurisprudence

For scholars of law and film, "cinematic jurisprudence" captures a way of reading films not just for what they say about law, but as their own projection of legality, sometimes an alternative legality that can be as powerful as the law that operates in formal legal institutions.[11] This approach to studying film "for its jurisprudential content" is necessarily attentive to how film projects its realities through framing, editing, narration, and sound.[12] Orit Kamir has noted the ways that law and film are both "pivotal discourses" that participate "in the construction of concepts such as subject, community, identity, memory, gender roles, justice, and truth; they offer major sociocultural arenas where collective hopes, dreams, beliefs, anxieties, and frustrations are publicly portrayed, evaluated, and enacted."[13]

11 See eg, Anthony Chase, *Movies on Trial: The Legal System on the Silver Screen* (The New Press 2002); Austin Sarat, Lawrence Douglas and Martha M. Umphrey, *Law on the Screen* (Stanford University Press 2005); Richard Sherwin, 'Law's Enchantment: The Cinematic Jurisprudence of Krzystztof Kieslowski' in Michael Freeman (ed), *Law and Popular Culture* (Oxford University Press 2005).

12 Austin Sarat, Lawrence Douglas and Martha Merrill Umphrey, 'On Law and Film: Broadening the Focus' in Austin Sarat, Lawrence Douglas and Martha Merrill Umphrey (eds), *Law on the Screen* (Stanford University Press 2005) 1,4.

13 Orit Kamir, 'Cinematic Judgment and Jurisprudence: A Woman's Memory, Recovery, and Justice in a Post-Traumatic Society (A Study of Polanski's Death and the Maiden)' in Austin Sarat, Lawrence Douglas and Martha Merrill Umphrey (eds), *Law on the Screen* (Stanford University Press 2005) 27–28.

This is the perspective from which I read the film OPPENHEIMER. I read it as a hearing on the two governmental hearings that are at the center of the film, as well as the two men at the center of those hearings. As a hearing, the film operates as an alternative legal discourse that, like judicial decisions, "constitute communities (of viewers) that are often engaged in judgment, legal-like reasoning, the pursuit of justice, and self-creation through judgment and justice."[14] Released during a period of political polarization and anxiety, the movie portrays a prior period of polarization and anxiety in which a national figure was subject to an unjust judgment. By enacting its own hearing, it engages its viewers in the role of collectively reconsidering the judgment passed on Oppenheimer, the public memory of that period, and the law and politics of the present. It also asks its viewers to consider their responsibility for the future by accepting the moral inheritance of Oppenheimer. This is cinematic jurisprudence, in which films don't simply portray legal judgment, but perform it.[15]

The cinematic jurisprudence of OPPENHEIMER is generated by inviting its audience to revisit and revise the national judgment against Oppenheimer and his complicated legacy. The movie is its own public reconsideration of McCarthyism and Oppenheimer's role in American history. Indeed, American Prometheus, the book on which the film is based,[16] is its own such reconsideration, revitalizing Oppenheimer as a complex American hero and exposing the "political gamesmanship, the vanity of petty men and the naked antisemitism of the Red scare" that undermined his public memory.[17] The film accepts this premise and at the same time engages its viewers in the act of judging the past anew by tying it to the urgency of the present.

To achieve jurisprudential judgment, the film brings the audience into Robert Oppenheimer's mind, it asks viewers to identify with his genius, his sense of moral responsibility, and his global legacy of destruction, which is bearable only because he is the one who already suffered for the sin. The cinematic jurisprudence of OPPENHEIMER is perhaps best articulated by the

14 Ibid. at 28.

15 Ibid. at 28.

16 Kai Bird and Martin J. Sherwin, *American Prometheus: The Triumph and Tragedy of J. Robert Oppenheimer* (Vintage Books 2005).

17 See eg, Manohla Dargis, '"Oppenheimer" Review: A Man for Our Time' *New York Times* (New York, 19 July 2023) <https://www.nytimes.com/2023/07/19/movies/oppenheimer-review-christopher-nolan.html> accessed 07 September 2025: "Yet Oppenheimer's genius, his credentials, international reputation and wartime service to the United States government cannot save him from political gamesmanship, the vanity of petty men and the naked antisemitism of the Red scare."

scientist Niels Bohr when he visits Oppenheimer at Los Alamos. Oppenheimer thinks he is there to participate, but Bohr announces,

> I'm here to talk about after. The power you are about to reveal will forever outlive the Nazis. And the world is not prepared. We have to make the politicians understand this is not a new weapon; it's a new world. You are the American Prometheus. The man who gave them the power to destroy themselves, and they'll respect that. Then your work really begins.

Indeed, the film takes pains to show that Oppenheimer took that post-war advocacy seriously.

Another crucial scene that helps guide viewers toward judgment connects the moral conflict of that past with the present and Oppenheimer's own unfinished business. Later in the film, at Los Alamos, when Hitler is dead and Germany close to surrender, a group of scientists discuss their ethical concerns about dropping the bomb. Oppenheimer walks in on the meeting of scientists, one of whom is saying, "it's no longer the enemy that is the greatest threat to mankind. It is our work." Someone else asks, "How do we justify using this weapon on human beings?" Oppenheimer responds:

> We are theorists, yes? We imagine the future and our imaginings horrify us. They won't fear it until they understand it, and they won't understand it until they use it. When the world learns the terrible secret of Los Alamos, our work here will ensure a peace mankind has never seen, a peace based on the kind of international cooperation that Roosevelt always envisioned.

Oppenheimer believed, as he attests later in conversation with Edward Teller, that once the atomic bomb is used, nuclear war, perhaps all war, becomes unthinkable.

The film's cinematic jurisprudence suggests that the work Oppenheimer took up after the war—advocating a ban on nuclear weapons and international treaties to ensure compliance rather than investing in still more lethal weapons—was cut short by the AEC Hearing judgment and remains unfinished. Like Prometheus, Oppenheimer was tortured by the dropping of the bomb, yet also by the judgment of the hearing. We see him suffering the visions of the charred and sick victims in Hiroshima and Nagasaki. But the audience has an opportunity to reach an alternative judgment, to collectively remember Oppenheimer differently, to clear his name, and to accept his legacy. That legacy comes with the burden of American responsibility for nuclear destruction and to finish the job of containment.

3.2 Trauma, Repetition and Visual Modernism

Visually and psychologically, the movie mirrors and performs the fragmentation and ruptures of modernism and allows its viewers to see and feel the crises of the time. The norms of narration recede, just as legality did in the context of the government hearings and the dropping of an atomic bomb. The movie escapes linearity, changes perspective, and portrays interior psychological states and experiences (the imploding universe, the images of Hiroshima and Nagasaki, Oppenheimer imagining testifying naked). Sometimes the film seems to portray the workings of the Freudian unconscious obsessively repeating a traumatic event.[18] So many episodes in the film operate like moments of obsessive repetition; the film revisits them, looks at them from different angles, and invokes for viewers the distortions of private and public memory.

Some of the repetition is visual, such as the multiple image fragments of Jean Tatlock's suicide that haunt Oppenheimer. The audience is also introduced to two pivotal moments for Strauss as he recounts them to the Senate Aide. The first is when Strauss meets Oppenheimer for the first time at Princeton, and the audience sees, from Strauss' perspective, the enigmatic encounter between Oppenheimer and Einstein by the pond, after which Strauss believes Oppenheimer had turned Einstein against him. It is also the day Strauss tells Oppenheimer his story, his rise from humble beginnings. Oppenheimer, a child of privilege, archly calls Straus "a lowly shoe salesman," to which Strauss responds coolly, "just a shoe salesman." The status differences between the two men are exacerbated later in a second encounter that is visually repeated. Oppenheimer publicly humiliates Strauss at an AEC hearing about the export of isotopes to Norway. Oppenheimer testifies against Strauss' position, playfully telling the Commission that isotopes are less useful than electronic components but more useful than a sandwich. The room breaks out laughing. That moment of humiliating laughter is visually recycled as evidence of Strauss' own trauma and resentment.

Other aspects of repetition in the film operate as verbal or rhetorical refrains. For example, early on the audience sees Oppenheimer read in Sanskrit from the Bhagavad Gita (while having sex with Jean Tatlock), where Vishnu reveals himself and says, "Now I am become Death, the Destroyer of

18 Sigmund Freud, *Beyond the Pleasure Principle and Other Writing* (Penguin Books 2003). The essay was originally published in 1920.

Worlds."[19] Oppenheimer famously repeats this phrase at the moment the test bomb explodes at Los Alamos, and the audio clip is dramatically juxtaposed against only the sound of Oppenheimer breathing. As one of the few dramatic moments without music, the auditory experience and the repetition are striking.

There is also an interesting refrain about power and the "rules of the game." When the Confirmation Hearing seems suddenly uncertain Strauss' instinct is to make his opposition to Oppenheimer seem patriotic. He wants to tell the Senators, "I fought Oppenheimer and the US won." The Aide resists this approach and seeks to reassure him: "This is just how the game is played. It's in the bag Lewis, so play nice." Strauss' face is in shadow, the viewer sees him think back again to being snubbed by Einstein after talking with Oppenheimer. This scene with the Aide is revisited much later at a climactic moment of disclosure, when Strauss reveals just how carefully he has studied the rules of the game. He has used his connections to get Time magazine to publish a favorable profile of him so he can change the dynamics of the Confirmation Hearing. In the profile, a caption of a photo of Strauss reads, "He fought Oppenheimer and the US won." The Aide realizes it was, in fact, Strauss who got Oppenheimer's file to the FBI and forced the AEC Hearing. It is also the moment when Strauss reveals how he designed the AEC Hearing, with its lack of trial-like procedural safeguards. Strauss turns to the Aide and says with chilling coldness: "What was it you said to me: this is just how the game is played. Amateurs seek the sun and get eaten. Power stays in the shadows." Strauss accumulated power and used it to manipulate the rules of the game against Oppenheimer, precisely at a moment when law was most fragile.

The film returns to all these moments again and again, like the psyche replaying a painful memory through traumatic repetition. The trauma for Strauss is his humble origins, his ambition, and his fear of always being an outsider and a source of ridicule. Strauss is finally undone when the scientist David Hill appears at the Confirmation Hearing to testify to Strauss' "vindictiveness against Dr. Oppenheimer." It is during this pivotal testimony that the images and the audio of the movie become momentarily delinked. As Hill speaks—describing how Oppenheimer was interrogated by a prosecutor "who used all the tricks of a rather ingenious legal background"—the visuals cut between the two hearings. These are the tricks of an ingenious visual jurisprudence. This is Strauss' poetic justice: he bet on power, but power is never

19 Swami Prabhavananda and Christopher Isherwood, *Bhagavad Gita: The Song of God* (Signet 2002) Chapter 11, Verse 32.

neutral; his traumatic humiliations are repeated in this final public failure to be confirmed.

The primary trauma for Oppenheimer is his role in developing a weapon of mass destruction. The third and final time we see the meeting between Einstein and Oppenheimer at Princeton, we hear their dialogue for the first time, and it has nothing to do with Strauss. It is also the film's closing statement. Oppenheimer says, "Albert, when I came to see you with those calculations, we thought we might start a chain reaction that could destroy the entire world. I think we did." This is the traumatic legacy that the film asks its viewers to inherit. Yet in its cinematic rehearing, it also offers us, its audience, an alternative legality, an opportunity to revisit our collective judgment of Oppenheimer and to revise his public memory. The film also invites us to consider the crisis of the present, and the instability and fragility of law that attends such moments of revolution and rupture, when paradigms are dying and the rules of the game are breaking down.

Acknowledgements

The author wishes to thank Walter Stoffel and Lucie Bader, for the invitation to participate in the Law Meets Film conference, and Gianmaria Ajani for hosting us at the University of Torino. She especially thanks Alex Parizot for his excellent research assistance.

References

Bird K. and Sherwin M.J., *American Prometheus: The Triumph and Tragedy of J. Robert Oppenheimer* (Vintage Books 2005).

Bremer E.S., 'Designing the Decider' (2018) 16 Geo JL & Pub Pol'y 67.

Chafetz J., 'Congressional Overspeech' (2020) 89 Fordham Law Review 529.

Chase A., *Movies on Trial: The Legal System on the Silver Screen* (The New Press 2002).

Dargis M., '"Oppenheimer" Review: A Man for Our Time' *New York Times* (New York, 19 July 2023) <https://www.nytimes.com/2023/07/19/movies/oppenheimer-review-christopher-nolan.html> accessed 07 September 2025.

Ellmann R. and Feidelson C.Jr., *The Modern Tradition: Backgrounds of Modern Literature* (Oxford University Press 1965).

Freud S., *Beyond the Pleasure Principle and Other Writings* (Penguin Books 2003).

Harrington B. and Sneffer D.J., 'Informal Administrative Adjudication: An Overview' (*Congress.Gov*, 10 October 2021) <https://www.congress.gov/crs-product/R46930> accessed 03 March 2025.

Kairys D., *The Politics of Law: A Progressive Critique* (3rd edn, Basic Books 1998).

Kamir O., 'Cinematic Judgment and Jurisprudence: A Woman's Memory, Recovery, and Justice in a Post-Traumatic Society (A Study of Polanski's Death and the Maiden)' in Austin Sarat, Lawrence Douglas and Martha Merrill Umphrey (eds), *Law on the Screen* (Stanford University Press 2005).

Linder D.O., 'The Oppenheimer Security Hearing: A Chronology' (*Famous Trials*) <https://famous-trials.com/oppenheimer/2690-the-oppenheimer-security-hearing-a-chronology> accessed 03 March 2025.

Letter from William Borden to J. Edgar Hoover (7 November 1953) in (*Famous Trials*) <https://famous-trials.com/oppenheimer/2711-borden-letter-to-hoover-regarding-oppenheimer> accessed 03 March 2025.

Letter from K. D. Nichols, General Manager, AEC, to Robert Oppenheimer (23 December 1953) in (*Famous Trials*) <https://famous-trials.com/oppenheimer/2691-charges-against-oppenheimer-dec-23-1953> accessed 03 March 2025.

Prabhavananda S. and Isherwood C., *Bhagavad Gita: The Song of God* (Signet 2002).

Sarat A., Douglas L. and Umphrey M.M., *Law on the Screen* (Stanford University Press 2005).

Sarat A., Douglas L. and Umphrey M.M., 'On Law and Film: Broadening the Focus' in Austin Sarat, Lawrence Douglas and Martha Merrill Umphrey (eds), *Law on the Screen* (Stanford University Press 2005).

Sherwin R., 'Law's Enchantment: The Cinematic Jurisprudence of Krzysztof Kieslowski' in Michael Freeman (ed), *Law and Popular Culture* (Oxford University Press 2005).

PART 3
Films Mirroring Law

CHAPTER 6

The Vulnerability of the Judiciary and the Fragility of the Rule of Law: a Socio-Legal Interpretation of Emin Alper's Burning Days

Ferdinando Spina

> This drama is loneliness; for in order to render judgment, the judge must be free from human bonds, he must be placed a step above his equals; at this level rarely does he find the affectionate friendship he desires, and if he sees it approaching he must be careful lest it be prompted only by the hope of his favors or lest it move him to betray his impartiality.[1]

1 Introduction

After several decades during which judicial power underwent a phase of significant expansion on a global scale[2]—gaining widespread public support and placing substantial constraints on the legislative and executive branches—we are now witnessing a reversal of this trend. In both consolidated and transitional democracies, as well as in hybrid regimes that appear constitutional and democratic but are authoritarian in nature, the administration of justice is under mounting pressure.[3] The institutions that safeguard the rule of law face growing threats from populist leaders, dominant majorities, powerful economic interests, and politically aligned news media.

The judiciary's role in society is among the most visible expressions of this tension. The ability of the judicial system to uphold individual rights and freedoms depends on the interaction of multiple factors: the type of political system and the role played by parties and their leaders; the balance of

1 Piero Calamandrei, *Eulogy of Judges* (Princeton University Press 1942) 72.
2 Carlo Guarnieri and Patrizia Pederzoli, *The Judicial System: The Administration and Politics of Justice* (Edward Elgar 2020) 152–180; Ran Hirschl, *Towards Juristocracy: The Origins and Consequences of the New Constitutionalism* (Harvard University Press 2004); C. Neal Tate and Torbjorn Vallinder, *The Global Expansion of Judicial Power* (New York University Press 1997).
3 Hans Petter Graver, 'On Judges When the Rule of Law Is under Attack' (2024) 15 Oñati Socio-Legal Series 369; James E. Moliterno and Peter Čuroš, 'Recent Attacks on Judicial Independence: The Vulgar, the Systemic, and the Insidious' (2021) 22 German Law Journal 1159.

© 2026 THE AUTHOR(S) | HTTPS://DOI.ORG/10.1163/9789004761704-007

power within society; the internal organisation of the judiciary, judges' role conceptions and professional performance; and the existing relationships within the "legal complex", including judges, prosecutors, lawyers, civil servants involved in the administration of justice, and academics.[4] Nor should we forget the judiciary's relationship with civil society, which may defend judicial independence—or, conversely, may adopt an attitude of "sullen tolerance",[5] indifference, or even open hostility.

All these interdependencies are complex and difficult for scholars to fully grasp—let alone for the general public, who may be easily swayed by oversimplified yet highly effective narratives about the role of the judiciary. It is against this backdrop that Emin Alper's 2022 film BURNING DAYS (Kurak Günler) commands our fullest attention. BURNING DAYS is an engaging and visually captivating film. Rich in insights, it is likely to enter the "law and film" canon—still largely composed of American films, though it has recently begun to be enriched by works from other parts of the world. Like other works of literature and popular culture that explore legal issues, BURNING DAYS raises fundamental questions for researchers and provides pedagogical value by stimulating critical discussion in the teaching of law and criminology. Emin Alper is not only a gifted and passionate filmmaker, and one of the most prominent Turkish directors of the new generation,[6] but also an accomplished scholar of modern history. His academic work has focused on social movements in Turkey, particularly the student protests of the 1968 era and their aspirations for modernisation.[7] It is therefore not surprising that BURNING DAYS offers a sincere representation of contemporary Turkey.

However, as I shall argue, the film addresses legal dilemmas that recur across modern state societies. Most notably, BURNING DAYS offers the general public a clearer view than many academic accounts of the dangers currently facing the administration of justice and the ongoing erosion of the rule of law,

4 Terence C. Halliday, Lucien Karpik and Malcom M. Feeley, *Fighting for Political Freedom: Comparative Studies of the Legal Complex and Political Liberalism* (Hart 2007).

5 Marc Hertogh, *Nobody's Law: Legal Consciousness and Legal Alienation in Everyday Life* (Palgrave Macmillan 2018).

6 Bilir İlknur, 'A Brief Descent into Liquid Fear in Emin Alper's Abluka' in Tage T.E. Luxembourgeus and Mumin Baris (eds), *The New Wave in Turkey's Cinema* (Proverbial Elephant 2018).

7 Emin Alper, 'Reconsidering Social Movements in Turkey: The Case of the 1968–71 Protest Cycle' (2010) 43 New Perspectives on Turkey 63; Emin Alper, 'Protest Diffusion and Rising Political Violence in the Turkish '68 Movement: The Arab-Israeli War, "Paris May" and The Hot Summer of 1968' in Lorenzo Bosi, Chares Demetriou and Stefan Malthaner (eds), *Dynamics of Political Violence* (Routledge 2014).

commonly referred to as "Rule of Law Backsliding",[8] not only in Turkey but across all liberal democracies.

2 The Hero, the Villains, and What Is at Stake

The protagonist of the story is the young public prosecutor, Emre Gündüz. His appearance and demeanour reflect the polished self-image of a cosmopolitan young professional from today's global upper-middle class. He maintains a firm and confident—at times almost arrogant—understanding of his institutional role as a judicial authority and representative of the law. In his office, during meetings and interrogations of suspects and witnesses, his black robe with its red collar hangs prominently behind him: a symbolic reminder of the solemnity and gravitas of his role.[9]

Coming from the big city, Emre is assigned at the start of his career to Yanıklar, a provincial town. Symbols of the local community's economic and cultural underdevelopment include the atavistic problem of water scarcity—the days themselves seem to burn with drought, and water rarely flows from the taps—as well as crumbling houses and the unsettling presence of rats within domestic spaces.

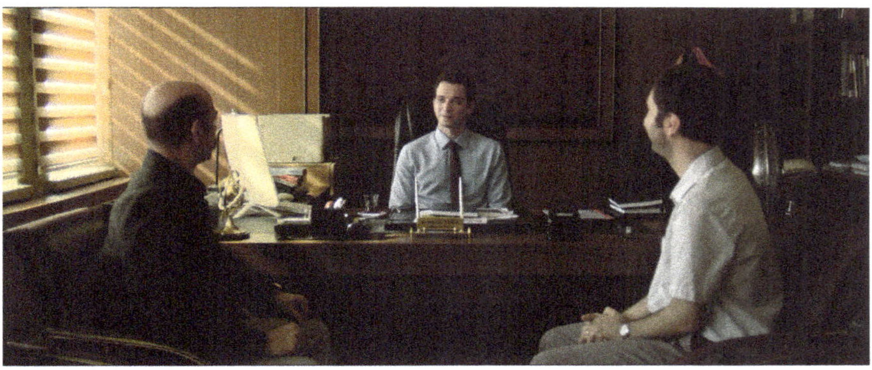

FIGURE 6.1 Emre Gündüz (Selahattin Paşalı), the public prosecutor, in his office (Film still by Cinema Galeries)

8 Laurent Pech and Kim Lane Scheppele, 'Illiberalism Within: Rule of Law Backsliding in the EU' (2017) 19 Cambridge Yearbook of European Legal Studies 3, 7.

9 Antoine Garapon, *Bien juger. Essai sur le rituel judiciaire* (Odile Jacob 1997) 71–91.

Emre has two helpers. The first is Murat Körükçü, a journalist critical of the local government, marginalised (possibly due to his implied homosexuality). Emre's association with Murat becomes a source of suspicion, ultimately undermining his legitimacy. The second helper is Sergeant Ilhan, a respectful and cautious police officer, who supports Emre despite being largely powerless against the town's dominant group.

The villains of the story emerge from this very group, led by the mayor, Selim Öztürk, and his son, the lawyer Şahin. Their defining characteristic is not their legal or formal status. Indeed, the lawyer is never visually represented with professional markers such as judicial robes, legal codes, or an office setting. Instead, they are portrayed, particularly towards the film's conclusion, though foreshadowed from the outset, as wielding rifles. The group thus resembles an armed, paramilitary formation, regularly handling firearms, whether for hunting, asserting dominance, or performing loud and chaotic displays of masculinity.

Among the hero's opponents, however, we must not forget another central actor in the story, whose role proves to be fundamental and to which I will return later: the town's community, figuratively represented in the disturbing form of the crowd. Another key character is Judge Zeynep, a female judge who, as the narrative unfolds, appears—at least in my reading—to play a dual role: that of a helper, but also, at times, an opponent to the hero, Emre.

The conflict at the centre of the film revolves around two interwoven enigmas. The first concerns the mysterious sinkholes near Yanıklar—described as both "frightening" and "marvellous"—which pose risks to infrastructure and public safety. Emre's predecessor had begun investigating them but mysteriously vanished. Two opposing narratives emerge: the mayor calls the sinkholes "a totally natural occurrence," while journalist Murat blames excessive groundwater extraction, used by the mayor to control the population.

The second enigma is the assault on Pekmez, a young Romani girl with cognitive disabilities, which takes place after a dinner hosted by Şahin at his home in Emre's honour. As the evening progresses, Emre loses consciousness—possibly because he drank too much raki or perhaps because his raki had been drugged—and the next morning, Pekmez is found raped and beaten. The perpetrators are unclear: Şahin, his friend Kemal, the musicians, or even Emre himself, as later insinuated.

These two mysteries drive the plot, with ambiguity carefully heightened through the film's script and editing. What initially appear to be moral certainties—the mayor's corruption and Şahin's guilt, are slowly destabilised, not only by the manipulations of the town's elite but also by the institutional fragility of the prosecutor's position.

3 A Guardian of the Constitution or an Enemy of the People?

Emin Alper has cited Henrik Ibsen's 1882 play *An Enemy of the People* as a source of inspiration.[10] In the play, Ibsen portrays the transformation of Dr Thomas Stockmann from civic hero to "enemy of the people". The irrefutable truth Stockmann asserts—based on scientific evidence, as he has discovered that the town's public water supply is contaminated—is progressively discredited through a false narrative orchestrated by the mayor, journalists, and members of the petty bourgeoisie, all more concerned with their own private interests than with the public good or the truth. The doctor becomes the target of insults, slander, and violence. As Francesco Gambino notes, the play exposes key structural weaknesses of modern democracies: declining trust in institutions as producers of truth, and widespread indifference to deception.[11]

BURNING DAYS brings these themes into the present. A compelling narrative choice makes this film especially relevant for those interested in the erosion of legal institutions: the protagonist who becomes an "enemy of the people" here is a public prosecutor. Bringing the truth about the sinkholes to light in court would mean holding the mayor accountable. Uncovering what happened to the Romani girl Pekmez would not only redress the abuse she suffered, both recent and past, but also challenge male domination and protect ethnic minorities. In this sense, the figure of Pekmez's grieving father, Yavuz, is symbolic: he places the greatest faith in, and shows the deepest gratitude toward, the prosecutor.

Against this background, I interpret prosecutor Emre as a cinematic embodiment of the conception of the judicial role defined by Guarnieri and Pederzoli,[12] drawing also on the work of Dworkin[13] and Pasquino,[14] as the "guardian of the Constitution." According to this conception, "the main task of the judge becomes the defence of individual or minority rights from abuses by the political branches and the majorities that control them".[15]

10 Sylvie Lazzarini and Teresa Vena, 'Emin Alper. Réalisateur de Burning Days' (*Cineuropa*, 2022) <https://cineuropa.org/fr/video/426102/> accessed 02 April 2025.

11 Francesco Gambino, *In sala con il diritto* (La Nave di Teseo 2023) 43–53.

12 Carlo Guarnieri and Patrizia Pederzoli, *The Judicial System: The Administration and Politics of Justice* (n 2).

13 Ronald Dworkin, *Taking Rights Seriously* (Harvard University Press 1977).

14 Pasquale Pasquino, 'Prolegomena to a Theory of Judicial Power: The Concept of Judicial Independence in Theory and History' (2003) 2 L.P.I.C.T. 11.

15 Carlo Guarnieri and Patrizia Pederzoli, *The Judicial System: The Administration and Politics of Justice* (n 2) 124.

This ideal-typical image of the judge's relationship to political power, or power *tout court*, as elaborated in legal philosophy and political science, finds a counterpart in popular legal culture: the "justice figure," defined as "a hero who tries to move man-made law ever closer to the ideal until it matches the justice template".[16] Prosecutor Emre is a compelling expression of this figure in its most heroic and intransigent form: that of the solitary lawman of the Western. BURNING DAYS consciously recalls classic Western tropes: arid landscapes, conflicts over water, the menace of lynch mobs, and the unchecked presence of firearms in town. In the classic frontier films of John Ford, such as YOUNG MR. LINCOLN (1939) or THE MAN WHO SHOT LIBERTY VALANCE (1962)—despite their differing messages and underlying themes[17]—the figure of the law enforcer enters a lawless wilderness and ultimately brings the law into existence. Through the imposition of law, he lays the foundations for order, civilisation, and peace.

This dynamic is illustrated by Emre's arrival in town, marked by a wild boar hunt: blood in the streets, celebratory cries, and rifle fire. The next day, Şahin and Kemal pay a courtesy visit to welcome the new prosecutor, casually dismissing the event as a harmless tradition in which the public display of firearms is taken for granted. Emre views the hunt as a barbaric affront to public order and immediately considers making arrests, startling the two men. He asserts the supremacy of law over custom, reaffirming his authority as a judicial figure.

And yet, unfortunately, BURNING DAYS is neither a courtroom drama nor a Western in the tradition of Ford's films, where the man of law averts a lynching or defeats the villain in a final duel. Although Emre appears to embody the justice figure, he ultimately fails, as he is unable to act as a true guardian of the rights of Yanıklar's citizens or to bring either of his two major cases to trial. Without a trial, only the truth of power remains, as the final scenes reveal: the mayor's armed gang parades through the town, celebrating victory with gunfire; Pekmez's Romani camp is burned; Murat's newspaper office is destroyed; Emre's home is besieged by a hostile crowd. He and Murat barely escape lynching, and Emre is even served with an arrest warrant for the assault he did not commit.

The administration of justice fails, its representative discredited, and law is reduced to a hollow bureaucratic shell concealing systemic injustice.

---

16 Nicole Rafter, *Shots in the Mirror: Crime Films and Society* (2nd edn, Oxford University Press 2006) 136.

17 Michael Böhnke, 'Myth and Law in the Films of John Ford' (2001) 28 Journal of Law and Society 47.

4 The Vulnerability of the Judiciary and the Challenge of Independence and Impartiality

Why does prosecutor Emre, so determined, authoritative, and aware of his role in delivering justice, ultimately lose his battle for truth, law and justice? The film offers valuable insight into the real and tangible processes through which the judiciary can be delegitimised within contemporary democratic systems.

The turning point—a kind of "narrative sinkhole"—occurs when Emre agrees to attend a dinner hosted by the mayor, Şahin and Kemal. In the opening scene, he confides to Judge Zeynep his reluctance to accept the invitation, aware of how much his reputation matters ("My reputation is everything," he later tells Şahin). Zeynep reassures him that such gatherings are common in small towns. Though he eventually agrees, Emre remains cold and uneasy, visibly unsettled by the attention he receives, nearly offending his hosts.

Gradually, the dinner turns into a trap from which the principled prosecutor will no longer be able to free himself. His independence is compromised: he has shared a meal with the main suspect in the sinkhole case, the mayor. Moreover, he begins to lose awareness of what happens around him, including the rape of Pekmez. The mere fact that he attended the dinner renders every suspicion plausible. This is precisely what his opponents exploit, launching a smear campaign in the compliant local press that places mounting pressure on the prosecutor during the pre-trial phase, discrediting his professional and moral integrity, and ultimately delegitimising his role altogether.

The dinner episode, which is actually the film's longest scene at 21 minutes, may seem a mere narrative device to shift the plot. Yet it carries significant explanatory weight, encapsulating the broader issue of conflicts of interest and the risk of undue influence from which all judicial actors must remain free. It invites reflection on how easily judicial independence, or its appearance, may be compromised in real life. Consider the Italian context. Section VII of the Code of Civil Procedure sets out safeguards for judicial impartiality, including abstention and recusal. Article 51, paragraph 2, for instance, requires a judge to abstain if he "usually has meals with one of the parties or one of the counsel in the proceeding".[18] This is not just a procedural concern, but also an ethical one. In this regard, I recall *Eulogy of Judges*, a collection of legal anecdotes that also serves as a guide to ethical conduct, written by the renowned jurist Piero Calamandrei.[19] Among its insights is a piece of advice to a young, unmarried magistrate newly assigned to a provincial town—much like Emre:

18 Simona Grossi and Maria Cristina Pagni, *Commentary on the Italian Code of Civil Procedure* (Oxford University Press 2010) 119.

19 (n 1).

> The judge is denied the hour of spiritual relaxation which other men may find in the conversation of friends at mealtime, for the law which forbids him to dine regularly with a person who may appear before him, compels him to take his repasts in ascetic solitude.
>
> The young graduate should bear this in mind and consider carefully whether he has found his true vocation before entering on a legal career, for during his novitiate, perhaps even before he is married, he will be assigned as the local judge in some provincial town where his table in the only restaurant must be set apart and where he must eat his meals in silence. The sole companion admitted there is invisible but ever present—his independence.[20]

Calamandrei's reasoning reflects a legal culture grounded in a strongly ethical, and almost sacerdotal conception of the magistrate: the judge as a "priest of justice".[21] Within this view, external guarantees of judicial independence are secondary to the judge's moral integrity.[22] This judicial habitus, still influential in 1960s Italy though already being contested at the time by younger magistrates, now seems outdated. Today, both dominant role conceptions and judicial practices reflect a vision of the magistrate as an active participant in the social, and, at times, political life of the community, a role increasingly accepted, if not actively promoted.

Yet the issue of public trust in judicial impartiality requires renewed attention—especially in an era of increasingly close ties between magistrates, politicians, lawyers, and journalists, and of pervasive, largely unregulated visibility through social media. At stake is the legitimacy of the judiciary: "the more the judicial power expands and penetrates both politics and society, the more it needs to be checked and held accountable".[23] This makes it all the more essential that judges not only exercise independence and impartiality, but also conduct themselves, both on and off the bench, in a manner that reinforces the public perception of their impartiality and independence.[24]

---

20 Ibid 68.

21 Michele Luminati, *Priester der Themis. Richterliches Selbstverständnis in Italien nach 1945* (Klostermann 2007).

22 Ezio Moriondo, *L'ideologia della magistratura italiana* (Laterza 1967) 225.

23 Daniela Piana, 'Beyond Judicial Independence: Rule of Law and Judicial Accountabilities in Assessing Democratic Quality' in Gianluigi Palombella and Leonardo Morlino (eds), *Rule of Law and Democracy: Inquiries into Internal and External Issues* (Brill 2010) 67.

24 Giuseppe Di Federico, 'Judicial Accountability and Conduct: An Overview' in Anja Seibert-Fohr (ed), *Judicial Independence in Transition* (Springer 2012); Keith J. Bybee and Angela G. Narasimhan, 'Courts and Judges: The Legitimacy Imperative and the Importance of Appearances' in Austin Sarat and Patricia Ewick (eds), *The Handbook of Law and Society* (Wiley-Blackwell 2015).

5 The Vulnerability of the Judiciary and the Challenge of Legality

There is another evident reason why the prosecutor Emre fails to embody the guardian of the Constitution and the justice figure, as outlined above. This, too, represents one of the key risks—closely linked to the challenges of independence and impartiality—that can contribute to the broader crisis of judicial legitimacy.

The film portrays the dilemma of a prosecutor who, in his quest for justice, ends up compromising the very principles of law and individual rights. During the investigation into Pekmez's case, Emre requests the pre-trial detention of Şahin (later extending it to Kemal) despite inconclusive evidence. Judge Zeynep expresses concern: the biological test results are pending, and the credibility of the victim's testimony, given her mental impairment, is uncertain. Significantly, the viewer never hears Pekmez's version of events—her exchanges with the prosecutor occur off-screen, a choice that appears to be a deliberate narrative strategy by the director. To justify the arrests, Emre cites the existence of a witness: himself. The conflation of prosecutor and witness violates the principle of impartiality and is legally indefensible. Worse still, Emre recalls nothing with certainty. He becomes obsessed with proving—above all to himself—that he was not involved in the assault. The use of noir-style flashbacks underlines the fragility of memory and the ambiguity of guilt. One key detail, however, confirms his presence at the crime scene: a pen, typically worn in his shirt pocket, is found in the grass. Emre discreetly retrieves it, concealing crucial evidence.

In short, Emre's conduct involves several procedural violations: arrests with weak justification, reliance on dubious testimony, the suppression of exculpatory evidence, and the distortion of due process. Literature, cinema, and television have offered numerous portrayals of prosecutors, judges, and lawyers who trample defendants' rights or manipulate the truth in pursuit of victory, money, or professional advancement. A classic example is Gérard de Villefort in *The Count of Monte Cristo* by Alexandre Dumas. In American popular culture, prosecutors are often depicted as cynical, dishonest, or overly ambitious.[25] Judges too, though less frequently, are cast in a similarly negative light, especially from the 1970s onward.[26]

---

25 Michael Asimow and Shannon Mader, *Law and Popular Culture: A Course Book* (2nd edn, Peter Lang 2013) 170–171.

26 David Ray Papke, 'From Flat to Round: Changing Portrayals of the Judge in American Popular Culture' (2007) 31 Journal of the Legal Profession 127; Steve Greenfield, Guy Osborn and Peter Robson, *Film and the Law* (Hart 2010) 128–29; Stefan Machura and Llewelyn

The case of prosecutor Emre nevertheless diverges from these examples. His actions—though exceeding the limits of criminal procedure and revealing the coercive power of his institutional role—are not driven by ambition, greed, or the desire for career advancement, but by a genuine pursuit of justice. In certain respects, BURNING DAYS reflects the way in which popular culture in countries with criminal justice systems rooted in the inquisitorial tradition tends to depict those responsible for enforcing penal norms—that is, the actors involved in the investigative and pre-trial phases of criminal proceedings, including prosecutors and instructing judges. One may think, for instance, of French cinema, in which the "procureur de la République" is most often portrayed as a cynical figure, lacking human empathy—indeed, as vindictive.[27] It is hard not to recall the aggressive stance of the *avocat général* during the trial in the film ANATOMY OF A FALL (2023, Justine Triet). A similar depiction is reserved for judges, who are frequently presented as stern and punitive, especially in contrast to defence lawyers and defendants.[28] I am thinking of the character of Jeanne Charmant-Kilmann—at last, a woman in the leading role—in COMEDY OF POWER (2007, Claude Chabrol). The examining magistrate is inebriated by her own power and abuses pre-trial detention as a means of exerting pressure on suspects.[29] Like Emre, she ultimately abandons the investigation, exhausted and unable to cleanse the system of what she herself calls, in one scene, "all the filth on both the right and the left". A similar ambivalence is found in the Italian film, IN THE NAME OF THE ITALIAN PEOPLE (1971, Dino Risi), where a young examining magistrate—far less glamorous than Emre and more caricatured in the spirit of "commedia all'italiana"—destroys exculpatory evidence in a murder case in order to strike back at the undeniable corruption and arrogance of the defendant, who is, however, innocent of the crime in question.

I have chosen to recall these few films—though they are in fact indicative of broader and well-established trends—in order to highlight the emergence, even within the cinema of liberal democracies with civil law jurisdictions, of a critique of the abuse of power by judicial actors involved in criminal

Davies, '"Law Is an Odd Thing"-Liberalism and Law in the TV-Series "The Good Wife"' (2013) 45 Kriminologisches Journal 279, 287–289.

27 Christian Guéry, *Les avocats au cinéma* (Presses Universitaires de France 2011) 107–110.

28 Ibid 114.

29 Christian Guéry, *Justices à l'écran* (Presses Universitaires de France 2007) para VIII; Magalie Flores-Lonjou and Nicolas Thirion, 'Le juge français et ses valeurs sous le regard cinématographique' (2022) 1 Les Cahiers de la Justice 131, 139.

prosecution, as well as the concern that they may overstep the bounds of the principle of legality.[30]

We all want Emre's triumph, justice for Pekmez, and freedom for the citizens of Yanıklar. But can substantive justice be achieved by violating the rules of formal justice? Between these two horns of the dilemma, which is more crucial for the legitimacy of the judiciary? Which offers the stronger safeguard against the erosion of the rule of law? And which is the more effective bulwark against the rise of populism and the authoritarian drift of constitutional regimes? Alper's film deserves recognition for posing these questions to the viewer, subtly suggesting that the judiciary itself may, at times, be tempted to overstep the legal boundaries it is meant to uphold in pursuit of substantive justice.

6 Final Reflections: the Challenge of the Judiciary's Interplay with Society

In light of these questions, another significant character in the film merits closer examination: Judge Zeynep. As noted, she maintains an ambivalent relationship with Emre—at times a helper, at others a quiet opponent. She questions the investigation, distrusts Emre's relationship with Murat, and ultimately orders the release of the two main suspects, citing insufficient evidence. In her institutional role as both a check on prosecutorial power and a guarantor of constitutional rights, Zeynep upholds the legal protections of the accused. She urges Emre to abandon his posture as a justice-seeker acting beyond the law: "Let go of all animosities … Start a new chapter in Yanıklar, okay?" Yet no sooner are these words spoken than the sound of gunfire is once again heard in the background—a stark symbol of law's defeat before raw power. Her defence of legality thus takes on a political dimension, halting the struggle against corruption that Emre has pursued.

Zeynep remains a complex figure, open to divergent readings. Is she a guardian of legality? Or a bureaucratic judge, faithful to formal rules but unwilling to resist dominant power or defend minority rights? Zeynep is neither corrupt nor directly connected to the town's dominant faction. Yet she appears career-conscious, seemingly intent on preserving her position of social privilege. She may thus be read as a symbol of a judiciary that cannot remain entirely independent from external pressures, and that must negotiate compromises in its relationship with political power, dominant groups, the legal

30 Antoine Garapon and Denis Salas, *La République pénalisée* (Hachette 1996); Antoine Garapon and Denis Salas, *Les nouvelles sorcières de Salem: leçons d'Outreau* (Seuil 2006); Sabino Cassese, *Il governo dei giudici* (Laterza 2022) 66–71.

professions, the media, and the expectations—or prejudices—of the broader community it serves.[31]

As Tomeo notes, in popular culture the hero of justice is expected to be “hopeful”, “actually an impossible role”[32] as evidenced by Emre’s contradictions. Rather, Zeynep emerges as a more realistic figure—one that reveals the judiciary’s institutional fragility within a regime best described as a democracy in transition, situated between advanced democracies and closed authoritarian systems.[33] Turkey exemplifies this condition, having undergone in the past decade a shift towards competitive authoritarianism, accompanied by a marked decline in judicial independence.[34] A series of institutional changes and constitutional amendments—particularly concerning the Constitutional Court and the High Council of Judges and Prosecutors—enabled the ruling party (AKP) to reshape the judiciary, consolidating its control over the courts. This reform was further facilitated by the judiciary’s loss of legitimacy, particularly after controversial decisions, such as the Constitutional Court’s rejection of a government-backed amendment allowing headscarves in public institutions, widely perceived as judicial overreach.[35] Such rulings fuelled the AKP’s strategy of court-packing and expanded executive influence over the judiciary.

Turkey thus stands as a case of a formal democracy in transition towards authoritarianism. Yet in this light, any democracy may be viewed as transitional, since the concentration of power in the hands of political, economic—and increasingly, military—elites remains a constant risk. In such scenarios, the judiciary’s role of oversight and resistance, like that of parties, the press, and intermediary institutions, is progressively dismantled. Judicial action becomes politicised, aligning with the goals of dominant power blocs and reinforcing broader projects of control and repression, an outcome clearly illustrated by Zeynep’s conduct in the film, which appears less as a personal choice than as

31 Lawrence Baum, *Judges and Their Audiences: A Perspective on Judicial Behavior* (Princeton University Press 2006).

32 Vincenzo Tomeo, *The Judge on the Screen: A Translation and Critical Edition* (Translated by Peter Robson, Fairleigh Dickinson University Press 2025) 114.

33 Nauman Reayat, Rhona K.M. Smith, and Moohyung Cho, *Judicial Independence in Transitional Democracies* (Routledge 2024).

34 Aslı Ü Bâlİ, ‘Constitutionalism in Turkey’ in Güneş Murat Tezcür (ed), The Oxford Handbook of Turkish Politics (Oxford University Press 2022); Nurullah Gorgen, ‘The Weakening of Judicial Independence Through the Transition From the Judicialization of Politics to the Politicization of the Judiciary: Turkish Case’ in Nauman Reayat, Rhona K.M. Smith, and Moohyung Cho (eds), *Judicial Independence in Transitional Democracies* (Routledge 2024); Berk Esen, ‘Judicial Transformation in a Competitive Authoritarian Regime: Evidence from the Turkish Case’ (2025) 47 Law & Pol. 1.

35 Berk Esen, ‘Judicial Transformation in a Competitive Authoritarian Regime: Evidence from the Turkish Case’ (n 34).

the result of structural pressures and constrained agency. However, such transitions are neither abrupt nor inevitable. The judiciary can preserve its oversight role and constitutional mandate—so long as it is supported and defended by civil society. The case of Turkey, along with other transitional democracies such as Hungary and Poland, illustrates that institutional independence alone is insufficient when courts lack public support, the legal complex is weak, and they face powerful political actors.[36]

These intricate matters cannot be explored in full here, but cinema once again provides a potent symbolic distillation. Several films include emblematic scenes depicting the encounter between a representative of the law and a hostile crowd—a narrative proxy for society at large. In THE YOUNG MR. LINCOLN, for instance, the figure of justice faces down a lynch mob and succeeds in ensuring that due process prevails. Similarly, in the Italian film IN THE NAME OF THE LAW (1949, Pietro Germi), a young judge stands before the resistant townsfolk and the mafiosi gathered in the square of a Sicilian town, compelling the crowd to submit to the law he represents. Despite differing historical and ideological contexts, these narratives converge in reaffirming law's value as a means of resisting criminal power and populist vigilantism. This message is embodied by the figure, lawyer or judge, who upholds justice without yielding to fear.

By contrast, BURNING DAYS reflects a much darker historical and ideological context. In the film's final scenes, the young prosecutor Emre is surrounded and attacked by a resentful mob, ready to lynch not someone else, but him (alongside Murat, who now stands with him). The scene recalls another with similar symbolic weight: THE CAIMAN (2006, Nanni Moretti), where judges are assaulted by a crowd after issuing a ruling against the populist leader in power—an explicit reference to Silvio Berlusconi. Like BURNING DAYS, THE CAIMAN powerfully captures today's climate of irritation and delegitimisation surrounding the judiciary.

Having escaped the lynching by the crowd of Yanıklar, Emre and Murat then encounter the armed group led by the mayor, his son, and their henchmen. What follows is a desperate attempt to flee from their pursuers: a nocturnal manhunt through the desolate landscape, as they run for their lives. The dynamic is reversed: it is no longer the judge who hunts the criminal, but the criminal who hunts the judge. Only at the very last moment do the prosecutor and the journalist escape. In my naïveté as a viewer, it felt almost as if a magical flying carpet had rescued them from the criminal gang.

---

36 Carlo Guarnieri and Patrizia Pederzoli, *The Judicial System: The Administration and Politics of Justice* (n 2) 174.

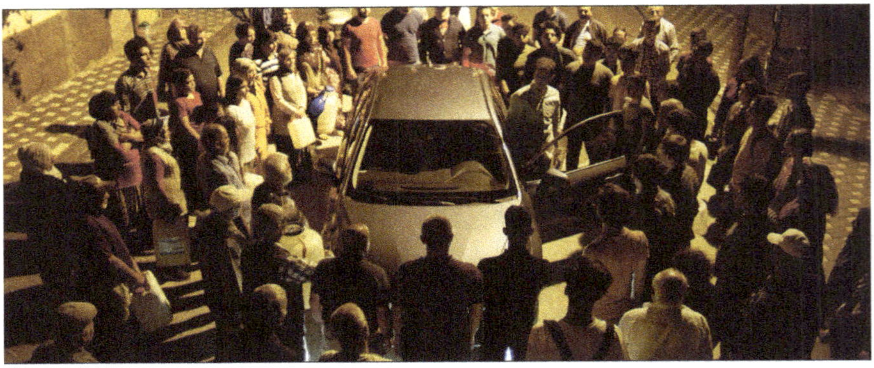

FIGURE 6.2 Emre Gündüz (Selahattin Paşalı), surrounded by the mob (Film still by Cinema Galeries)

The film concludes with a faint glimmer of hope—the result of a brilliant, poetic invention that the director presents not as an idealistic vision, but as a lesson learned from history, grounded in the understanding of historical patterns. Something, perhaps, can still happen to consign authoritarian leaders, mafias, and vengeful crowds to the sinkhole—and make them vanish from sight. Something can still happen to reinforce, both from within and without, the fragile position of the judiciary and the broader legal complex, including lawyers, law professors, officials, and others, in support of a more stable liberal order.

But if something can still happen, it will not be thanks to the intervention of a magical flying carpet: it will depend on the political will of all of us. BURNING DAYS invites not only reflection, but also mobilisation.

References

Alper E., 'Reconsidering Social Movements in Turkey: The Case of the 1968–71 Protest Cycle' (2010) 43 New Perspectives on Turkey 63.

Alper E., 'Protest Diffusion and Rising Political Violence in the Turkish '68 Movement: The Arab-Israeli War, "Paris May" and The Hot Summer of 1968' in Lorenzo Bosi, Chares Demetriou and Stefan Malthaner (eds), *Dynamics of Political Violence: A Process-Oriented Perspective on Radicalization and the Escalation of Political Conflict* (Routledge 2014).

Asimow M. and Mader S., *Law and Popular Culture: A Course Book* (2nd edn, Peter Lang 2013).

Bâlİ A.Ü., 'Constitutionalism in Turkey' in Güneş Murat Tezcür (ed), *The Oxford Handbook of Turkish Politics* (Oxford University Press 2022).

Baum L., *Judges and Their Audiences: A Perspective on Judicial Behavior* (Princeton University Press 2006).

Bilir İ., 'A Brief Descent into Liquid Fear in Emin Alper's Abluka' in Tage T.E. Luxembourgeus and Mumin Baris (eds), *The New Wave in Turkey's Cinema* (Proverbial Elephant 2018).

Böhnke M., 'Myth and Law in the Films of John Ford' (2001) 28 Journal of Law and Society 47.

Bybee K.J. and Narasimhan A.G., 'Courts and Judges: The Legitimacy Imperative and the Importance of Appearances' in Austin Sarat and Patricia Ewick (eds), *The Handbook of Law and Society* (Wiley-Blackwell 2015).

Calamandrei P., *Eulogy of Judges* (Princeton University Press 1942).

Cassese S., *Il governo dei giudici* (Laterza 2022).

Di Federico G., 'Judicial Accountability and Conduct: An Overview' in Anja Seibert-Fohr (ed), *Judicial Independence in Transition* (Springer 2012).

Dworkin R., *Taking Rights Seriously* (Harvard University Press 1977).

Esen B., 'Judicial Transformation in a Competitive Authoritarian Regime: Evidence from the Turkish Case' (2025) 47 Law and Policy 1.

Flores-Lonjou M. and Thirion N., 'Le juge français et ses valeurs sous le regard cinématographique' (2022) 1 Les Cahiers de la Justice 131.

Gambino F., *In sala con il diritto* (La Nave di Teseo 2023).

Garapon A., *Bien juger. Essai sur le rituel judiciaire* (Odile Jacob 1997).

Garapon A. and Salas D., *La République pénalisée* (Hachette 1996).

Garapon A. and Salas D., *Les nouvelles sorcières de Salem: leçons d'Outreau* (Seuil 2006).

Gorgen N., 'The Weakening of Judicial Independence Through the Transition From the Judicialization of Politics to the Politicization of the Judiciary: Turkish Case' in Nauman Reayat, Rhona K.M. Smith, and Moohyung Cho (eds), *Judicial Independence in Transitional Democracies* (Routledge 2024).

Graver H.P., 'On Judges When the Rule of Law Is under Attack' (2024) 15 Oñati Socio-Legal Series 369.

Greenfield S., Osborn G. and Robson P., *Film and the Law* (Hart 2010).

Grossi S. and Pagni M.C., *Commentary on the Italian Code of Civil Procedure* (Oxford University Press 2010).

Guarnieri C. and Pederzoli P., *The Judicial System: The Administration and Politics of Justice* (Edward Elgar 2020).

Guéry C., *Justices à l'écran* (Presses Universitaires de France 2007).

Guéry C., *Les avocats au cinéma* (Presses Universitaires de France 2011).

Halliday T.C., Karpik L. and Feeley M.M., *Fighting for Political Freedom: Comparative Studies of the Legal Complex and Political Liberalism* (Hart 2007).

Hertogh M., *Nobody's Law: Legal Consciousness and Legal Alienation in Everyday Life* (Palgrave Macmillan 2018).

Hirschl R., *Towards Juristocracy: The Origins and Consequences of the New Constitutionalism* (Harvard University Press 2004).

Lazzarini S. and Vena T., 'Emin Alper. Réalisateur de Burning Days' (*Cineuropa*, 2022) <https://cineuropa.org/fr/video/426102/> accessed 2 April 2025.

Luminati M., *Priester der Themis. Richterliches Selbstverständnis in Italien nach 1945* (Klostermann 2007).

Machura S. and Davies L., '"Law Is an Odd Thing"-Liberalism and Law in the TV-Series "The Good Wife"' (2013) 45 Kriminologisches Journal 279.

Moliterno J.E. and Čuroš P., 'Recent Attacks on Judicial Independence: The Vulgar, the Systemic, and the Insidious' (2021) 22 German Law Journal 1159.

Moriondo E., *L'ideologia della magistratura italiana* (Laterza 1967).

Papke D.R., 'From Flat to Round: Changing Portrayals of the Judge in American Popular Culture' (2007) 31 Journal of the Legal Profession 127.

Pasquino P., 'Prolegomena to a Theory of Judicial Power: The Concept of Judicial Independence in Theory and History' (2003) 2 Law and Practice of International Courts and Tribunals 11.

Pech L. and Scheppele K.L., 'Illiberalism Within: Rule of Law Backsliding in the EU' (2017) 19 Cambridge Yearbook of European Legal Studies 3.

Piana D., 'Beyond Judicial Independence: Rule of Law and Judicial Accountabilities in Assessing Democratic Quality' in Gianluigi Palombella and Leonardo Morlino (eds), *Rule of Law and Democracy: Inquiries into Internal and External Issues* (Brill 2010).

Rafter N., *Shots in the Mirror: Crime Films and Society* (2nd edn, Oxford University Press 2006).

Reayat N., Smith R.K.M. and Cho M., *Judicial Independence in Transitional Democracies* (Routledge 2024).

Tate C.N. and Vallinder T., *The Global Expansion of Judicial Power* (New York University Press 1997).

Tomeo V., *The Judge on the Screen: A Translation and Critical Edition* (Translated by Peter Robson, Fairleigh Dickinson University Press 2025).

CHAPTER 7

Politics, Law and Tradition—a Film Talk with the Film Director Emin Alper about Burning Days (Kurak Günler)

Lucie Bader

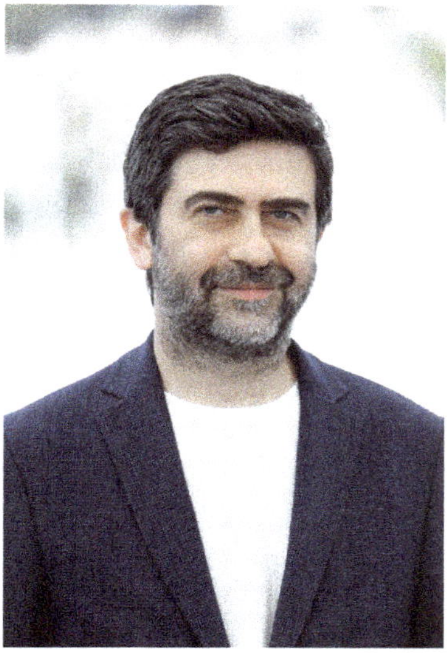

FIGURE 7.1
Emin Alper (Photo by ZUMA Press)

EMIN ALPER, Turkey
Born 1974 in Ermenek in the Turkish province of Karaman, Emin Alper studied economics and history at Bogazici University in Istanbul. He holds a Ph.D in Modern Turkish History and teaches at the Faculty of Humanities and Social Sciences at Istanbul Technical University.
His first film, BEYOND THE HILL (Tepenin Ardi), has received many awards, including the Caligari Prize at the 2012 Berlinale and Best Film in the Asia Pacific Screen Awards. In 2015, FRENZY (Abluka) received the Special Jury Prize in Venice. In 2019, A TALE OF THREE SISTERS was in competition at the Berlinale and received several awards at the Istanbul Film Festival: Best Turkish Film, Best Director, Best Actress and FIPRESCI Award. His latest film BURNING DAYS was nominated for the Queer Palm Award in Cannes in the section Un Certain Regard. It has received awards at many festivals, including Pula and Thessaloniki, as well as eight awards at the Antalya Golden Orange Film Festival 2022, and the 2022 European Film Award for Best Editing.

© 2026 THE AUTHOR(S) | HTTPS://DOI.ORG/10.1163/9789004761704-008

Lucie Bader: *Emin Alper, you have made some great films about politics, law and tradition. Your latest film,* BURNING DAYS, *deals with these important social issues too. It tells the story of a public prosecutor who is appointed to a small town in the countryside. What was the initial idea?*

Emin Alper: First of all, my family is full of lawyers. I grew up in a small town, and my father was a lawyer too. So I know this context well.

But what inspired me most to make this film is of course what we have experienced in Turkey during the last decade.

For those who are not very familiar with what has been going on in Turkey, can you say more about these experiences?

The huge civilian coup staged by Erdoğan took special aim at the justice system. When a third of the judges and the prosecutors were expelled from their offices in 2016 and 2017, the judiciary became a mere tool in the hands of Erdoğan. And everyone, even his supporters, lost their trust and confidence to the justice system.

The law has always been very important for Turkish people. Especially if you are an intellectual, if you are a little bit interested in politics, you need to understand the law, even to understand the newspaper you read. That's because political oppression has always had a legal guise in Turkey.

I see. So the law played a more important role in the Turkish society before the coup?

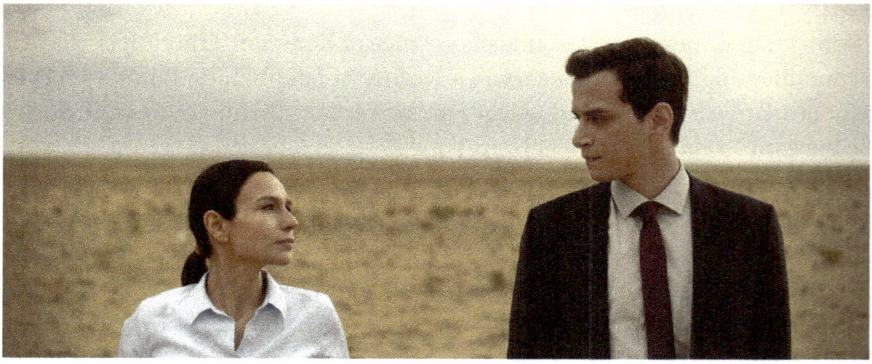

FIGURE 7.2 The judge Zeynep (Selin Yeninci) and the public prosecutor Emre (Selahattin Paşalı) (Film still by Trigon Film)

Turkey has always been a kind of semi-authoritarian country, but it was still the case that everything was done according to the law. I mean, Turkey is not a kind of arbitrary dictatorship, and never has been. Everything fits somehow into the law. So law has always been the realm of a power struggle, as it is now. It became the tool for the oppressors and, at the same time, a way of protecting people's civil rights as well. Those holding power attack our rights by interpreting the law according to their own interests, and we defend our rights with our own interpretations.

The situation has deteriorated now. The previous judiciary establishment, which was more Kemalist, was quite opposed to Erdoğan in the 2000s, and Erdoğan fought this establishment in order to turn the judiciary into a mere tool of power. The old establishment was not democratic either, but it did at least more or less respect legal procedures. Now, the judiciary is completely in the service of Erdoğan, and enjoys no such respect. It can openly defy the Constitutional Court and ignore the European Court of Human Rights. That's why today in Turkey many people think that they are not protected by law at all. Erdoğan's decisions are above the law. If he thinks that you should go to jail, you go to jail. Simple as that. And unfortunately, this issue is of global significance.

So would you say that your film deals with a universal issue?

Definitely. I am convinced about the universality of this story. It concerns the rise of populism around the world. I think this is not only an issue for Turkey, but also in Trump's America, in Hungary, in India.

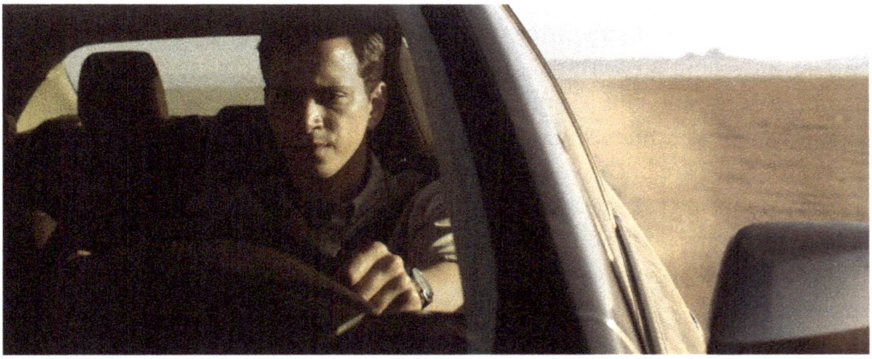

FIGURE 7.3 Emre (Selahattin Paşalı), the young prosecutor, in his car (Film still by Trigon Film)

All around the world we see similar situations: the rise of certain figures who gain power through elections and then think that this gives them the right to throw the law and the constitution into the bin of history. They think that they are above the law. This is my main source of inspiration. I wanted the film to be a microcosmos of such political situations.

The opening scene of BURNING DAYS *shows the arrival of a young public prosecutor in a small village where he is called upon to solve problems that are difficult and unfamiliar to him. After an unfriendly reception, he is repeatedly prevented from investigating. Can you comment on the role of this public prosecutor?*

A very important keyword in my film is loneliness. My aim is to investigate the spirit of loneliness and the desperation not only of the judge and prosecutor, but any modern intellectual, in the face of rising populism.

I wanted to show the confrontation between a young and unexperienced person who regards himself as "civilized" and educated, and the elite of a small town which is completely corrupt. Although their corruption is known to everyone, they are re-elected again and again.

As Ferdinando Spina said in his analysis, I also interpreted the story as a kind of western: I really owe a lot to westerns. The film might also be set in a southern part of the United States, for example, with a young judge coming to a town that is governed by a corrupt and powerful sheriff.

One of the big conflicts is around the shortage of water. Are sinkholes caused by water shortages specific to Anatolia?

The sinkholes are mainly in central Anatolia, very close to my home town. So I'm quite familiar with this phenomenon. It is, of course, related to the structure of the soil, but as I present it in the film, the main reason is the overconsumption of underground water. The problem is increasing day by day; these sinkholes are becoming really dangerous.

The experts always point to future developments and possible catastrophes, but as with many environmental problems, people want immediate solutions. They don't care about overconsumption because they want water in the here and now.

Film financing is not easy in Turkey. How did you finance your film?

At first, we were able to get funding from the Ministry of Culture. But when they saw the film, they didn't like it and wanted the money to be paid back.

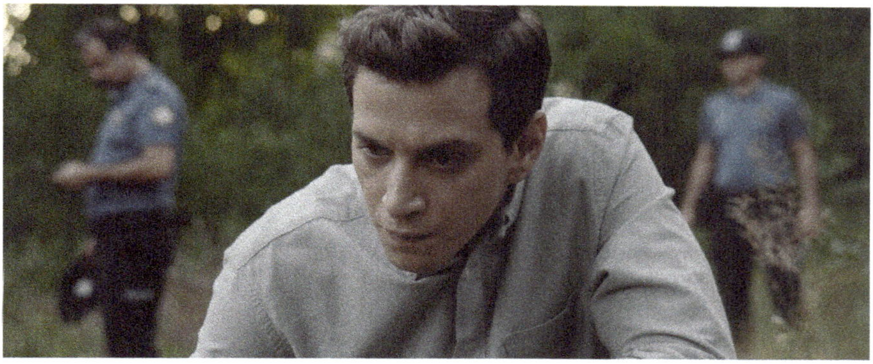

FIGURE 7.4 Emre (Selahattin Paşalı) on investigation (Film still by Trigon Film)

The funding was withdrawn, which was itself a scandal: nothing like this could happen in the European funding system.
Suddenly, the film became very popular in Turkey: audiences were very angry with the governmental decision and its policies of censorship, and started buying tickets. In fact, admissions were so high that, in at the end, we were able to pay the money back.

That was fine for the production company, but not for me. I didn't receive state funding for my next project, and now I am on a kind of blacklist. I doubt that I will get any money from the state in the near future.

You also expressed your political opinion at the film festival in Cannes when you presented the film for the first time in 2022. You mentioned that your executive producer had been arrested. What has happened?

This person is a friend, first of all, who helped in the production of the film as executive producer.

Erdoğan's crackdown on the opposition started with the 2013 Gezi protests which he thought represented a huge conspiracy to overthrow him. He didn't consider it to be a kind of social movement, but something inspired and manipulated by foreign elements, the CIA, Mossad or something like that. His judges and his prosecutors identified some people as collaborators in this conspiracy.

That's scary!

Yes: in what has become a very famous court case, our friend Çiğdem Mater was named as one of the so-called collaborators. She was sentenced to 18 years of imprisonment, without any evidence. Osman Kavala, who was considered the main conspirator, was sentenced to life imprisonment. He received the highest possible punishment in law, just because he was a part of social movement. He didn't even organize it: Gezi was a completely spontaneous movement.

Such sentences handed down in Turkey have been rejected by the European Court of Human Rights several times, but Turkey does not comply with the findings of the court, and Europe does nothing to force Turkey to do so.

What does this mean for your situation in the country? You have to deal with a certain censorship and a strong control and you are blacklisted. How can you work as a filmmaker?

There is a kind of censorship, but it is not like in Iran. In Turkey, the censorship is rather indirect: if the government does not give you money, as in my case, one can try to find private investors. They can also be bullied because of supporting you, and I have witnessed this indirect kind of pressure and censorship. For now, however, I have not found it difficult to release my films.

It is not common to ban films in Turkey, although a couple of weeks ago, Luca Guadagninos last film QUEER was banned in Istanbul. We will see what will happen in the future.

Due to the success of your films, you have a big network all over Europe. In what respect is that useful for you?

Of course, the support of some private investors and the help of European producers are both very important. My last films were co-productions between Greece, Netherlands and France. With this support and with the funds from Eurimages, we can still survive.

Let's come back to the story of your film. The dinner scene lasts twenty minutes. That's a very long time for a scene in a dark garden.

Actually, the scene was even longer, but I cut some dialogue in the editing process. I really enjoyed writing and shooting it.

This kind of dinner draws on my childhood memories. As I said, my father was a lawyer, and we were always together with judges and prosecutors in the small town. But unlike the picture in Turkey now, these people were part of the same elite. That there is a rift between them is something new. There is a populist, local elite and there are the state representatives on the other side. When I was a child, they were happy all together.

And this has changed?

State representatives have always had to ask themselves to what degree they will build a relationship with the local elite. If these representatives, coming from Istanbul or Ankara, become too close to the local elite, they can lose trust amongst the population. This was already a problem. My father did not want to go too far in such relationships with judges and prosecutors because he was quite honest and he hated to be considered as a corrupt lawyer. Today civil servants need to show that they are supporting Erdoğan as well as having ties with the local elite. Even if they cannot show sympathy to the government, they have to avoid being seen as opponents.

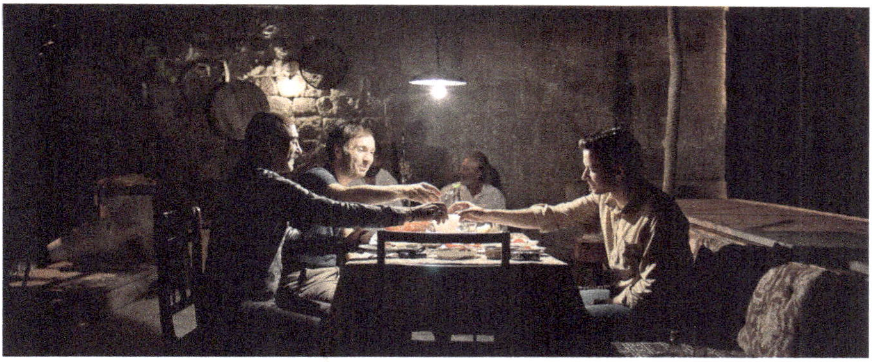

FIGURE 7.5 Dinner with Şahin (Erol Babaoğlu), Kemal (Erdem Şebicak) and Emre (Selahattin Paşalı) (Film still by Trigon Film)

In the film, we can feel the hesitation of the public prosecutor, his reticence to accept the invitation for the dinner. Why does he go along with it?

Emre suffers a lot in this dilemma. He can either choose to act like a high-nosed, cold prosecutor who comes from the city and is hated by the people, or to foster contacts with the locals. It is a delicate balance. At one point he realizes that he loses this balance and starts reprimanding the lawyer and the dentist again, and then a tension arises between them and the relationship becomes a trap for him.

Emre tries to memorise his past, but he can't trust his own memories. Is there a message that you want to convey here too?

Of course. In the hospital he says that the girl should remember what happened last night, and then, some minutes later, he realises that he is not able to remember his own past. Actually, there are two reasons why I put Emre in such a situation: first, I wanted to add some psychological depth to the character.

And secondly, I wanted to avoid a simple contrast between good and evil. I wanted to show that finding the truth is not so easy. Although the prosecutor tries to convince himself that he has nothing to do with the alleged rape, he finds himself in a position in which it is impossible to be confident about the truth.

Emre is never sure about what really happened?

I just wanted to show that the judge as well as the prosecutor are human beings and that they can also be the criminals. Despite Emre's idealistic appearance, he does not refrain from hiding evidence and misusing his power.

I think these elements make the story more nuanced and deepened the characters. You very often leave us in doubt about what has happened, and what is the truth. For example, what is the relationship between the prosecutor and the journalist? How should we understand that?

The dinner is also crucial here. Not only does it trigger a search for the truth about the crime, but it is also an investigation into Emre's own sexual desires. The dinner is very important, as it is instrumental in infuriating the villagers.

It gives the mayor the opportunity to incite their hatred of the prosecutor and the journalist, not least by using the homophobia which is still (or again) common and relevant in the Turkish context. Within the last five or six years,

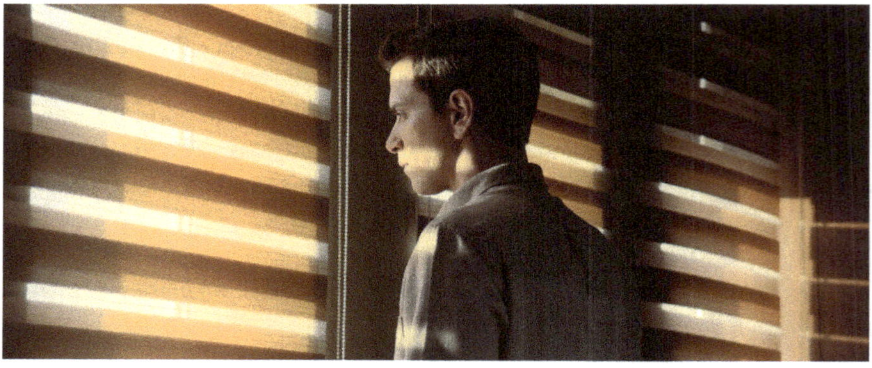

FIGURE 7.6 Emre (Selahattin Paşalı) looks out of the window (Film still by Trigon Film)

homophobia has become part of Erdoğan's official policy. One of the top priorities of the government is to ban all kinds of LGBTQIA+ activities.

In my case, this element of homosexuality was the main reason for the Ministry of Culture to withdraw funding from the production of the film.

In that respect, this film has also relevance for the debate on homophobia in Turkey. Was it appreciated by the LGBTQIA+ community?

No, not always. Some people appreciated it, but others had hoped to see more obvious and open scenes and were disappointed. Perhaps their expectations had been raised by the film being put forward for the Queer Palm.

I would like to come to the sinkhole in the powerful last sequence of the film. It presents similarities with the opening scene. In the beginning, people hunt the boars and at the end they hunt people. The narrative structure is the same. Is this the message of the film?

I have been asked this question many times. Even on the street, people stop me, asking how the prosecutor and the journalist crossed the sinkhole in this short time.

It is the final image which interests me most. It shows that there is an enormous sinkhole between the hunted and the pursuers. The latter, the corrupt and villainous pursuers, are stopped by the sinkhole which, just like the wars, economic crises or other catastrophes created by the autocrats, has become a hindrance to them. As a historian, I tend to believe that popular dictators generally prepare the ground for their own endings by themselves.

PART 4

Perspectives

CHAPTER 8

The Future of Law and Film in Context

Peter Robson and Michael Randall

1 Introduction

This chapter has a simple aim. It notes approaches to films dealing with law and justice and their persistence. It seeks to indicate why such films have been examined by scholars. It focuses initially on English language films and scholarship. There are, however, significant contributions from other jurisdictions which are also covered. On the basis of what has been the focus of film and law scholarship in the past, and the trends and directions which have been present, possible directions for the future are suggested along with how future scholars might learn about and expand the field.

2 The Importance of Law in Film in Society

An initial response to the significance of films is that they seek to entertain audiences, or inform them of the experience of others. However, film, and the process of not only capturing, but distributing moving images has carried a broader significance. From the infancy of moving pictures, those wanting to influence members of society for socio-political reasons recognised the significance of cinema. This was seen in the Soviet era cinema of Eisenstein[1] and the Nazi propaganda work supported by Josef Goebbels.[2] By a similar token, those wishing to prevent the populace from seeing certain kinds of material have sought to do so on grounds of them being deemed immoral, subversive or in some way unsuitable. From the early days of the cinema there have been attempts to censor what films get made and shown. The most celebrated of these attempts is probably the Hays Code introduced in 1933 in the United

---

1 The portrayal in BATTLESHIP POTEMKIN (USSR, 1925, director: Sergei Eisenstein) of the failed 1905 Revolution, for example, remains inspirational. See also Zoe Beloff, *A World Redrawn: Eisenstein and Brecht in Hollywood* (Christine Burgin 2016) for Eisenstein's encounter with Hollywood.

2 Antonella Argenio, *I film del nazismo: Süss l'ebreo, L'ebreo errante, Terezin* (Editoriale Scientifica 2017).

© 2026 THE AUTHOR(S) | HTTPS://DOI.ORG/10.1163/9789004761704-009

States.[3] While superficially restrictive, there is an argument that the creativity of film makers in testing the limits of the code, have carried greater significance in advancing film making techniques and genres.[4] For example, the prevalence of musical theatre and dance movies was, in part, due to a perception that more revealing costumes and movements were socially acceptable relative to other genres of film, owing to the necessary costumes for the genre.[5] The notion that film can be of significance in establishing and maintaining social order is one of the background factors informing the interest by scholars of law in society.

3 The Cinema of Justice

One of the major strands in film for as long as cinema has been in operation has been coverage in films of the operation of the justice system. These include all aspects from the apprehension of lawbreakers by the police through the adjudication phase in courtroom dramas to disposal with prison films an ever-present feature.[6] There are many other films which include areas of legal interest and representations of justice and ethics on screen. These range from contentious issues such as capital punishment,[7] abortion,[8] environmental pollution,[9] racism,[10] rape,[11] divorce[12] and child welfare.[13] The treatments range

3 Gregory D. Black, *Hollywood Censored: Morality Codes, Catholics and the Movies* (Cambridge University Press 1996).

4 See for example Nora Gilbert, *Better Left Unsaid: Victorian Novels, Hays Code Films, and the Benefits of Censorship* (Stanford University Press 2013).

5 This forms a large part of the discussion in documentaries of Hollywood responses to the Hays Code. See for example HOLLYWOOD CENSORED (USA, 2015 Wichita films, directors: Clara Kuperberg and Julia Kuperberg).

6 Suzanne Bouclin, *Women, Film and the Law: Cinematic Representation of Female Incarceration* (UBC Press 2021).

7 EIGHT O'CLOCK WALK (Great Britain, 1954, director: Lance Comfort).

8 VERA DRAKE (UK, 1998, director: Mike Leigh).

9 A CIVIL ACTION (USA, 1998, director: Steven Zaillian); ERIN BROCKOVICH (USA, 2000, director: Steven Soderbergh).

10 SAPPHIRE (Great Britain, 1959, director Basil Dearden).

11 LIPSTICK (USA, 1976, director: Lamont Johnson); ROB ROY (Great Britain, 1995, director: Michael Caton-Jones).

12 KRAMER V KRAMER (USA, 1979, director: Robert Benton).

13 LOSING ISAIAH (USA, 1995, director: Stephen Gyllenhaal); THE CHILDREN ACT (Great Britain/USA, 2017, director: Richard Eyre).

from serious dramas[14] through melodrama,[15] romantic comedy,[16] farce[17] to satire.[18] There have been trends and developments in the kinds of issues covered and personnel involved. In order to trace how, for instance, women's oppression has been dealt with in film over time,[19] it is important to have some notion of boundaries. Themes such as the absence of women,[20] ethnic minority[21] and gay[22] protagonists in law films also required delineation of the field of study. Various attempts have been made to characterise what constitutes a "law film" to clarify what trends there have been in coverage of issues and personnel as well as style.[23] As this essay suggests, however, identifying such scholarship requires some detective work due to the variety of locations in which such "law" films are often discussed.[24] Furthermore, films create a form of polysemy with the same image carrying multiple meanings and significance for different viewers, leading to detailed discussions and debates about the intention of film makers, and what audiences experience from engaging with films, particularly in the field of law and justice.

---

14 JUDGMENT AT NUREMBERG (USA, 1961, director: Stanley Kramer); INHERIT THE WIND (USA, 1960, director: Stanley Kramer).

15 THE PARADINE CASE (USA, 1947, director: Alfred Hitchcock).

16 LEGAL EAGLES (USA, 1986, director: Ivan Reitman); LEGALLY BLONDE (USA, 2001, director: Robert Luketic).

17 MY COUSIN VINNY (USA, 1992, director: Jonathan Lynn).

18 ... AND JUSTICE FOR ALL (USA, 1979, director: Norman Jewison).

19 Louise Everett Graham and Geraldine Maschio, 'A False Public Sentiment: Narrative and Visual Images of Women Lawyers in Film' (1996) 84 Ky Law J 1027; Carole Shapiro, 'Women Lawyers in Celluloid: Why Hollywood Skirts the Truth' (1995) 25 University of Toledo Law Review 955; Cynthia Lucia, 'Women on Trial: The Female Lawyer in the Hollywood Courtroom' in Martha Fineman and Martha T. McCluskey (eds), *Feminism, Media and the Law* (Oxford University Press 1997); Martha Fineman and Martha T. McCluskey, *Feminism, Media and the Law* (Oxford University Press 1997); Orit Kamir, *Framed: Women in Law and Film* (Duke University Press 2006); Cynthia Lucia, *Framing Female Lawyers: Women on Trial In Film* (University of Texas Press 2006); Rebecca Korzec, 'Viewing North Country: Sexual Harassment Goes to the Movie' (2007) 36 University of Baltimore Law Review 303.

20 Steve Greenfield, Guy Osborn and Peter Robson, *Film and the Law: the cinema of justice* (Hart 2010) ch14.

21 Steve Greenfield, Guy Osborn and Peter Robson, *Film and the Law* (Cavendish 2001) 119–122.

22 Leslie Moran, 'Heroes and Brothers in Love: the male homosexual as lawyer in popular culture' (1998) 18 Studies in Law, Politics and Society 3.

23 Steve Greenfield, Guy Osborn and Peter Robson, *Film and the Law* (n 21); Steve Greenfield, Guy Osborn and Peter Robson, 'Genre, Iconography and British Film' (2007) 36 Baltimore Law Review 371; Steve Greenfield, Guy Osborn and Peter Robson, *Film and the Law: the cinema of justice* (n 20).

24 See below at section 10.

4 The Emergence of Law and Film an Area of Scholarship

Before, however, we find widespread attention being paid to the world of law in film, there was an important intervention linking law and film with the innovative research and writing between 1968 and 1973 of Vincenzo Tomeo from Italy.[25] It is fair to say, however, that this work went largely unnoticed for the next 40 years. It is referred to in Conference papers and books from 2010 onwards.[26] The first Anglophone recognition of the importance of film comes in the mid 1980s from two American scholars. In unconnected articles in different locations Anthony Chase[27] and Stewart Macaulay[28] made the case for legal scholars to examine popular culture and its significance for a richer understanding of the justice system. This theme was given a clear focus with a special issue of the Yale Law Journal in 1989 in which a clear outline of the academic basis for the role of popular culture was provided, particularly by Lawrence Friedman.[29]

This theme was taken up in a Law and Popular Culture Conference in 1993.[30] This looked at why lawyers should study popular culture across film, literature and television from a variety of perspectives. From the contribution by Paul Mastrangelo it is clear that there was writing about individual films and the relationship between law and film in trade papers and journals, on a sporadic basis, principally from 1990 onwards.[31]

25 Vincenzo Tomeo, *Il giudice sullo schermo* (Laterza 1973). See also Vincenzo Tomeo, *The Judge on the Screen* (Translated by Peter Robson, Fairleigh Dickinson 2024).

26 Peter Robson, 'Judges on Screen' (Research Committee on Sociology of Law Annual Meeting, Gothenburg, July 2010); Peter Robson and Jessica Silbey, *Law and Justice on the Small Screen* (Hart 2012); Peter Robson and Jennifer Schulz, *A Transnational Study of Law and Justice on TV* (Hart 2016); Peter Robson and Jennifer Schulz, *Ethnicity, Gender and Diversity: Law and Justice on TV* (Fairleigh Dickinson University Press 2018).

27 Anthony Chase, 'Towards a Legal Theory of Popular Culture' (1986) Wisconsin Law Review 527.

28 Stewart Macaulay, 'Images of Law in Everyday Life: The Lessons of School Entertainment and Spectator Sports' (1987) 21 Law and Society Review 185.

29 Lawrence Friedman, 'Law, Lawyers and Popular Culture' (1989) 98 The Yale Law Journal 1579.

30 David L. Gunn, *The Lawyer and Popular Conference: Proceedings of a Conference* (Fred B Rothman 1993).

31 Paul Mastrangelo, 'Creating a Filmography' in David L. Gunn (ed), *The Lawyer and Popular Conference: Proceedings of a Conference* (Fred B Rothman 1993) 73.

5 The Nature of Early Scholarship

The first forays into discussions on law and film tended to focus on courtroom dramas.[32] Within this field there was selectivity in the coverage. For instance, Harris in 1987 only dealt with what he regarded as the 8 classic courtroom films.[33] Bergman and Asimow also focused on the trial movie in their pioneering overview in 1996 Reel Justice: the courtroom goes to the movies.[34] They selected 68 films of interest. This compendium style can also be seen in Strickland, Foster and Banks' *Screening Justice*[35] and Gibney's *Watching Human Rights*[36] and most recently by Stanley Fish.[37] Non-Anglophone scholars also adopted a similar approach. Rivaya and de Cima selected the best one hundred law films to discuss in *Cien Peliculas de Derecho y Cine*[38] and Ollé-Laprune took this path with *Le Cinéma Policier Francais: 100 films, 100 réalisateurs*[39] from 2020. A rather more personalised perspective was taken in the first journal Special Issue[40] with one section devoted to some eighteen scholars writing on "One Movie No Lawyer Should Miss".[41]

6 The Focus of Scholarship

The scholars looking at law and film over the years have come from a variety of backgrounds. The majority have been from legal backgrounds and linking their scholarship with a range of goals. Some sought to make their doctrinal legal focus simply more entertaining. Others looked at the light these films shed

32 *Pace* the pioneering study of Vincenzo Tomeo from 1973 noted above and in Vincenzo Tomeo, *The Judge on the Screen* which focused on the role of the Continental Examining magistrate.

33 Thomas J. Harris, *Courtroom's Finest Hour in American Cinema* (Scarecrow Press 1987).

34 Paul Bergman and Michael Asimow, *Reel Justice: the courtroom goes to the movies* (Andrews McMeel Publishing 1996).

35 Rennard Strickland, Teree E. Foster and Taunya Lovelle Banks, *Screening Justice—The Cinema of Law: Significant Films of Law, Order and Social Justice* (Hein 2006).

36 Mark Gibney, *Watching Human Rights: The 101 Best Films* (Routledge 2013).

37 Stanley Fish, *Law at the Movies: Turning Legal Doctrine into Art* (Oxford University Press 2024).

38 Benjamin Rivaya and Pablo de Cima, *Derecho y Cine en 100 peliculas* (Tirant Lo Blanch 2004).

39 Jean Ollé-Laprune, *Le Cinéma Policier Francais: 100 films, 100 réalisateurs* (Hugo Image 2020).

40 Richard K. Sherwin, 'Symposium: Picturing Justice: Images of Law and Lawyers in the Visual Media' (1996) 30 University of San Francisco Law Review 891.

41 Ibid., 1051–1247.

on different social practices in relation to gender,[42] ethnicity[43] and sexuality[44] through to social policy conflicts[45] as well as utilising the notion of the *auteur*.[46] Socio-legal approaches[47] are encountered alongside literary ones.[48] So we find coverage of the ethnic minority experience as shown in British film emerging from a discrimination law class.[49]

There has also been a link with the world of film theory. These perspectives informed David A Black's early work *Law in Film*[50] in which he drew attention to the lack of theoretical sophistication of lawyers writing on film along with noting how film can have a reflective or refractive impact. In Britain, *Law's Moving Image* provided an introduction to the complex issues and debates in the field of law and film.[51] It brought together work on visual culture, criminology, social and cultural studies. The essays covered an amazing range of films from HENRY V, TOY STORY 2, THE CASTLE and the films about Oscar Wilde. The focus is principally on the filmic elements in these products but there are also essays on more traditional fare such as censorship, copyright and national film policies. United States scholars in *Law on the Screen* also urged those looking at the representation of law to pay attention to questions of reception.[52] There was also a broadening out found beyond both the Hollywood focus[53]

---

42 Orit Kamir, *Framed: Women in Law and Film* (n 19).

43 R. Sheffield, 'A social history of black lawyers in popular culture' (1991) 7 Focus on Law Studies 4.

44 Leslie Moran, 'Heroes and Brothers in Love: the male homosexual as lawyer in popular culture' (n 22).

45 Matthias Kuzina, 'The social issue courtroom drama as an expression of American popular culture' in Stefan Machura and Peter Robson (eds), *Law and Film* (Blackwell 2001).

46 Peter Robson, 'The justice films of Sidney Lumet' in Steve Greenfield and Guy Osborn (eds), *Readings in Law and Popular Culture* (Routledge 2006).

47 Hilary Sommerlad and Peter Sanderson, 'Talk of the Town' in Steve Greenfield and Guy Osborn (eds), *Readings in Law and Popular Culture* (Routledge 2006).

48 William MacNeil and Peter Hutchings, 'Law's Cultural Mediations: An Introduction by Way of Introduction' (2001) 10 Griffith Law Review 1.

49 Peter Robson, 'Fade to Grey: portraying the ethnic minority experience in British film' (2002) 30 International Journal of the Sociology of Law 235.

50 David Alan Black, *Law in Film: Resonance and Representation* (University of Illinois Press 1999).

51 Leslie Moran and others, *Laws Moving Image* (Glasshouse 2004).

52 Austin Sarat, Lawrence Douglas and Martha Umphrey, *Law on the Screen* (University of Massachusetts Press 2005).

53 Peter Robson, 'Law, Hollywood and the European Experience' in Austin Sarat (ed), *Studies in Law, Politics and Society* (Vol 46, Emerald Publishing 2009).

into actual practice in the courtroom[54] and into a concern with impact.[55] There was also a noted burst of films with women lawyers as, for once, the protagonists.[56]

The development of law and film scholarship, to a large extent, stemmed from the increased awareness and familiarity of available films, but also increased accessibility to watch, and re-watch films away from cinema screens. Another major factor in the development of law and film scholarship, particularly in the 1990s, can be tied to the increased frequency and prominence of law and justice films. In the mid-1990s law and justice became prime time viewing and 'entertainment' with the trial of OJ Simpson where the court room and its characters and roles were more accessible to audiences.[57] Films such as A TIME TO KILL[58] and PRIMAL FEAR,[59] released in the wake of the OJ Simpson trial, and with box office success, led to more court room films being made.[60]

7 Law and the Small Screen

One crucial area of the scholarship in the area of law and popular culture has been the extension from a principal focus on film into television. This was

54 Philip Meyer, 'Why a jury trial is more like a movie than a novel' in Stefan Machura and Peter Robson (eds), *Law and Film* (Blackwell 2001); Richard Sherwin, 'What screen do you have in mind? Contesting the Visual Context of Law and Film Studies' (2009) 46 Studies in Law, Politics and Society 3.

55 Jessica Silbey, 'A Witness to Justice' in Austin Sarat (ed), *Studies in Law, Politics and Society* (Vol 46, Emerald Publishing 2009); Ruth Buchanan and Rebecca Johnson, 'Strange Encounters: Exploring Law and Film in the Affective Register' (2009) 46 Studies in Law, Politics, and Society 33.

56 Orit Kamir, *Framed: Women in Law and Film* (n 19); Steve Greenfield, Guy Osborn and Peter Robson, *Film and the Law: the cinema of justice* (n 20) Ch14 on JAGGED EDGE (USA, 1985, director: Richard Marquand); SUSPECT (USA, 1987, director: Peter Yates) ; THE ACCUSED (USA, 1988, director: Jonathan Kaplan); MUSIC BOX (USA, 1989, director: Costa-Gavras) culminating in LEGALLY BLONDE (USA, 2000, director: Robert Luketic).

57 On the cultural significance of the OJ Simpson Trials see Janice E. Schuetz and Lin S. Lilley, *The OJ Simpson Trials: Rhetoric, Media, and the Law* (Southern Illinois University Press 1999).

58 USA, 1996, director: Joel Schumacher.

59 USA, 1996, director: Gregory Hoblit.

60 Including A CIVIL ACTION (USA, 1998, director: Steven Zaillian); ERIN BROCKOVICH (USA, 2000, director: Steven Soderbergh); THE EXORCISM OF EMILY ROSE (USA, 2005, director: Scott Derrickson); THE JUDGE (USA, 2014, director: David Dobkin).

always something in the early shift of lawyers beyond the black letter doctrinal focus of legal education. This has produced a number of Collections[61] as well as separate essays.[62] It has to some extent transformed into a quite distinct area of study, with the differences between the products and how they are consumed demanding different analytical techniques.[63]

There are high-profile cinematic releases which demonstrate a continued interest in law and justice films on screen, for example OPPENHEIMER,[64] ANATOMY OF A FALL,[65] and JOKER: FOLIE À DEUX.[66] It is arguable that there is an increasing re-emergence of the impact of the small screen on representations of law. In an age of streaming services producing their own original content, there has been an increase in the number of TV series which are easily accessible to a wide range of audiences. For example, these include THE LINCOLN LAWYER[67] and BETTER CALL SAUL,[68] REASONABLE DOUBT,[69] PRESUMED INNOCENT,[70] THE KILLING KIND,[71] and YOUR HONOR.[72] These series also prompt an immediate response from audiences through online posts and reviews (e.g. Rotten Tomatoes and IMDB), bringing the discussion of law and film to a wider and more mainstream audience. These offer a new

61 Robert M. Jarvis and Paul R. Joseph, *Prime Time Law: Fictional television as legal narrative* (Carolina University Press 1998); Michael Asimow, *Lawyers in Your Living Room!: Law on Television* (American Bar Association 2009); Peter Robson and Jessica Silbey, *Law and Justice on the Small Screen* (n 26); Peter Robson and Jennifer Schulz, *A Transnational Study of Law and Justice on TV* (n 26); Peter Robson and Jennifer Schulz, *Ethnicity, Gender and Diversity: Law and Justice on TV* (n 26).

62 Paul Bergman, 'EMERGENCY!: Send a TV show to Rescue Paramedic Services!' (2007) 36 University of Baltimore Law Review 347; Peter Robson, 'Lawyers and the legal system on TV: the British experience' (2007) 2 International Journal of Law in Context 333; Peter Robson, 'Developments in Law and Popular Culture: The Case of the TV Lawyer' in Antoine Masson and Kevin O'Connor (eds), *Representations of Justice* (Peter Lang 2007); Peter Robson 'Cathy Come Home Today' in Eamon Keane and Peter Robson (eds), *The Ian Willock Collection on Law and Justice in the Twenty-First Century* (Fairleigh Dickinson University Press 2023); Adam Andrzejewski and Mateusz Salwa, *Law and TV Series* (Brill 2018); Jennifer Schulz 'Law and TV' in Russell Sandberg and Daniel Newman (eds), *Law and Humanities* (Anthem Press 2024).

63 John Fiske, *Television Culture* (2nd edn, Routledge 2010).

64 USA, 2023, director: Christopher Nolan.

65 France, 2023, director: Justine Triet.

66 USA, 2024, director: Todd Phillips.

67 USA Netflix 2022–.

68 USA AMC 2013–2022.

69 USA Disney+ 2022–.

70 USA Apple TV 2024–.

71 Great Britain Paramount + 2023.

72 USA Paramount + 2020–2023.

dimension for scholars beyond professional critics and other law and film writers.

8 Developments in Film and Law Scholarship

8.1 The Shift from Hollywood to a Local Focus

In terms of volume there has been the pre-eminence in the field by American writers on Hollywood. Along with an interest in English language cinema and the continued dominance of Hollywood on screens worldwide, scholars have started to focus on the products in their own jurisdictions. There has also been, for instance, British scholarship on British films, both in general[73] and specialist areas and themes.[74] Some areas like Canada have been overshadowed by their neighbours in terms of film production. The extensive Canadian scholarship by prominent writers like Schulz[75] and Johnson and Buchanan[76] has principally looked beyond their own borders but not exclusively.[77] There

73 Steve Greenfield, Guy Osborn and Peter Robson, 'Genre, Iconography and British Film' (2007) 36 Baltimore Law Review 371.

74 Peter Robson, 'Future Directions in Law and Popular Culture: a British perspective' in Jacqueline Visconti (ed), *Handbook of Communication in the Legal Sphere* (Walter de Gruyter Inc 2018); Peter Robson, 'Law in War—The Wind that Shakes the Barley and the Republican Court Experiment. Justice in the Time of War in Popular Culture' in Stefan Machura (ed), *Law and War in Popular Culture* (Nomos Verlags GmbH 2024); Peter Robson, 'From Bloodbath to Parody: Western Cinema's Uneasy Relationship with Rape-Revenge Themes—a fresh approach?' in Christine Künzel and Manuel Bolz (eds), *Rape and Revenge: Rache-Kulturen und sexualisierte Gewalt in intermedialer Perspektive* (V&R Unipress 2024).

75 Jennifer Schulz, 'Monsters & Madwomen? Neurosis, Ambition and Mothering in Women Lawyers in Film' (2016) 16 Journal of Law, Culture and the Humanities 1; Jennifer Schulz, 'Using Film to Teach ADR' in Christine Corcos (ed), *The Media Method: Teaching Law With Popular Culture* (Carolina Academic Press 2019).

76 Rebecca Johnson and Ruth Buchanan, 'Getting the Insider Getting the Insider's Story Out: What Popular Film Can Tell Us about Legal Method's Dirty Secrets' (2001) 20 Windsor Yearbook of Access to Justice 87; Ruth Buchanan and Rebecca Johnson, 'Strange Encounters: Exploring Law and Film in the Affective Register' (n 55).

77 Rebecca Johnson, 'Justice and the Colonial Collision: Reflections on Stories of Intercultural Encounter in Law, Literature, Sculpture and Film' (2012) 9 No Foundations 68; Rebecca Johnson, 'Notes on Using Film to Engage with Philosophy of Law in the Arctic' in Dawid Bunikowski, *Philosophy of Law in the Arctic* (The University of the Arctic, The Arctic Law Thematic Network, The Sub-group of Philosophy of Law in the Arctic 2016); Rebecca Johnson, 'Intercultural Cinema and the (Re)Envisioning of Law: Exploring Life, Death and

has also been discussion of issues traditionally outwith the boundaries of law and film.[78]

Australia has been rather luckier with a more dynamic film industry,[79] in turn producing more work on locally produced film.[80] From individual essays in journals and collected works a shift from American material has occurred. The topics range from blockbusters films with implications for an understanding of justice[81] to those with a more modest international profile,[82] as well as the colonial experience.[83] Some areas are rather more local.[84] Others address

---

Law in *Atanarjuat* and *Before Tomorrow*' in Timothy D. Peters and Karen Crawley (eds), *Envisioning Legality: Law, Culture and Representation* (Routledge 2018).

78 Jennifer Schulz, 'The Mediator as Cook: Mediation Metaphors at the Movies' (2007) 2 Journal of Dispute Resolution 455; Jennifer Schulz, 'Law & Film: Where are the Mediators?' (2008) 58 University of Toronto Law Journal 233; Jennifer Schulz, 'The Cook, the Mediator, the Feminist, and the Hero' (2009) 21 Canadian Journal of Women and the Law 177; Jennifer Schulz, 'Law and TV' in Russell Sandberg and Daniel Newman (eds), *Law and Humanities* (Anthem Press 2024).

79 Ian Craven, *Australian Cinema in the 1990s* (Routledge 2000); Ben Goldsmith, Susan Ward and Thomas O'Regan, *Local Hollywood: Global Film Production and the Gold Coast* (University of Queensland Press 2010).

80 Timothy D. Peters and Karen Crawley, *Envisioning Legality: Law, Culture and Representation* (Routledge 2018); Kim D. Weinert, Karen Crawley and Kieran Tranter, *Law, Lawyers and Justice: Through Australian Lenses* (Routledge 2020); Kim D. Weinert, Karen Crawley and Kieran Tranter, 'Australian Lenses on Law, Lawyers and Justice' in Kim D. Weinert, Karen Crawley and Kieran Tranter (eds), *Law, Lawyers and Justice: Through Australian Lenses* (Routledge 2020) 3.

81 Timothy D. Peters, 'Seeing' Justice Done: Envisioning Legality in Christopher Nolan's The Dark Knight Trilogy' in Timothy D. Peters and Karen Crawley (eds), *Envisioning Legality: Law, Culture and Representation* (Routledge 2018); Penny Crofts and Honni van Rijswijk, 'Picnic at Hanging Rock: Coming of age as a girl in the Gothic colonial institution' in Kim D. Weinert, Karen Crawley and Kieran Tranter (eds), *Law, Lawyers and Justice: Through Australian Lenses* (Routledge 2020); Kieran Tranter, 'Justice at the end of *Fury Road*' in Kim D. Weinert, Karen Crawley and Kieran Tranter (eds), *Law, Lawyers and Justice: Through Australian Lenses* (Routledge 2020); Alison Young, 'Ambivalence and the Spectatorship of Violence: Viewing *Inglourious Basterds*' in Timothy D. Peters and Karen Crawley (eds), *Envisioning Legality: Law, Culture and Representation* (Routledge 2018).

82 Kim D. Weinert, 'Romper Stomper: a critique of neoliberalism in Australia' in Kim D. Weinert, Karen Crawley and Kieran Tranter (eds), *Law, Lawyers and Justice: Through Australian Lenses* (Routledge 2020); Jack Quirk and Julian R. Murphy, 'Whose country? Colonialism and the rule of law in Sweet Country and Charlie's Country' in Kim D. Weinert, Karen Crawley and Kieran Tranter (eds), *Law, Lawyers and Justice: Through Australian Lenses* (Routledge 2020).

83 Thalia Anthony and Kieran Tranter, 'Taking a Lens to the Chase in Australian Settler State Colonialism' in Kim D. Weinert, Karen Crawley and Kieran Tranter (eds), *Law, Lawyers and Justice: Through Australian Lenses* (Routledge 2020).

84 Kirsty Duncanson, 'Being Engaged in Colonial Critique by Mojo Juju's Native Tongue' in Kim D. Weinert, Karen Crawley and Kieran Tranter (eds), *Law, Lawyers and Justice: Through Australian Lenses* (Routledge 2020).

topics of great interest across the field of law and popular culture including ethnicity[85] and vigilantism.[86]

8.2 Extending the Field in Non-Anglophone Scholarship

In a survey of the directions of law and film scholarship in *Film and the Law* in 2010[87] Greenfield, Osborn and Robson also briefly noted a range of work being carried out in the non-Anglophone world. This work has since expanded considerably. In Germany, for instance, inspired by Stefan Machura, from German scholars in the 21st century there have been examinations of American law films[88] and engagement with major Hollywood and European fare from a German perspective.[89] There have also been reviews of the scope and methodology[90] of the "law and film movement".[91] The whole area of film in law-related areas such as war has also engaged the scholarly community.[92] In addition, there has been a joint interest in both film and television. *Strafrecht*

85 David Callahan, 'His Natural Whiteness: Modes of Ethnic Presence and Absence in Some Recent Australian Films' in Ian Craven (ed), *Australian Cinema in the 1990s* (Routledge 2000).

86 Lili Pâquet, 'Vigilante Frontier Communities on Australian Screens: Bushrangers, Bikies, and Bogans in Vigilante Justice' in Peter Robson and Ferdinando Spina (eds), *Vigilante Justice in Society and Popular Culture* (Fairleigh Dickinson University Press 2022).

87 Steve Greenfield, Guy Osborn and Peter Robson, *Film and the Law: the cinema of justice* (n 20) 285–292.

88 Matthias Kuzina, *Der amerikanische Gerichtsfilm: Justiz, Ideologie, Dramatik* (Vandenhoek and Ruprecht 2000); Stefan Machura and Stefan Ulbrich, 'Law in film: Globalizing the Hollywood courtroom drama' (2001) 28 Journal of Law and Society 117; Stefan Machura, 'Recht im Film– Themen und Formen des Unterrichts' (2016) 3 ZDRW Zeitschrift für Didaktik der Rechtswissenschaft 363; Frans-Willem Korsten, 'Öffentlichkeit (open-ness) and the Law's Behind the Scenes: Theatrical and Dramatic Appearance in European and US, American Criminal Law' (2017) 18 German Law Journal 399.

89 Stefan Machura and Stefan Ulbrich, *Recht im Film* (Nomos Verlagsgesellschaft 2002); Stefan Machura, 'German Response to 12 Angry Men' (2007) 82 Chicago-Kent Law Review 777; Stefan Machura, 'Patton—Ein biographischer Kriegsfilm und der Mythos des amerikanischen Soldaten' in Stefan Machura and Rüdiger Voigt (eds), *Krieg im Film* (Lit 2005).

90 Stefan Machura, 'An Analysis Scheme for Law Films' (2007) 36 University of Baltimore Law Review 329.

91 Stefan Machura, 'Law and Cinema Movement' in Caroline Joan Picart, Michael Hviid Jacobsen and Cecil Greek (eds), *Framing Law and Crime: An Interdisciplinary Anthology* (Rowman and Littlefield 2016).

92 Stefan Machura and Rüdiger Voigt, *Krieg im Film* (Lit 2005); Matthias Kuzina, 'Das Kriegsgerichtsverfahren als Filmsujet: US-amerikanische Erzählmuster' in Stefan Machura and Rüdiger Voigt (eds), *Krieg im Film* (Lit 2005); Stefan Machura and Rüdiger Voigt, 'Krieg im Film. Der ewige Kampf des "Guten" gegen das "Böse"' in Stefan Machura and Rüdiger Voigt (eds), *Krieg im Film* (Lit 2005).

in Film und Fernsehen (Criminal Law in Film and on TV)[93] for instance from 2016 consists of a mix of essays mainly on various German TV shows and their impact as well as coverage of film.

It is clear that law and film also thrives in France with both courses[94] and Seminars as well as tangible evidence of a strong engagement with the field through traditional publications and the internet. Similar themes crop up as have been encountered in the Anglophone and German work such as the hegemony of Hollywood—the Atticus Finch effect. In 2015 a seminar on Law and Cinema[95] suggested that the role of the United States also appears as dominant and involves nothing less than "the americanisation".[96] The themes of the literature have included the symbols of justice and their function both past and present including their representation in film.[97] Censorship and the controls on film link legal and cultural themes.[98] There have also been wide-ranging surveys with a French series, from the publishers Mare and Martin.[99] Within the overall heading of *Droit et Cinema* there have been monographs covering the family in film[100] individual directors, both French[101] and British,[102] TV comic amateur vigilantes,[103] the juridical thought of Sheldon Cooper from THE BIG

93 Hauke Brettel, Matthias Rau and Jannik Rienhoff, *Strafrecht in Film und Fernsehen* (Springer 2016).

94 Master Droit du cinéma, de l'audiovisuel et de la communication numérique (anciennement Droit du cinéma et de l'audiovisuel) (*Université Lyon III Jean Moulin*) <https://facdedroit.univ-lyon3.fr/master-droit-du-cinema-et-de-l-audiovisuel-2> accessed 06 December 2024.

95 Droit et Cinéma Printemps 2015.

96 'Droit et cinéma' (*Marie-Anne Frison Roche*) <https://mafr.fr/en/enseignements/droit-et-cinema/> accessed 06 December 2024.

97 Wanda Mastor and Lionel Miniato, *Les figures du procès au-delà des frontières* (Dalloz 2014). See also Magalie Flores-Lonjou, 'Le juge français mis en images: images officielles versus images documentaires' (2018) 1 Revue de droit et de criminologie de l'ULB 1 <https://hal-univ-rochelle.archives-ouvertes.fr/hal-02389883/document> accessed 06 December 2024.

98 Frédéric Hervé, *Censure et Cinéma dans la France des Trente Glorieuses* (Nouveau Monde Éditions 2015); Christophe Triolle, *Le contrôle cinématographique en France. Quand le sexe, la violence, et la religion font encore débat* (L'Harmattan 2015).

99 'Collection Droit et Cinéma' (*Mare et Martin*) <https://www.mareetmartin.com/les-editions-mare-et-martin/les-collections/collection-droit-cinema> accessed 06 December 2024.

100 Magalie Flores-Lonjou and Estelle Épinoux, *La famille au cinéma: Regards juridiques et esthétiques* (Mare et Martin 2016).

101 Fabrice Defferrard, *La pensée juridique de Sheldon Cooper ou Comment faire du droit avec The Big Bang Theory* (Mare et Martin 2019).

102 Arnaud Coutant, *Les lois d'Alfred Hitchcock* (Mare et Martin 2018).

103 Arnaud Coutant, *Juridiquement vôtre: Brett Sinclair et Danny Wilde, un duo au service du droit* (Mare et Martin 2020).

BANG THEORY,[104] Disney films[105] as well as interdisciplinary engagement with the humanities on specific themes.[106] Add to this a volume on police films[107] and the broad field of law and film has come a long way from the limited material from the early part of the 21st century.[108] In addition to traditional sources there are also internet sources including a fascinating blog entitled *Le Blog Droit et Cinéma*.[109]

Spanish scholars in the field have continued to focus almost exclusively on film rather than television. There has been a slight shift away from the earlier focus on Hollywood which was found in the first volumes of the *Cine y Derecho* series. There is also evidence that the interest in film goes beyond the academy into the legal profession. For example, the professional body for lawyers in Aragon, the *Real y Ilustre Colegio de Abogados de Zaragoza*, reveal in their Journal a series of presentations with accompanying literature, entitled *Ciclo de Cine Juridico*. These have covered *Matar a un ruiseñor* (TO KILL A MOCKINGBIRD) in May 2019, *Doce Hombres sin Piedad* (12 ANGRY MEN) in December 2019, *Acusados* (THE ACCUSED) in June 2020 as well as *Testigo de cargo*, (WITNESS FOR THE PROSECUTION 1957) in December 2022.[110] There is also a book from a commercial lawyer looking at a range of thirteen films related to this field from classics like LLOYD'S OF LONDON (1936), DOUBLE INDEMNITY (1944), GILDA (1946), and IT'S A WONDERFUL LIFE (1946), to

104 Fabrice Defferrard, *La pensée juridique de Sheldon Cooper ou Comment faire du droit avec The Big Bang Theory* (n 101).

105 Quention Le Pluard and Marion Talbot, *Du droit dans Disney* (Mare et Martin 2020).

106 Magalie Flores-Lonjou, Estelle Épinoux and Vincent Lefebve, *Frontière(s) au cinéma* (Mare et Martin 2019).

107 Jean Ollé-Laprune, *Le Cinéma Policier Francais: 100 films, 100 réalisateurs* (n 39).

108 Françoise Puaux, *La Justice à L'Écran* (CinemAction 2002); Christian Delage, 'Image as evidence and mediation: The Experience of the Nuremberg Trials' in Michael Freeman (ed), *Law and Popular Culture* (Oxford University Press 2005).

109 Andrea Grunert, 'Vérité et mensonge dans Distance/Disutansu de Hirokazu Kore-Eda (Japon, 2001)' (*Le Blog Droit et Cinéma*, 22 January 2024) <https://lesmistons.typepad.com/blog/2024/01/index.html> accessed 06 December 2024. It includes coverage of traditional fare for cineastes such as RASHOMON. It also looks at the role of Isabelle Huppert in the controversial rape film ELLE as well as the feted vigilante film THE REVENANT and the State v Family rights film PHILOMENA (2013). We find traditional concerns such as censorship as well as more unexpected topics such as the law in STAR TREK. The directors' work examined ranges wide well beyond the standard coverage of law and film studies into the cinema of Hitchcock, Woody Allen and Clint Eastwood.

110 'Testigo de cargo. Witness for the Prosecution Billy Wilder (1957)' (*Standum est chartae*) <http://revista.reicaz.es/numeros-anteriores/n-012/cine-y-derecho/> accessed 27 November 2022.

more modern films such as WALL STREET (1987), THE INSIDER (1999) and THE SOCIAL NETWORK.[111]

The Tirant Lo Blanch publishing house in Valencia have produced over 70 volumes in their Cine y Derecho series. Commencing in 2002 there has been a steady stream of works. These can be divided into three broad categories—individual films, thematic works and overviews or guides. Firstly, those which focus on a single film and are generally quite short with an average of 115 pages—the shortest 66 pages and the longest 240. They have covered a wide range of films and have been dominated by material from the United States. Of the 44 individual film monographs, 30 are on American material and only 1 on a Spanish film. The remaining 13 examine British (6), Italian (3), French (1), Danish (1), Polish (1) and Palestinian (1). There is in the volumes produced in the series only one work on television—*The West Wing: Politica Como Promesa*[112] (Politics as Promise).

These individual films covered range from classics which one might expect in a series dedicated to law and film like ANATOMY OF A MURDER (1959), JUDGMENT AT NUREMBERG (1961), TO KILL A MOCKINGBIRD (1962), and A FEW GOOD MEN (1999). Some of the early coverage was, however, on slightly less obvious films like BLADE RUNNER (1982), THREE COLOURS: RED (1994), THE SCARLET LETTER (1995), MACBETH (1971), THE MATRIX (1999) and THE SHOES OF THE FISHERMAN (1968).

There are 21 volumes centred on specific themes. These range from the death penalty, torture, prostitution, rape, strikes, and euthanasia to the rights of the child, films on life in the office and factory, prison films and the impact of Francoism. These are rather longer averaging 240 pages. There is also a volume from 2012 on the scholarship on law and film with a focus on migration—*Fotogramas para la multiculturaidad.*[113] They consist of essays by a collection of authors. Straying from film, one volume also offers a perspective taking in not only film but also literature and comics—*Derechos, Cine, Literatura y Cómics. Cómo y por qué.*[114] The approaches in these collections vary from a legal focus through a cultural assessment to a mixture. There is also a volume from 2020 by the driving force behind the output from Spain, Javier de

111 Pablo Fernadez Carballo Calero, *Derecho Mercantil y Cine* (Editorial Aranzadi 2016).

112 Miguel Ángel Presno Linares, *The West Wing: la política como promessa* (Tirant Lo Blanch 2016).

113 Mónica Cantero-Exojo, Maria Van Liew and José Carlos Suarez, *Fotogramas para la multiculturalidad: Migraciones y alteridad en el cine español contemporáneo* (Tirant Lo Blanch 2012).

114 Miguel Ángel Ramiro Avilés, *Derechos, cine, literatura y cómics: como y porqué* (Tirant Lo Blanch 2014).

Lucas. It looks at the impact of the image of To Kill A Mockingbird's protagonist, Atticus Finch—*Nosotros, que quisimos tanto a Atticus Finch*—What we love so much about Atticus Finch. This addresses, *inter alia*, revisionist perspectives on the iconic defence lawyer.[115]

The remaining six volumes involve overviews of the field of law in film. By their very nature they are longer averaging 350 pages. One of the earliest was a guide to law and film in 100 films from 2004 *Derecho y Cine en 100 peliculas*.[116] It focused on films which encapsulated a specific legal concept rather than artistic quality. Again, US cinema dominated with 73 films and 9 from Spain. The remainder were from Italy (7), Great Britain (4), France (3), Japan (2), Colombia (1) and Germany (1). The films included standards like Young Mr Lincoln (1939), 12 Angry Men (1957) and Anatomy of a Murder (1959) as well as less discussed films like the prison film Birdman of Alcatraz (1962) and the notorious Straw Dogs (1971). 2006 saw the publication of a collection of essays providing a Cinematic Introduction to the Law—*Una Introducción Cinematográfica al Derecho*[117]—which consisted of individual areas of law being illustrated through film. There is also a guide to the law in modern Spanish cinema—*El Derecho en el Cine Español Contemporaneo* (2009)—recounting the changes in Spanish social, political and cultural life since the arrival of democracy in 1975. This guide is provided by twenty different writers on how this can be seen through film.[118]

This heuristic division between individual films, themes and overviews does not accommodate every single volume perfectly. There is, for example a volume on law in the cinema focusing on constitutional law—*Derecho al cine: Una Introducciòn cinematográfica al Derecho constitucional*[119]—seeking to provide a guide to a broad theme. The same kind of engagement with the underlying concepts in constitutional law as found in film, is the theme of another 2012 volume—*Proyecciones de Derecho Consitucional*.[120]

A more clear-cut example of a guide can be found in another 2012 offering—A Judicial Handbook: cinema for judges—*Un vademécum judicial:*

115 Javier de Lucas, *Nosotros, que quisimos tanto a Atticus Finch* (Tirant Lo Blanch 2020).

116 Benjamin Rivaya and Pablo de Cima, *Derecho y Cine en 100 peliculas* (n 38).

117 Miguel Ángel Presno Linera and Benjamin Rivaya, *Una Introducción cinematográfica al derecho* (Tirant Lo Blanch 2006).

118 Ricardo Garcia Manrique and Mario Ruiz Sainz, *El Derecho en el Cine Español Contemporáneo* (Tirant Lo Blanch 2009).

119 Abraham Barrero Ortega and others, *Derecho al Cine: Una introducción cinematográfica al Derecho Constitucional* (Tirant Lo Blanch 2011).

120 Fernando Reviriego Picón, *Proyecciones de Derecho Constitucional* (Tirant Lo Blanch 2012).

Cine para jueces.[121] This seeks to put the case for why judges ought to study the seventh art. Film offers the opportunity to observe different perspectives on the judicial process.

The major pioneering work by Benjamin Rivaya and Pablo de Cima has been revised and expanded by Rivaya from its original 502 to an even weightier 659 pages. The title, however remains Law and Film in 100 films—*Derecho y cine en 100 peliculas*.[122] The impact of film on people's understanding of law is examined. It looks at the field of the cinema of justice including film and legal theory as well as how law and film studies can be used. It is clear that the world of film and law in both in terms of publications and engagement is thriving in Spain.

Law and film has also been subject to major work across Latin America from Argentina[123] to Peru.[124] The coverage includes not only traditional Hollywood films[125] but also local material.[126] Significant debate with other Spanish speaking writers and researchers also takes place within the *Red Iberoamericana de Cine y Derecho* (Spanish American Network on Film and the Law) which takes in Argentina, Bolivia, Brazil, Chile, Colombia, Ecuador, Mexico, Peru and Spain.[127] The issues include a focus at one Meeting in 2020 on criminals in film in such Hollywood products as MY COUSIN VINNY, THE JOKER, THE

121 Benjamin Rivaya, *Un Vademécum Judicial: Cine para jueces* (Tirant Lo Blanch 2012).

122 Benjamin Rivaya and Pablo de Cima, *Derecho y Cine en 100 peliculas* (Tirant Lo Blanch 2004); Benjamin Rivaya, *Derecho y Cine en 100 peliculas* (Tirant Lo Blanch 2021).

123 Rafael de Mendizábal Allende, *Cine y Derecho: togas en la gran pantalla* (Berenice 2021).

124 Cecilia O'Neill de la Fuente, *El derecho va al cine: intersecciones entre la visión artística y la visión jurídica de los problemas sociales* (Universidad del Pacífico 2013); José Ramón Narváez Hernández, *Los jueces en el cine. La administración de justicia y la argumentación en el séptimo arte* (Fondo Editorial del Poder Judicial del Perú/Red Iberoamericana de Cine y Derecho Editorial 2016); Eddy Huanca Chávez and Helder Domínguez Haro, *Los tribunales de justicia en el cine* (Fondo Editorial del Poder Judicial del Perú/Red Iberoamericana de Cine y Derecho 2018); Luis Pásara and Manuel Alcántara, *La justicia en la pantalla: Un reflejo de jueces y tribunales en cine y TV* (Pontificia Universidad Católica del Perú, Fondo Editorial 2019).

125 Eg WITNESS FOR THE PROSECUTION (1957); JUDGMENT AT NUREMBERG (1961).

126 Eg Manuel Iturralde, 'Justicia de bagatela: sistema penal y desigualdad en un documental colombiano' in Eddy Huanca Chávez and Helder Domínguez Haro (eds), *Los tribunales de justicia en el cine* (Fondo Editorial del Poder Judicial del Perú/Red Iberoamericana de Cine y Derecho 2018); Sebastián Linares, 'El secreto de sus ojos: justicia por mano propia y legitimidad del Estado' in Eddy Huanca Chávez and Helder Domínguez Haro (eds), *Los tribunales de justicia en el cine* (Fondo Editorial del Poder Judicial del Perú/Red Iberoamericana de Cine y Derecho 2018).

127 '27th Meeting—28 September to 3 October 2020' (*Nitter*) <https://nitter.fdn.fr/pic/media%2FEf7R9FpWAAATZED.jpg%3Fname%3Dorig> accessed 21 December 2024.

GODFATHER as well as the Italian Mafia film IL TRADITORE and the Peruvian SIN COMPASIÓN.[128] This Network is described as a space to share experiences stemming from the intersection between law and film. By October 2021 it had held some 29 meetings. The material covered in the 29th meeting, for instance, held under the auspices of the National Autonomous University of Mexico went beyond film analysis into locating film's role in struggles for social and human rights.[129] The 30th meeting was held in May 2023 in Quito, Ecuador with themes including the law of damages in film, the TV drama SUITS and the impact of filmic representations on law teaching.[130]

There is also extensive work in Italy. From 2017 there has been a series of 18 monographs from Editoriale Scientifica of Naples. Most of these are quite short with an average of just over 60 pages and only 4 in excess of 100 pages. These range across a wide range of topics from the threat to liberty under McCarthyism[131] and neoliberalism in a modern world[132] to taxation issues,[133] bio-medical issues raised by films like BLADE RUNNER,[134] the Italian family in film,[135] consumerism[136] and the 20th century Balkan Wars.[137] There has also been work on how film represents immigration[138] and medically assisted

---

128 '13–15 October 2021' (*Nitter*) <https://nitter.fdn.fr/pic/media%2FFBhtWOZVgAIMCog.jpg%3Fname%3Dorig> accessed 10 February 2025.

129 'CINE EN LA UNAM PROGRAMACIÓN' (*Culturaunam*) <https://www.filmoteca.unam.mx/290-congreso-de-cine-y-derecho-iv-muestra-internacional-de-cine-derechos-humanos-y-justicia/> accessed 10 February 2025. The papers presented at the Meeting can be viewed on YouTube.

130 Mariella Toranzos, 'Congreso de Cine y Derecho se dará en la Universidad Andina' (*Expreso*, 10 May 2023) <https://www.expreso.ec/actualidad/cine-leyes-160044.html> accessed 16 December 2024.

131 Claudio De Fiores, *Il fragile scudo della Costituzione: L'occhio del cinema sulla violazione dei diritti al tempo del maccartismo* (Editoriale Scientifica 2017).

132 Salvatore D'Acunto and Valeria Nuzzo, *Fotogrammi dal dominio della lotta: L'occhio del cinema sulla società neoliberista* (Editoriale Scientifica 2017).

133 Fabrizio Amatucci and Anna Rita Ciarcia, *Il cinema come evasione … fiscale* (Editoriale Scientifica 2017); Anna Rita Ciarcia, *Il cinema e le tasse* (Editoriale Scientifica 2017); Adriana Salvati, *Timema e Thanatos: Tasse e morte* (Editoriale Scientifica 2017).

134 Roberta Catalano and Carlo Venditti, *Questioni di biodiritto nella filmografia cyberpunk* (Editoriale Scientifica 2017).

135 Filomena D'Alto and Marianna Pignata, *Le forme della legge e le forme dell'arte: La famiglia italiana nel racconto cinematografico* (Editoriale Scientifica 2017).

136 Alessia Fachechi, *Storie di facili consumi* (Editoriale Scientifica 2017).

137 Maria Chiara Vitucci, *La guerra dietro casa: Lo sguardo del cinema sulla Jugoslavia in fiamme* (Editoriale Scientifica 2017).

138 M. Eugenia Bartoloni and Luigi Valentino, *Il fenomeno migratorio fra immagini e norme* (Editoriale Scientifica 2017).

birth.[139] More recently we have seen coverage of the representation of the legal process through the reflective lens of film.[140]

There are also volumes focusing on individual films including the 1963 Italian film LE MANI SULLA CITTÀ about political corruption in the urban development process[141] and the representation of law in the films of the Italian comic actor *Totò*.[142] Also the Steve McQueen version of Ibsen's ENEMY OF THE PEOPLE (1978)[143] comes under the spotlight as well as the more conventional American courtroom drama FRACTURE from 2007.[144] Three very different films about Nazism are also examined. They are the Nazi propaganda historical drama JUD SŰ3 (1940) along with the post War Italian adaptation of the tale of the wandering Jew. Here this story of redemption, L'EBREO ERRANTE (1948), is adapted to include coverage of the Nazi concentration camps and the German Nazi propaganda documentary THERESIENSTADT (1944) which sought to show how the camps were happy and well run.[145] Despite the title of the series being *Cine e Diritto*, there has also been coverage of TV with a work on the US prison drama ORANGE IS THE NEW BLACK.[146]

There is also a selection of films from some five hundred deemed by the authors to be on a legal theme. They include in their coverage popular and classical Italian film as well as international material.[147] A later collection of essays from 2020 covered a number of distinct issues from Italian comedy films between the 1970s to 1990s, multiculturalism in film, cinema and human rights to parenting and well-being as well as animal rights and the film industry. There was also coverage of the 2000 Canadian-American docudrama (IL PROCESSO DI NORIMBERGA).[148] Traditionally, there was a strong interest in

139 Maria Pia Iadicicco, *La procreazione medicalmente assistita al cinema* (Editoriale Scientifica 2017).

140 Osvaldo Sacchi, *Lo scudo riflettente di Perseo. Archetipi del giuridico nel cinema contemporaneo* (Editoriale Scientfica 2019).

141 Fernando Flores, *Le mani sulla città. Il capitalismo: la democrazia in ostaggio* (Editoriale Scientifica 2018).

142 Fluvio Corso, *Totò Il lavoro e ... la legge* (Editoriale Scientifica 2019).

143 Carlo Lanza and Luciano Minieri, + *Nemici del popolo* (Editoriale Scientifica 2017).

144 Teresa Bene and Giorgio Spangher, *Un processo americano: Il caso Thomas Crawford* (Editoriale Scientifica 2017).

145 Antonella Argenio, *I film del nazismo: Süss l'ebreo, L'ebreo errante, Terezin* (Editoriale Scientifica 2017).

146 Andreana Esposito, *Dal nero all'arancio: anatomia penitenziaria di una serie TV* (Editoriale Scientifica 2017).

147 Giovanni Ziccardi, *Il diritto al cinema: Cent'anni di courtroom drama e melodrammi giudiziari* (Giuffrè 2010).

148 Orlando Roselli, *Cinema e diritto. La comprensione della dimensione giuridica attraverso la cinematografia* (Giappichelli 2020).

Hollywood[149] although, more recently, there has been a focus on Italian films dealing with legal issues.[150] Such is the nature of the links between politics and law generally, and in Italy in particular, that some studies go beyond a narrow focus on the justice system,[151] including the Mafia.[152] Some titles which appear dedicated to film alone also cover other elements of the media. For example the fascinating collection *In nome della legge. La giustizia nel cinema italiano*[153] in addition to considering why there has been no Italian courtroom drama also contains essays on literature and television. Again, as in Spain and France, there is availability of courses on film and law such as the course *Communication, Crime, Deviance,* (Comunicazione, Crimine, Devianza) at the University of Salento which has been looking at films, as well as TV, for more than ten years.[154]

9 Locating Law and Film Scholarship within Broader Disciplines

The approaches taken over the years by scholars in law and film have changed from an almost "diversionary" approach by law teachers seeking to simply engage their students more effectively with doctrinal and practical issues. Rather more seriously, the interest was on what legal errors there were in specific films.[155] The relationship with the humanities is, thereafter, symbiotic or perhaps more accurately parasitic.[156] This stems from the critical methods that

149 Paolo Cattorini, *L'occhio che uccide. Criminologi al cinema* (FrancoAngeli 2006); Ennio Amodio, *Estetica della giustizia penale. Prassi, media, fiction* (Giuffrè 2016).

150 Luigi Pannarale, 'La verità degli avvocati: un'indagine sul cinema italiano' (2021) 3 Sociologia del Diritto 33.

151 Anton Giulio Mancino, *Il processo della verità: le radici del film politico-indiziario italiano* (Kaplan 2008).

152 Roberto Curti, *Italian Crime Filmography, 1968–1980* (McFarland 2013); Marcello Ravveduto, *Lo spettacolo della mafia. Storia di un immaginario tra realtà e finzione* (Edizioni Gruppo Abele 2019).

153 Guido Vitiello, *In nome della legge. La giustizia nel cinema italiano* (Rubbettino 2013).

154 'Ferdinando Spina' (*Uni Salento*) <https://www.unisalento.it/people/ferdinando.spina/didattica/1256842020/scheda> accessed 30 August 2025.

155 Paul Bergman and Michael Asimow, *Reel Justice: the courtroom goes to the movies* (n 34).

156 Anne Bottomley and Nathan Moore, 'Law, Diagram, Film: Critique Exhausted' (2012) 23 Law Critique 163; Melissa de Zwart, Bernadette Richards and Suzanne Le Mire, *Law and Popular Culture in Australia* (LexisNexis 2015); Costas Douzinas, 'A Humanities of Resistance: Fragments for a Legal History of Humanity' in Austin Sarat, Matthew Anderson and Cathrine O. Frank (eds), *Law and Humanities: An Introduction* (Cambridge University

are central.[157] From early days there had been interest in historical elements[158] along with some limited engagement with empirical approaches.[159] There has been little obvious engagement with literature which has operated in its own silo.[160] Much the same can be said about law and linguistics with its own specialist journal,[161] and publications focused on linguistics.[162] It is clear from the material we have noted above that the area of law and film has developed its own set of interests and criteria and has become self-sustaining and self-referential whilst drawing on some of the cognate areas of the humanities noted below.[163] One volume from the field of law, semiotics and visual studies produced fifteen out of 46 essays on film and TV.[164] Law and Popular Culture also featured early on as an area around which scholars with related interests coalesced. So we find film analysis of the *auteur* notion in justice films[165] alongside

Press 2009); Lieve Gies, 'Law as Popular Culture: Cross-Disciplinary Encounters' (2005) 19 Continuum 165; Priska Gisler, Sara Steinert Borella, Caroline Wiedmer, *Intersections of Law and Culture* (Palgrave Macmillan 2012); Kathy Laster, *Law as Culture* (Federation Press 2011); Marett Leiboff and Cassandra Sharp, 'Cultural Legal Studies and Law's Popular Cultures' in Cassandra Sharp and Marett Leiboff (eds), *Cultural Legal Studies Law's Popular Cultures and the Metamorphosis of Law* (Routledge 2015); William MacNeil and Peter Hutchings, 'Law's Cultural Mediations: An Introduction by Way of Introduction' (2001) 10 Griffith Law Review 1; Cassandra Sharp and Marett Leiboff, *Cultural Legal Studies: Law's Popular Cultures and the Metamorphosis of Law* (Routledge 2015).

157 Guyora Binder and Robert Weisberg, 'Cultural Criticism of Law' (1997) 49 Stanford Law Review 1149; Simon Stern, Maksymilian Del Mar and Bernadette Meyler, *The Oxford Handbook of Law and Humanities* (Oxford University Press 2019).

158 Francis Nevins, 'Through the Great Depression on Horseback: legal themes in Western films of the 1930s' in John Denvir (ed), *Legal Reelism: Movies as Legal Texts* (University of Illinois Press 1996).

159 Michael Asimow and others, 'Perceptions of lawyers: a transnational study of student views on law and lawyers' (2005) 12 International Journal of the Legal Profession 407.

160 Kieran Dolin, *Critical Introduction to Law and Literature* (Cambridge University Press 2007); Kieran Dolin, *Fiction and the Law: Legal Discourse in Victorian and Modernist Literature* (Cambridge University Press 2009); Kieran Dolin, *Law and Literature* (Cambridge University Press 2018); Margaret Thornton, *Romancing the Tomes: Popular Culture, Law and Feminism* (Routledge 2002).

161 International Journal for the Semiotics of Law (from 1988 to date—thus far 35 volumes).

162 Jacqueline Visconti, *Handbook of Communication in the Legal Sphere* (Walter de Gruyter Inc 2018).

163 Russell Sandberg and Daniel Newman, *Law and Humanities* (Anthem 2024).

164 Anne Wagner and Richard K. Sherwin, *Law, Culture and Visual Studies* (Springer 2014).

165 Peter Robson, 'The justice films of Sidney Lumet' in Steve Greenfield and Guy Osborn (eds) (n 46).

writing on literature, music and sport.[166] Other work appeared under this banner dealing with a range of issues from reality TV.[167]

Law and film ultimately depicts social values, which go beyond the accuracy of legal processes and systems. For example, biopics document the experience of an individual, or a collective, in their interactions with rule makers and authority. This can often highlight high-profile miscarriage of justice cases, but can also be used as an avenue to discuss disciplines such as human rights, environmental law, and public health. However, the majority of the films ultimately present ethical dilemmas—what position do the characters find themselves in? What is the desired outcome? What obstacles do they face, and what steps should they take to get to the desired outcome?

10 Current Trends

Another place in which film scholarship is found has been within discrete themes where film, along with other areas like television and literature has been used as a focal point. One Collection published in 2024 centres on the theme of rape revenge.[168] Of the 15 essays 7 are on film.[169] The approaches involve in some instances interrogating films in detail. The films include both the traditional sources such as Hollywood and other Anglophone products[170]

---

166 Steve Greenfield and Guy Osborn, *Readings in Law and Popular Culture* (Routledge 2006).

167 Austin Sarat, *Imagining Legality: When Law Meets Popular Culture* (University of Alabama Press 2011).

168 Christine Künzel and Manuel Bolz, *Rape and Revenge: Rache-Kulturen und sexualisierte Gewalt in intermedialer Perspektive* (V&R Unipress 2024).

169 Five are in English—see below—the two in German are Jakob Larisch, 'Rape-and-Revenge -Filme im Kontext strafrechtlicher Verbotpraxis' in Christine Künzel and Manuel Bolz (eds), *Rape and Revenge: Rache-Kulturen und sexualisierte Gewalt in intermedialer Perspektive* (V&R Unipress 2024) and Sarah K. Becker, 'Rape/Revenge/Suicide. Zum Verhältnis von Fremd-und Autoaggression in BIG LITTLE LIES und 13 REASONS WHY' in Christine Künzel and Manuel Bolz (eds), *Rape and Revenge: Rache-Kulturen und sexualisierte Gewalt in intermedialer Perspektive* (V&R Unipress 2024).

170 Robson P., 'From Bloodbath to Parody: Western Cinema's Uneasy Relationship With Rape-Revenge Themes—A Fresh Approach?' in Christine Künzel and Manuela Bolz (Eds), *Rape and Revenge: Rache-Kulturen und sexualisierte Gewalt in intermedialoer Perspaktice* (V&R Unipress 2024); Sarah K. Becker, 'Rape/Revenge/Suicide. Zum Verhältnis von Fremd-und Autoaggression in BIG LITTLE LIES und 13 REASONS WHY' in Christine Künzel and Manuel Bolz (eds) (n 346); Lisa Haegele, 'Popfeminist Approaches to Rape-and-Revenge: Avenging with Awkwardness in Emerald Fennell's PROMISING YOUNG WOMAN (UK/ USA 2020) and Ziska Riemann's LOLLIPOP MONSTER (GER 2011)' in Christine Künzel and Manuel Bolz (eds), *Rape and Revenge: Rache-Kulturen und sexualisierte Gewalt in*

as well as India's Bollywood[171] and Nigeria's Nollywood.[172] The material includes dark comedies and teen dramas,[173] as well as serious examinations of the phenomenon of revenge in response to rape. Some focus on the shifting narrative elements within recent portrayals of rape and revenge.[174]

More recently, Stefan Machura has edited a collection on Law and War in Popular Culture[175] covering a range of different issues in this area including war crimes and military justice in film.[176] There are also contributions on justice in civil war situations,[177] as well as slightly more unexpected essays on crime and law in Music and Bollywood Drama.[178] A leading figure in the development of scholarship, Austin Sarat, has also edited a collection focusing on impact of

---

intermedialer Perspektive (V&R Unipress 2024); Sabine Sielke, 'Return with a Vengeance? The Serial Debate on Sexual Harassment and Sexual Violence, or: What's New About #MeToo—and What Film Can (Still) Do' in Christine Künzel and Manuel Bolz (eds), *Rape and Revenge: Rache-Kulturen und sexualisierte Gewalt in intermedialer Perspektive* (V&R Unipress 2024).

171 Sanchari Basu Chaudhuri, 'Neoliberal Avenging Moms? Examining Rape-and-Revenge in Bollywood Movies' in Christine Künzel and Manuel Bolz (eds), *Rape and Revenge: Rache-Kulturen und sexualisierte Gewalt in intermedialer Perspektive* (V&R Unipress 2024).

172 Helen Ufuoma Ugah, 'Reconfiguring Victimhood: Rape Culture and Rape-Revenge in Nollywood Movies' in Christine Künzel and Manuel Bolz (eds), *Rape and Revenge: Rache-Kulturen und sexualisierte Gewalt in intermedialer Perspektive* (V&R Unipress 2024).

173 Sarah K. Becker, 'Rape/Revenge/Suicide. Zum Verhältnis von Fremd-und Autoaggression in BIG LITTLE LIES und 13 REASONS WHY' in Christine Künzel and Manuel Bolz (eds) (n 169).

174 Robson P., 'From Bloodbath to Parody: Western Cinema's Uneasy Relationship With Rape-Revenge Themes—A Fresh Approach?' in Christine Künzel and Manuela Bolz (Eds), *Rape and Revenge: Rache-Kulturen und sexualisierte Gewalt in intermedialoer Perspaktice* (V&R Unipress 2024).

175 Stefan Machura, *Law and War in Popular Culture* (Nomos Verlags GmbH 2024).

176 Ann Ching, 'Depictions of War Crimes in Film' in Stefan Machura (ed), *Law and War in Popular Culture* (Nomos Verlags GmbH 2024); Michael Asimow, 'All's Fair in Love and War. Military Justice in the Movies' in Stefan Machura (ed), *Law and War in Popular Culture* (Nomos Verlags GmbH 2024); Nathan Abrams and Michael Lipiner, 'Macho–Menschlichkeit Law and War in Stanley Kubrick's Paths of Glory (1957)' in Stefan Machura (ed), *Law and War in Popular Culture* (Nomos Verlags GmbH 2024).

177 Ferdinando Spina, 'Through the Law, Beyond the Law Dealing with Fascism and Civil War in Italian Cinema' in Stefan Machura (ed), *Law and War in Popular Culture* (Nomos Verlags GmbH 2024); Iker Nabaskues Martínez de Eulate, 'War, Film, Memory and Trauma: the Bosnian case in Quo Vadis Aida?' in Stefan Machura (ed), *Law and War in Popular Culture* (Nomos Verlags GmbH 2024); Peter Robson, 'Law in War—The Wind that Shakes the Barley and the Republican Court Experiment. Justice in the Time of War in Popular Culture' in Stefan Machura (ed) (n 170).

178 Stefan Machura and John Cunnigham, 'Law and War in the Opera' in Stefan Machura (ed), *Law and War in Popular Culture* (Nomos Verlags GmbH 2024); John Cunningham, 'That's When I Reach for My Revolver. War Crimes and Popular Music' in Stefan Machura (ed), *Law and War in Popular Culture* (Nomos Verlags GmbH 2024); Steven Greenfield, 'The

modern technology. These six essays examine how the power of the state can now be made visible to a much wider audience and the implications of this.[179]

Extending the coverage into wider fields of popular culture, Sandberg and Newman covered the wider field of law and humanities.[180] In the last thirty to forty years, interdisciplinary scholarship on law has significantly increased. Law has a number of different potential disciplinary bedfellows. It can be seen as a social science but also as part of the humanities. Given how ubiquitous social scientific theories and methods are within legal studies, this collection explores law's place within the humanities. It examines a number of 'law and' interactions in turn with the aim of exploring what these different fields can learn from each other and what this reveals about the law and humanities approach in general. The Collection from 2024, *Law and Humanities*, provides an accessible, introductory but critical guide to this emerging area of scholarship. Unlike the existing works that adopt a thematic approach, this is the only edited collection that explores law and humanities field by field. Experts in each 'law and' field analyse the nature, development and future of their respective fields, placing this within the law and humanities context for the first time. Each chapter provides a seminal contribution to the respective field while the volume as a whole represents a major work in the development of law and humanities, as well as to interdisciplinary legal studies generally. One earlier law and popular culture Collection, by contrast, had some 6 of the twenty-four essays covering film and four covering TV.[181]

A combination of both a non-Hollywood focus and a specific issue is found in a book dealing with Indian cinema (across geographic regions, languages and formats) and human rights.[182] It analyses Indian cinema from multiple human rights perspectives, such as freedom of expression and censorship, socio-economic rights, caste rights, women's and children's rights and LGBTQIA+ equality. The book bridges human rights law and cinema studies, and opens up new research areas within sociocultural and socio-legal academic contexts. It also contributes to academic disciplines beyond Law and Cinema, including Media, Cultural, Gender, Socio-economic and Sociology studies and is relevant for Liberal Arts curricula, Law Schools and as a reference book in university libraries in India and internationally, especially in film institutes.

Rising: Mangal Pandey and India's First War of Independence' in Stefan Machura (ed), *Law and War in Popular Culture* (Nomos Verlags GmbH 2024).

179 Austin Sarat, *Law and the Visible* (University of Massachusetts Press 2021).

180 Russell Sandberg and Daniel Newman, *Law and Humanities* (n 163).

181 Michael Asimow, Kathryn Brown and David Papke, *Law and Popular Culture: International Perspectives* (Cambridge Scholars Publishing 2014).

182 Adam D. Dubin, Ruchira Goswami and Ishita Sharma, *Indian Cinema and Human Rights: An Intersectional Tale* (Springer 2025).

Finally, the book offers practical implications for human rights activists and policymakers exploring how rights can be advanced through cinema and pop culture.

11 Conclusions

From an apparently narrow focus on how accurately the American legal profession and its legal system has been portrayed in film, the scholarship on law and film has developed into a vast and sprawling field within many disciplines. The interest has spread from what individual films have to say about justice to surveys of how different social issues have altered over the years. The initial tendency to focus on the products from Hollywood has also changed. There is now considerable interest from scholars outwith the English-speaking world. Not only that but the areas within which this work is carried out has gone beyond the Law School. Despite efforts to suggest some kind of common approach[183] it might seem that all that will continue to be the unifying factor in future scholarship is its sheer diversity. Films will probably be used both as a conduit into their internal meaning as well as to illustrate changes in social practices and politics. They will be used to explore very specific political and social issues particularly at a local level. It is clear that the films around justice will continue to be produced and that there will be accompanying analysis. Within which of the fields of scholarship this is located is likely to depend on the individual whims of scholars. There does not seem to have emerged any central focal set of criteria separating "good" work from "weak" scholarship. Films seem likely to continue to be plucked from the shelf and used by scholars with different goals and methodologies. That has been both the charm and curse of law and film. There is though, we would suggest, a rather more positive alternative.

12 Ways Forward

The issue can be broken into different components when considering the future of law and film scholarship. What could we do, what can we do, and what is currently possible? We have access to more content than ever before, and more content is being made available. There is a temptation to stick with

183 Stefan Machura, 'An Analysis Scheme for Law Films' (n 90).

the existing canon and demonstrate the historical significance of films such as TO KILL A MOCKINGBIRD and 12 ANGRY MEN to younger audiences. This overview has, rightly, given credit to the scholarship which has established the framework for law and film discussions.

While there is a merit to this approach, law and film scholarship needs to adapt and modernise, in part to recognise the changing market around film creation and distribution. It may be that the discussion progresses to consideration of the importance of the small screen, and this may increase the engagement with materials considering adaptations of literature, or remakes of existing law and justice media. This could lead to more genre-specific discussions on the differences between, for example, legal comedies and biopics.

The examples of the varying nature of scholarship internationally regarding law and film tend to lean towards more commonwealth and civil law jurisdictions, with a westernized production and audience. Part of the reason for this is the investment that is put into script and film development across the world. Therefore, where possible, law and film scholarship needs to highlight the increasing prominence of films and TV series from other jurisdictions—in particular, East Asian countries such as Korea (JUROR 8,[184] a Korean version of 12 ANGRY MEN in a setting where a jury verdict is advisory), South American countries like Argentina (CARANCHO,[185] a film in which a literal ambulance chaser works with people to deliberately get run over to make an insurance claim), and African countries such as Nigeria (TV series CASTLE AND CASTLE).[186] Where there is a good example, this should be celebrated in order to attract more discussion. It may be the case that law and film scholarship needs to look at short films in order to broaden its horizon and find a wider range of examples.

Yet there remain obstacles to this approach which put a significant caveat and ultimately leads us to the question of what can be done. Awareness of a film is one thing. Access to the film is another. For example, are there licensing restrictions and a lack of distribution in a particular territory? If intellectual property is used which dates back to indigenous legal traditions, how is this utilised in a manner that does not exploit a community? How can we ensure that a translation is accurate and an appropriate reflection of content in another language? As a collective, increased diversity in law and film scholarship should create a 'rising tide raises all ships' scenario where everyone

184 South Korea, 2019, director: Hong Seung-wan.

185 Argentina/Chile/Spain/France/South Korea, 2010, director: Pablo Trapero.

186 2018 Nigeria Netflix 2 series.

benefits. However, this will require greater collaboration between scholars and significant promotion or good practice in order to advance the discourse in the field.

This scholarship can be advanced in two primary ways. The first is to identify those who are already engaged in scholarship and teaching activities that actively use and embrace art and media as a way in which to disseminate and teach legal concepts and values. This has some forerunners in the United States[187] and Germany,[188] albeit with a local focus. There are tangible examples of a new crop of academics that clearly engage in the themes of law and film, but branch out further into other areas of media, art and law. While not an exhaustive list, examples of research groups in the UK include Rosie Fox and James Greenwood-Reeves' 'Law's a Drag' from the University of Leeds.[189] Sophie Doherty of the Open University's use of art and imagery both in teaching (e.g. on modules such as jurisprudence) and collaborating with artists in creating exhibitions and installations that are visible to the wider public. These include reviews of exhibitions as publications.[190] Furthermore, scholarship in the field is interdisciplinary and identification of, for example, anthropologists, in particular legal anthropologists, like Saskia Vermeylen,[191] will advance the need to promote greater diversity in identifying materials. The challenge here is maintaining existing and creating new forums to allow scholars to find each other.

The second way is to look to encourage newcomers into the field, through highlighting how the themes of law and film can be used beneficially in existing teaching practices. Legal education discourse highlights the rich variety of teaching and assessment, and this includes finding ways to engage learners through, for example, finding methods to support visual learning. Throughout the study of law, students are learning cases, all with their own in-built story and narrative. The infamous *Donoghue v Stevenson* "who is my neighbour?" case,[192]

187 Christine Corcos, *The Media Method: Teaching Law With Popular Culture* (Carolina Academic Press 2019); Michael Asimow and Jessica Silbey, *Law and Popular Culture: a course book* (3rd edn, Vandeplas Publishing 2020).

188 Stefan Machura, 'Recht im Film- Themen und Formen des Unterrichts' (2016) (n 88).

189 'Laws's a Drag' (*Law's a Drag*) <https://lawsadrag.org.uk#:~:text=We%20are%20a%20network%20of,faced%20by%20the%20drag%20community.&text=We%20make%20sure%20we%20pay,expertise%20at%20our%20collaborative%20events> accessed 30 August 2025.

190 Sophie Doherty, 'Framing Women in Revolt! As a Feminist Expression of Women's Lived Experiences of Law' (2024) 18 Law and Humanities 313.

191 Saskia Vermeylen, 'Space Art as a Critique of Space Law' (2021) 54 Law, People and Policy 115.

192 [1932] A.C. 562.

for example, can be summarized by a single image of a snail and a drinking vessel. Cases can easily be recalled, like FRIENDS[193] episode titles, as 'the one with the ...', or 'the one where ...'. It is naive to make simple assumptions about the roles we play when presenting the merits of law and film scholarship to a wider audience.[194] For example, when we engage with academic associations such as The Association for the Study of Law,[195] Culture and the Humanities, The Association of Law Teachers and Connecting Legal Education, we cannot presume that fellow academics are automatically understanding of these arguments. There are, of course, many other groupings whose interests also encompass law and film albeit tangentially like the Law and Society Association and the Research Committee on Sociology of Law. They might be loath to ask newcomers to adopt law and film modules in their entirety. Examples of potential avenues for integrating some law and film depictions into other modules include a consideration of the rights of workers in the gig economy through showing SORRY WE MISSED YOU,[196] consideration of children's ability to consent to medical treatment through THE CHILDREN ACT[197] and to using RASHŌMON[198] when teaching evidence as a way to ask if there is a way to identify the definitive truth of events.

Of course any such shifts in focus require commitment and structures. Academics and scholars, by their nature are reluctant to what might be perceived as any kind of central direction. There are, however, as we have indicated above already existing groupings in different countries who are engaged with the interface between law and film.[199] Bringing such groups together in the world of Zoom is more feasible than it has ever been before. Channelling the enthusiasm and commitment we have observed in our own countries for this kind of work should enrich the field of inquiry so that it can engage more effectively than perhaps it has in the past with a wider audience.

193 USA NBC 1994–2004.

194 Founded in the United States in 1997 LCH convenes annual meetings in the United States and sponsors a quarterly peer-reviewed journal, Law Culture and the Humanities. See 'The Association for the Study of Law, Culture, and the Humanities' (*Law, Culture and Humanities*) <https://lawculturehumanities.com> accessed 30 August 2025.

195 Founded in the United Kingdom in 1965 it engages with largely with university based legal education running an annual conference and sponsoring The Law Teacher: the International Journal of Legal Education.

196 Great Britain/France/Belgium, 2019, director: Ken Loach.

197 Great Britain, 2017, director: Richard Eyre.

198 Japan, 1950, director Akira Kurusawa.

199 Our linguistic skills limit us to the countries we have noted but there is, no doubt work going on in other jurisdictions which others may be able to identify.

References

Abrams N. and Lipiner M., 'Macho–Menschlichkeit Law and War in Stanley Kubrick's Paths of Glory (1957)' in Stefan Machura (ed), *Law and War in Popular Culture* (Nomos Verlags GmbH 2024).

Amatucci F. and Ciarcia A.R., *Il cinema come evasione ... fiscale* (Editoriale Scientifica 2017).

Amodio E., *Estetica della giustizia penale. Prassi, media, fiction* (Giuffrè 2016).

Andrzejewski A. and Salwa M., *Law and TV Series* (Brill 2018).

Anthony T. and Tranter K., 'Taking a Lens to the Chase in Australian Settler State Colonialism' in Kim D. Weinert, Karen Crawley and Kieran Tranter (eds), *Law, Lawyers and Justice: Through Australian Lenses* (Routledge 2020).

Argenio A., *I film del nazismo: Süss l'ebreo, L'ebreo errante, Terezin* (Editoriale Scientifica 2017).

Asimow M., *Lawyers in Your Living Room!: Law on Television* (American Bar Association 2009).

Asimow M., 'All's Fair in Love and War. Military Justice in the Movies' in Stefan Machura (ed), *Law and War in Popular Culture* (Nomos Verlags GmbH 2024).

Asimow M., Brown K. and Papke D., *Law and Popular Culture: International Perspectives* (Cambridge Scholars Publishing 2014).

Asimow M. and others, 'Perceptions of lawyers: a transnational study of student views on law and lawyers' (2005) 12 International Journal of the Legal Profession 407.

Asimow M. and Silbey J., *Law and Popular Culture: a course book* (3rd edn, Vandeplas Publishing 2020).

Barrero Ortega A. and others, *Derecho al Cine: Una introducción cinematográfica al Derecho Constitucional* (Tirant Lo Blanch 2011).

Bartoloni M.E. and Valentino L., *Il fenomeno migratorio fra immagini e norme* (Editoriale Scientifica 2017).

Becker S.K., 'Rape/Revenge/Suicide. Zum Verhältnis von Fremd-und Autoaggression in BIG LITTLE LIES und 13 REASONS WHY' in Christine Künzel and Manuel Bolz (eds), *Rape and Revenge: Rache-Kulturen und sexualisierte Gewalt in intermedialer Perspektive* (V&R Unipress 2024).

Beloff Z., *A World Redrawn: Eisenstein and Brecht in Hollywood* (Christine Burgin 2016).

Bene T. and Spangher G., *Un processo americano: Il caso Thomas Crawford* (Editoriale Scientifica 2017).

Bergman P., 'EMERGENCY!: Send a TV show to Rescue Paramedic Services!' (2007) 36 University of Baltimore Law Review 347.

Bergman P. and Asimow M., *Reel Justice: the courtroom goes to the movies* (Andrews McMeel Publishing 1996).

Binder G. and Weisberg R., 'Cultural Criticism of Law' (1997) 49 Stanford Law Review 1149.

Black D.A., *Law in Film: Resonance and Representation* (University of Illinois Press 1999).

Black G.D., *Hollywood Censored: Morality Codes, Catholics and the Movies* (Cambridge University Press 1996).

Bottomley A. and Moore N., 'Law, Diagram, Film: Critique Exhausted' (2012) 23 Law Critique 163.

Bouclin S., *Women, Film and the Law: Cinematic Representation of Female Incarceration* (UBC Press 2021).

Brettel H., Rau M. and Rienhoff J., *Strafrecht in Film und Fernsehen* (Springer 2016).

Buchanan R. and Johnson R., 'Strange Encounters: Exploring Law and Film in the Affective Register' (2009) 46 Studies in Law, Politics, and Society 33.

Bunikowski D., *Philosophy of Law in the Arctic* (The University of the Arctic, The Arctic Law Thematic Network, The Sub-group of Philosophy of Law in the Arctic 2016).

Callahan D., 'His Natural Whiteness: Modes of Ethnic Presence and Absence in Some Recent Australian Films' in Ian Craven (ed), *Australian Cinema in the 1990s* (Routledge 2000).

Cantero-Exojo M., Van Liew M. and Suarez J.C., *Fotogramas para la multiculturalidad: Migraciones y alteridad en el cine español contemporáneo* (Tirant Lo Blanch 2012).

Catalano R. and Venditti C., *Questioni di biodiritto nella filmografia cyberpunk* (Editoriale Scientifica 2017).

Cattorini P., *L'occhio che uccide. Criminologi al cinema* (FrancoAngeli 2006).

Chase A., 'Towards a Legal Theory of Popular Culture' (1986) Wisconsin Law Review 527.

Chaudhuri S.B., 'Neoliberal Avenging Moms? Examining Rape-and-Revenge in Bollywood Movies' in Christine Künzel and Manuel Bolz (eds), *Rape and Revenge: Rache-Kulturen und sexualisierte Gewalt in intermedialer Perspektive* (V&R Unipress 2024).

Ching A., 'Depictions of War Crimes in Film' in Stefan Machura (ed), *Law and War in Popular Culture* (Nomos Verlags GmbH 2024).

Ciarcia A.R., *Il cinema e le tasse* (Editoriale Scientifica 2017).

'CINE EN LA UNAM PROGRAMACIÓN' (*Culturaunam*) <https://www.filmoteca.unam.mx/290-congreso-de-cine-y-derecho-iv-muestra-internacional-de-cine-derechos-humanos-y-justicia/> accessed 10 February 2025.

'Collection Droit et Cinéma' (*Mare et Martin*) <https://www.mareetmartin.com/les-editions-mare-et-martin/les-collections/collection-droit-cinema> accessed 06 December 2024.

Corcos C., *The Media Method: Teaching Law With Popular Culture* (Carolina Academic Press 2019).

Corso F., *Totò Il lavoro e ... la legge* (Editoriale Scientifica 2019).

Coutant A., *Les lois d'Alfred Hitchcock* (Mare et Martin 2018).

Coutant A., *Juridiquement vôtre: Brett Sinclair et Danny Wilde, un duo au service du droit* (Mare et Martin 2020).

Craven I., *Australian Cinema in the 1990s* (Routledge 2000).

Crofts P. and van Rijswijk H., 'Picnic at Hanging Rock: Coming of age as a girl in the Gothic colonial institution' in Kim D. Weinert, Karen Crawley and Kieran Tranter (eds), *Law, Lawyers and Justice: Through Australian Lenses* (Routledge 2020).

Cunningham J., 'That's When I Reach for My Revolver. War Crimes and Popular Music' in Stefan Machura (ed), *Law and War in Popular Culture* (Nomos Verlags GmbH 2024).

Curti R., *Italian Crime Filmography, 1968–1980* (McFarland 2013).

D'Acunto S. and Nuzzo V., *Fotogrammi dal dominio della lotta: L'occhio del cinema sulla società neoliberista* (Editoriale Scientifica 2017).

D'Alto F. and Pignata M., *Le forme della legge e le forme dell'arte: La famiglia italiana nel racconto cinematografico* (Editoriale Scientifica 2017).

De Fiores C., *Il fragile scudo della Costituzione: L'occhio del cinema sulla violazione dei diritti al tempo del maccartismo* (Editoriale Scientifica 2017).

Defferrard F., *La pensée juridique de Sheldon Cooper ou Comment faire du droit avec The Big Bang Theory* (Mare et Martin 2019).

Defferrard F., *Les Lois de Michel Audiard: Liberté, Fraternité, Égalité* (Mare et Martin 2021).

Delage C., 'Image as evidence and mediation: The Experience of the Nuremberg Trials' in Michael Freeman (ed), *Law and Popular Culture* (Oxford University Press 2005).

de Lucas J., *Nosotros, que quisimos tanto a Atticus Finch* (Tirant Lo Blanch 2020).

Denvir J., *Legal Reelism: Movies as Legal Texts* (University of Illinois Press 1996).

de Zwart M., Richards B. and Le Mire S., *Law and Popular Culture in Australia* (LexisNexis 2015).

Doherty S., 'Framing Women in Revolt! As a Feminist Expression of Women's Lived Experiences of Law' (2024) 18 Law and Humanities 313.

Dolin K., *Critical Introduction to Law and Literature* (Cambridge University Press 2007).

Dolin K., *Fiction and the Law: Legal Discourse in Victorian and Modernist Literature* (Cambridge University Press 2009).

Dolin K., *Law and Literature* (Cambridge University Press 2018).

Douzinas C., 'A Humanities of Resistance: Fragments for a Legal History of Humanity' in Austin Sarat, Matthew Anderson and Cathrine O. Frank (eds), *Law and Humanities: An Introduction* (Cambridge University Press 2009).

'Droit et cinéma' (*Marie-Anne Frison Roche*) <https://mafr.fr/en/enseignements/droit-et-cinema/> accessed 06 December 2024.

Dubin A.D., Goswami R. and Sharma I., *Indian Cinema and Human Rights: An Intersectional Tale* (Springer 2025).

Duncanson K., 'Being Engaged in Colonial Critique by Mojo Juju's Native Tongue' in Kim D. Weinert, Karen Crawley and Kieran Tranter (eds), *Law, Lawyers and Justice: Through Australian Lenses* (Routledge 2020).

Esposito A., *Dal nero all'arancio: anatomia penitenziaria di una serie TV* (Editoriale Scientifica 2017).

Fachechi A., *Storie di facili consumi* (Editoriale Scientifica 2017).

'Ferdinando Spina' (*Uni Salento*) <https://www.unisalento.it/people/ferdinando.spina/didattica/1256842020/scheda> accessed 30 August 2025.

Fernadez Carballo Calero P., *Derecho Mercantil y Cine* (Editorial Aranzadi 2016).

Fineman M. and McCluskey M.T., *Feminism, Media and the Law* (Oxford University Press 1997).

Fish S., *Law at the Movies: Turning Legal Doctrine into Art* (Oxford University Press 2024).

Fiske J., *Television Culture* (2nd edn, Routledge 2010).

Flores F., *Le mani sulla città. Il capitalismo: la democrazia in ostaggio* (Editoriale Scientifica 2018).

Flores-Lonjou M., 'Le juge français mis en images: images officielles versus images documentaires' (2018) 1 Revue de droit et de criminologie de l'ULB 1 <https://hal-univ-rochelle.archives-ouvertes.fr/hal-02389883/document> accessed 06 December 2024.

Flores-Lonjou M. and Épinoux E., *La famille au cinéma: Regards juridiques et esthétiques* (Mare et Martin 2016).

Flores-Lonjou M., Épinoux E. and Lefebve V., *Frontière(s) au cinéma* (Mare et Martin 2019).

Freeman M., *Law and Popular Culture* (Oxford University Press 2005).

Friedman L., 'Law, Lawyers and Popular Culture' (1989) 98 The Yale Law Journal 1579.

Garcia Manrique R. and Ruiz Sainz M., *El Derecho en el Cine Español Contemporáneo* (Tirant Lo Blanch 2009).

Gibney M., *Watching Human Rights: The 101 Best Films* (Routledge 2013).

Gies L., 'Law as Popular Culture: Cross-Disciplinary Encounters' (2005) 19 Continuum 165.

Gilbert N., *Better Left Unsaid: Victorian Novels, Hays Code Films, and the Benefits of Censorship* (Stanford University Press 2013).

Gisler P. and others, *Intersections of Law and Culture* (Palgrave Macmillan 2012).

Gisler P. and others, 'Setting the Stage: Reading Law and Culture' in Priska Gisler, Sara Steinert Borella, Caroline Wiedmer (eds), *Intersections of Law and Culture* (Palgrave Macmillan 2012).

Goldsmith B., Ward S. and O'Regan T., *Local Hollywood: Global Film Production and the Gold Coast* (University of Queensland Press 2010).

Graham L.E. and Maschio G., 'A False Public Sentiment: Narrative and Visual Images of Women Lawyers in Film' (1996) 84 Ky Law J 1027.

Greenfield S., 'The Rising: Mangal Pandey and India's First War of Independence' in Stefan Machura (ed), *Law and War in Popular Culture* (Nomos Verlags GmbH 2024).
Greenfield S. and Osborn G., *Readings in Law and Popular Culture* (Routledge 2006).
Greenfield S., Osborn G. and Robson P., *Film and the Law* (Cavendish 2001).
Greenfield S., Osborn G. and Robson P., 'Genre, Iconography and British Film' (2007) 36 Baltimore Law Review 371.
Greenfield S., Osborn G. and Robson P., *Film and the Law: the cinema of justice* (Hart 2010).
Greenfield S., Osborn G. and Robson P., 'Law and Film' in Russell Sandberg and Daniel Newman (eds), *Law and Humanities* (Anthem Press 2024).
Greenfield S., Osborn G. and Robson P., 'Genre and Cinematic Justice: Towards a "Rights-Based" Analysis' in Adam Dubin, Ruchira Goswami and Ishita Sharma, *Indian Cinema and Human Rights: An Intersectional Tale* (Springer 2025).
Grunert A., 'Vérité et mensonge dans Distance/Disutansu de Hirokazu Kore-Eda (Japon, 2001)' (*Le Blog Droit et Cinéma*, 22 January 2024) <https://lesmistons.typepad.com/blog/2024/01/index.html> accessed 06 December 2024.
Gunn D.L., *The Lawyer and Popular Conference: Proceedings of a Conference* (Fred B Rothman 1993).
Haegele L., 'Popfeminist Approaches to Rape-and-Revenge: Avenging with Awkwardness in Emerald Fennell's PROMISING YOUNG WOMAN (UK/USA 2020) and Ziska Riemann's LOLLIPOP MONSTER (GER 2011)' in Christine Künzel and Manuel Bolz (eds), *Rape and Revenge: Rache-Kulturen und sexualisierte Gewalt in intermedialer Perspektive* (V&R Unipress 2024).
Harris T.J., *Courtroom's Finest Hour in American Cinema* (Scarecrow Press 1987).
Hervé F., *Censure et Cinéma dans la France des Trente Glorieuses* (Nouveau Monde Éditions 2015).
Huanca Chávez E. and Domínguez Haro H., *Los tribunales de justicia en el cine* (Fondo Editorial del Poder Judicial del Perú/Red Iberoamericana de Cine y Derecho 2018).
Iadicicco M.P., *La procreazione medicalmente assistita al cinema* (Editoriale Scientifica 2017).
Iturralde M., 'Justicia de bagatela: sistema penal y desigualdad en un documental colombiano' in Eddy Huanca Chávez and Helder Domínguez Haro (eds), *Los tribunales de justicia en el cine* (Fondo Editorial del Poder Judicial del Perú/Red Iberoamericana de Cine y Derecho 2018).
Jarvis R.M. and Joseph P.R., *Prime Time Law: Fictional television as legal narrative* (Carolina University Press 1998).
Johnson R., 'Justice and the Colonial Collision: Reflections on Stories of Intercultural Encounter in Law, Literature, Sculpture and Film' (2012) 9 No Foundations 68.
Johnson R., 'Notes on Using Film to Engage with Philosophy of Law in the Arctic' in Dawid Bunikowski, *Philosophy of Law in the Arctic* (The University of the Arctic,

The Arctic Law Thematic Network, The Sub-group of Philosophy of Law in the Arctic 2016).

Johnson R., 'Intercultural Cinema and the (Re)Envisioning of Law: Exploring Life, Death and Law in *Atanarjuat* and *Before Tomorrow*' in Timothy D. Peters and Karen Crawley (eds), *Envisioning Legality: Law, Culture and Representation* (Routledge 2018).

Johnson R. and Buchanan R., 'Getting the Insider's Story Out: What Popular Film Can Tell Us about Legal Method's Dirty Secrets' (2001) 20 Windsor Yearbook of Access to Justice 87.

Kamir O., *Framed: Women in Law and Film* (Duke University Press 2006).

Keane E. and Robson P., *The Ian Willock Collection on Law and Justice in the Twenty-First Century* (Fairleigh Dickinson University Press 2023).

Korsten F.-W., 'Öffentlichkeit (open-ness) and the Law's Behind the Scenes: Theatrical and Dramatic Appearance in European and US, American Criminal Law' (2017) 18 German Law Journal 399.

Korzec R., 'Viewing North Country: Sexual Harassment Goes to the Movies' (2007) 36 University of Baltimore Law Review 303.

Künzel C. and Bolz M., *Rape and Revenge: Rache-Kulturen und sexualisierte Gewalt in intermedialer Perspektive* (V&R Unipress 2024).

Kuzina M., *Der amerikanische Gerichtsfilm: Justiz, Ideologie, Dramatik* (Vandenhoek and Ruprecht 2000).

Kuzina M., 'The social issue courtroom drama as an expression of American popular culture' in Stefan Machura and Peter Robson (eds), *Law and Film* (Blackwell 2001).

Kuzina M., 'Das Kriegsgerichtsverfahren als Filmsujet: US-amerikanische Erzählmuster' in Stefan Machura and Rüdiger Voigt (eds), *Krieg im Film* (Lit 2005).

Lanza C. and Minieri L., + *Nemici del popolo* (Editoriale Scientifica 2017).

Larisch J., 'Rape-and-Revenge-Filme im Kontext strafrechtlicher Verbotpraxis' in Christine Künzel and Manuel Bolz (eds), *Rape and Revenge: Rache-Kulturen und sexualisierte Gewalt in intermedialer Perspektive* (V&R Unipress 2024).

Laster K., *Law as Culture* (Federation Press 2011).

'Laws's a Drag' (*Law's a Drag*) <https://lawsadrag.org.uk#:~:text=We%20are%20a%20network%20of,faced%20by%20the%20drag%20community.&text=We%20make%20sure%20we%20pay,expertise%20at%20our%20collaborative%20events> accessed 30 August 2025.

Le Pluard Q. and Talbot M., *Du droit dans Disney* (Mare et Martin 2020).

Leiboff M. and Sharp C., 'Cultural Legal Studies and Law's Popular Cultures' in Cassandra Sharp and Marett Leiboff (eds), *Cultural Legal Studies Law's Popular Cultures and the Metamorphosis of Law* (Routledge 2015).

Linares S., 'El secreto de sus ojos: justicia por mano propia y legitimidad del Estado' in Eddy Huanca Chávez and Helder Domínguez Haro (eds), *Los tribunales de justicia en el cine* (Fondo Editorial del Poder Judicial del Perú/Red Iberoamericana de Cine y Derecho 2018).

Lucia C., 'Women on Trial: The Female Lawyer in the Hollywood Courtroom' in Martha Fineman and Martha T. McCluskey (eds), *Feminism, Media and the Law* (Oxford University Press 1997).

Lucia C., *Framing Female Lawyers: Women on Trial In Film* (University of Texas Press 2006).

Macaulay S., 'Images of Law in Everyday Life: The Lessons of School, Entertainment and Spectator Sports' (1987) 21 Law and Society Review 185.

Machura S., 'Patton—Ein biographischer Kriegsfilm und der Mythos des amerikanischen Soldaten' in Stefan Machura and Rüdiger Voigt (eds), *Krieg im Film* (2005).

Machura S., 'Procedural unfairness in real and film trials: Why do audiences understand stories placed in foreign legal systems?' in Michael Freeman (ed), *Law and Popular Culture* (Oxford University Press 2005).

Machura S., 'An Analysis Scheme for Law Films' (2007) 36 University of Baltimore Law Review 329.

Machura S., 'German Response to 12 Angry Men' (2007) 82 Chicago-Kent Law Review 777.

Machura S., 'Law and Cinema Movement' in Caroline Joan Picart, Michael Hviid Jacobsen and Cecil Greek (eds), *Framing Law and Crime: An Interdisciplinary Anthology* (Rowman and Littlefield 2016).

Machura S., 'Recht im Film- Themen und Formen des Unterrichts' (2016) 3 ZDRW Zeitschrift für Didaktik der Rechtswissenschaft 363.

Machura S., *Law and War in Popular Culture* (Nomos Verlags GmbH 2024).

Machura S. and Cunningham J., 'Law and War in the Opera' in Stefan Machura (ed), *Law and War in Popular Culture* (Nomos Verlags GmbH 2024).

Machura S. and Robson P., *Law and Film* (Blackwell 2001).

Machura S. and Ulbrich S., 'Law in film: Globalizing the Hollywood courtroom drama' (2001) 28 Journal of Law and Society 117.

Machura S. and Ulbrich S., *Recht im Film* (Nomos Verlagsgesellschaft 2002).

Machura S. and Voigt R., *Krieg im Film* (Lit 2005).

Machura S. and Voigt R., 'Krieg im Film. Der ewige Kampf des "Guten" gegen das "Böse"' in Stefan Machura and Rüdiger Voigt (eds), *Krieg im Film* (Lit 2005).

MacNeil W. and Hutchings P., 'Law's Cultural Mediations: An Introduction by Way of Introduction' (2001) 10 Griffith Law Review 1.

Mancino A.G., *Il processo della verità: le radici del film politico-indiziario italiano* (Kaplan 2008).

Masson A. and O'Connor K., *Representations of Justice* (Peter Lang 2007).

Master Droit du cinéma, de l'audiovisuel et de la communication numérique (anciennement Droit du cinéma et de l'audiovisuel) (*Université Lyon III Jean Moulin*) <https://facdedroit.univ-lyon3.fr/master-droit-du-cinema-et-de-l-audiovisuel-2> accessed 06 December 2024.

Mastor W. and Miniato L., *Les figures du procès au-delà des frontières* (Dalloz 2014).

Mastrangelo P., 'Creating a Filmography' in David L. Gunn (ed), *The Lawyer and Popular Conference: Proceedings of a Conference* (Fred B Rothman 1993).

Mendizábal Allende R. de, *Cine y Derecho: togas en la gran pantalla* (Berenice 2021).

Meyer P., 'Why a jury trial is more like a movie than a novel' in Stefan Machura and Peter Robson (eds), *Law and Film* (Blackwell 2001).

Moran L., 'Heroes and Brothers in Love: the male homosexual as lawyer in popular culture' (1998) 18 Studies in Law, Politics and Society 3.

Moran L. and others, *Laws Moving Image* (Glasshouse 2004).

Nabaskues Martínez de Eulate I., 'War, Film, Memory and Trauma: the Bosnian case in Quo Vadis Aida?' in Stefan Machura (ed), *Law and War in Popular Culture* (Nomos Verlags GmbH 2024).

Narváez Hernández J.R., *Los jueces en el cine. La administración de justicia y la argumentación en el séptimo arte* (Fondo Editorial del Poder Judicial del Perú/Red Iberoamericana de Cine y Derecho Editorial 2016).

Nevins F., 'Through the Great Depression on Horseback: legal themes in Western films of the 1930s' in John Denvir (ed), *Legal Reelism: Movies as Legal Texts* (University of Illinois Press 1996).

Ollé-Laprune J., *Le Cinéma Policier Francais: 100 films, 100 réalisateurs* (Hugo Image 2020).

O'Neill de la Fuente C., *El derecho va al cine: intersecciones entre la visión artística y la visión jurídica de los problemas sociales* (Universidad del Pacífico 2013).

Pannarale L., 'La verità degli avvocati: un'indagine sul cinema italiano' (2021) 3 Sociologia del Diritto 33.

Pâquet L., 'Vigilante Frontier Communities on Australian Screens: Bushrangers, Bikies, and Bogans in Vigilante Justice' in Peter Robson and Ferdinando Spina (eds), *Vigilante Justice in Society and Popular Culture* (Fairleigh Dickinson University Press 2022).

Pásara L. and Alcántara M., *La justicia en la pantalla: Un reflejo de jueces y tribunales en cine y TV* (Pontificia Universidad Católica del Perú, Fondo Editorial 2019).

Peters T.D., 'Seeing' Justice Done: Envisioning Legality in Christopher Nolan's The Dark Knight Trilogy' in Timothy D. Peters and Karen Crawley (eds), *Envisioning Legality: Law, Culture and Representation* (Routledge 2018).

Peters T.D. and Crawley K., *Envisioning Legality: Law, Culture and Representation* (Routledge 2018).

Presno Linares M.A., *The West Wing: la política como promessa* (Tirant Lo Blanch 2016).

Presno Linares M.A. and Rivaya B., *Una Introducción cinematográfica al derecho* (Tirant Lo Blanch 2006).

Puaux F., *La Justice à L'Écran* (CinemAction 2002).

Quirk J. and Murphy J.R., 'Whose country? Colonialism and the rule of law in Sweet Country and Charlie's Country' in Kim D. Weinert, Karen Crawley and Kieran Tranter (eds), *Law, Lawyers and Justice: Through Australian Lenses* (Routledge 2020).

Ramiro Avilés M.A., *Derechos, cine, literatura y cómics: como y porqué* (Tirant Lo Blanch 2014).

Ravveduto M., *Lo spettacolo della mafia. Storia di un immaginario tra realtà e finzione* (Edizioni Gruppo Abele 2019).

Reviriego Picón F., *Proyecciones de Derecho Constitucional* (Tirant Lo Blanch 2012).

Rivaya B., *Un Vademécum Judicial: Cine para jueces* (Tirant Lo Blanch 2012).

Rivaya B., *Derecho y Cine en 100 peliculas* (2nd edn, Tirant Lo Blanch 2021).

Rivaya B. and de Cima P., *Derecho y Cine en 100 peliculas* (Tirant Lo Blanch 2004).

Robson P., 'Fade to Grey: portraying the ethnic minority experience in British film' (2002) 30 International Journal of the Sociology of Law 235.

Robson P., 'The justice films of Sidney Lumet' in Steve Greenfield and Guy Osborn (eds), *Readings in Law and Popular Culture* (Routledge 2006).

Robson P., 'Lawyers and the legal system on TV: the British experience' (2006) 2 International Journal of Law in Context 333.

Robson P., 'Developments in Law and Popular Culture: The Case of the TV Lawyer' in Antoine Masson and Kevin O'Connor (eds), *Representations of Justice* (Peter Lang 2007).

Robson P., 'Law, Hollywood and the European Experience' in Austin Sarat (ed), *Studies in Law, Politics and Society* (Vol 46, Emerald Publishing 2009).

Robson P., 'Judges on Screen' (Research Committee on Sociology of Law Annual Meeting, Gothenburg, July 2010).

Robson P., 'Future Directions in Law and Popular Culture: a British perspective' in Jacqueline Visconti (ed), *Handbook of Communication in the Legal Sphere* (Walter de Gruyter Inc 2018).

Robson P., 'Cathy Come Home Today' in Eamon Keane and Peter Robson (eds), *The Ian Willock Collection on Law and Justice in the Twenty-First Century* (Fairleigh Dickinson University Press 2023).

Robson P., 'Law in War—The Wind that Shakes the Barley and the Republican Court Experiment. Justice in the Time of War in Popular Culture' in Stefan Machura (ed), *Law and War in Popular Culture* (Nomos Verlags GmbH 2024).

Robson P., 'From Bloodbath to Parody: Western Cinema's Uneasy Relationship with Rape-Revenge Themes—a fresh approach?' in Christine Künzel and Manuel Bolz (eds), *Rape and Revenge: Rache-Kulturen und sexualisierte Gewalt in intermedialer Perspektive* (V&R Unipress 2024).

Robson P. and Silbey J., *Law and Justice on the Small Screen* (Hart 2012).

Robson P. and Schulz J., *A Transnational Study of Law and Justice on TV* (Hart 2016).

Robson P. and Schulz J., *Ethnicity, Gender and Diversity: Law and Justice on TV* (Fairleigh Dickinson University Press 2018).

Robson P. and Spina F., *Vigilante Justice in Society and Popular Culture: A Global Perspective* (Fairleigh Dickinson University Press 2022).

Robson P., Osborn G. and Greenfield S., 'The Impact of Film and Television On Perceptions of Law and Justice: Towards a Realisable Methodology' in Anne Wagner and Richard K. Sherwin (eds), *Law, Culture and Visual Studies* (Springer 2014).

Roselli O., *Cinema e diritto. La comprensione della dimensione giuridica attraverso la cinematografia* (Giappichelli 2020).

Sacchi O., *Lo scudo riflettente di Perseo. Archetipi del giuridico nel cinema contemporaneo* (Editoriale Scientfica 2019).

Salvati A., *Timema e Thanatos: Tasse e morte* (Editoriale Scientifica 2017).

Sandberg R. and Newman D., *Law and Humanities* (Anthem 2024).

Sarat A., Douglas L. and Umphrey M., *Law on the Screen* (University of Massachusetts Press 2005).

Sarat A., Douglas L. and Umphrey M., *Studies in Law, Politics and Society* (Vol 46, Emerald Publishing 2009).

Sarat A., Douglas L. and Umphrey M., *Imagining Legality: When Law Meets Popular Culture* (University of Alabama Press 2011).

Sarat A., Douglas L. and Umphrey M., *Law and the Visible* (University of Massachusetts Press 2021).

Schuetz J.E. and Lilley L.S., *The OJ Simpson Trials: Rhetoric, Media, and the Law* (Southern Illinois University Press 1999).

Schulz J., 'The Mediator as Cook: Mediation Metaphors at the Movies' (2007) 2 Journal of Dispute Resolution 455.

Schulz J., 'Law & Film: Where are the Mediators?' (2008) 58 University of Toronto Law Journal 233.

Schulz J., 'The Cook, the Mediator, the Feminist, and the Hero' (2009) 21 Canadian Journal of Women and the Law 177.

Schulz J., 'Monsters & Madwomen? Neurosis, Ambition and Mothering in Women Lawyers in Film' (2016) 16 Journal of Law, Culture and the Humanities 1.

Schulz J., 'Using Film to Teach ADR' in Christine Corcos (ed), *The Media Method: Teaching Law With Popular Culture* (Carolina Academic Press 2019).

Schulz J., 'Contemplating Law, Film and Mennonites' (2021) 20 Law, Culture and Humanities 421.

Schulz J., 'Law and TV' in Russell Sandberg and Daniel Newman (eds), *Law and Humanities* (Anthem Press 2024).

Shapiro C., 'Women Lawyers in Celluloid: Why Hollywood Skirts the Truth' (1995) 25 University of Toledo Law Review 955.

Sharp C. and Leiboff M., *Cultural Legal Studies: Law's Popular Cultures and the Metamorphosis of Law* (Routledge 2015).

Sheffield R., 'A social history of black lawyers in popular culture' (1991) 7 Focus on Law Studies 4.

Sherwin R.K., 'Symposium: Picturing Justice: Images of Law and Lawyers in the Visual Media' (1996) 30 University of San Francisco Law Review 891.

Sherwin R.K., *When Law Goes Pop: The Vanishing Line between Law and Popular Culture* (University of Chicago Press 2000).

Sherwin R.K., 'What screen do you have in mind? Contesting the Visual Context of Law and Film Studies' (2009) 46 Studies in Law, Politics and Society 3.

Sielke S., 'Return with a Vengeance? The Serial Debate on Sexual Harassment and Sexual Violence, or: What's New About #MeToo—and What Film Can (Still) Do' in Christine Künzel and Manuel Bolz (eds), *Rape and Revenge: Rache-Kulturen und sexualisierte Gewalt in intermedialer Perspektive* (V&R Unipress 2024).

Silbey J., 'A Witness to Justice' in Austin Sarat (ed), *Studies in Law, Politics and Society* (Vol 46, Emerald Publishing 2009).

Sommerlad H. and Sanderson P., 'Talk of the Town' in Steve Greenfield and Guy Osborn (eds), *Readings in Law and Popular Culture* (Routledge 2006).

Spina F., 'Through the Law, Beyond the Law Dealing with Fascism and Civil War in Italian Cinema' in Stefan Machura (ed), *Law and War in Popular Culture* (Nomos Verlags GmbH 2024).

Stern S., Del Mar M. and Meyler B., *The Oxford Handbook of Law and Humanities* (Oxford University Press 2019).

Strickland R., Foster T.E. and Lovelle Banks T., *Screening Justice—The Cinema of Law: Significant Films of Law, Order and Social Justice* (Hein 2006).

'Testigo de cargo. Witness for the Prosecution Billy Wilder (1957)' (*Standum est chartae*) <http://revista.reicaz.es/numeros-anteriores/n-012/cine-y-derecho/> accessed 27 November 2022.

'The Association for the Study of Law, Culture, and the Humanities' (*Law, Culture and Humanities*) <https://lawculturehumanities.com> accessed 30 August 2025.

Thornton M., *Romancing the Tomes: Popular Culture, Law and Feminism* (Routledge 2002).

Tomeo V., *Il giudice sullo schermo* (Laterza 1973).

Tomeo V., *The Judge on the Screen* (Translated by Peter Robson, Fairleigh Dickinson 2024).

Toranzos M., 'Congreso de Cine y Derecho se dará en la Universidad Andina' (*Expreso*, 10 May 2023) <https://www.expreso.ec/actualidad/cine-leyes-160044.html> accessed 16 December 2024.

Tranter K., 'Justice at the end of *Fury Road*' in Kim D. Weinert, Karen Crawley and Kieran Tranter (eds), *Law, Lawyers and Justice: Through Australian Lenses* (Routledge 2020).

Triolle C., *Le contrôle cinématographique en France. Quand le sexe, la violence, et la religion font encore débat* (L'Harmattan 2015).

Ugah H.U., 'Reconfiguring Victimhood: Rape Culture and Rape-Revenge in Nollywood Movies' in Christine Künzel and Manuel Bolz (eds), *Rape and Revenge: Rache-Kulturen und sexualisierte Gewalt in intermedialer Perspektive* (V&R Unipress 2024).

University of Baltimore Law Review (2007) Law and Cinema Special Issue Vol 36 No 3 299–391.

Vermeylen S., 'Space Art as a Critique of Space Law' (2021) 54 Law, People and Policy 115.

Visconti J., *Handbook of Communication in the Legal Sphere* (Walter de Gruyter Inc 2018).

Vitiello G., *In nome della legge. La giustizia nel cinema italiano* (Rubbettino 2013).

Vitucci M.C., *La guerra dietro casa: Lo sguardo del cinema sulla Jugoslavia in fiamme* (Editoriale Scientifica 2017).

Wagner A. and Sherwin R.K., *Law, Culture and Visual Studies* (Springer 2014).

Weinert K.D., 'Romper Stomper: a critique of neoliberalism in Australia' in Kim D. Weinert, Karen Crawley and Kieran Tranter (eds), *Law, Lawyers and Justice: Through Australian Lenses* (Routledge 2020).

Weinert K.D., Crawley K. and Tranter K., 'Australian Lenses on Law, Lawyers and Justice' in Kim D. Weinert, Karen Crawley and Kieran Tranter (eds), *Law, Lawyers and Justice: Through Australian Lenses* (Routledge 2020).

Weinert K.D., Crawley K. and Tranter K., *Law, Lawyers and Justice: Through Australian Lenses* (Routledge 2020).

Young A., 'Ambivalence and the Spectatorship of Violence: Viewing *Inglourious Basterds*' in Timothy D. Peters and Karen Crawley (eds), *Envisioning Legality: Law, Culture and Representation* (Routledge 2018).

Ziccardi G., *Il diritto al cinema: Cent'anni di courtroom drama e melodrammi giudiziari* (Giuffrè 2010).

'13–15 October 2021' (*Nitter*) <https://nitter.fdn.fr/pic/media%2FFBhtWOZVgAIMCog.jpg%3Fname%3Dorig> accessed 10 February 2025.

'27th Meeting—28 September to 3 October 2020' (*Nitter*) <https://nitter.fdn.fr/pic/media%2FEf7R9FpWAAATZED.jpg%3Fname%3Dorig> accessed 21 December 2024.

Index of Films Cited

© 2026 THE AUTHOR(S) | HTTPS://DOI.ORG/10.1163/9789004761704-010

www.ingramcontent.com/pod-product-compliance
Lightning Source LLC
Chambersburg PA
CBHW071341230926
51846CB00002B/406
* 9 7 8 9 0 0 4 7 6 1 6 9 8 *